Reconstructing Sociology

Critical realism is a philosophy of science that positions itself against the major alternative philosophies underlying contemporary sociology. This book offers a general critique of sociology, particularly sociology in the United States, from a critical realist perspective. It also acts as an introduction to critical realism for students and scholars of sociology. Written in a lively, accessible style, Douglas V. Porpora argues that sociology currently operates with deficient accounts of truth, culture, structure, agency, and causality that are all better served by a critical realist perspective. This approach argues against the alternative sociological perspectives, in particular the dominant positivism which privileges statistical techniques and experimental design over ethnographic and historical approaches. However, the book also compares critical realism favorably with a range of other approaches, including poststructuralism, pragmatism, interpretivism, practice theory, and relational sociology. Numerous sociological examples are included, and each chapter addresses well-known and current work in sociology.

DOUGLAS V. PORPORA is a professor of Sociology at Drexel University, Philadelphia. His previous publications include *Post-Ethical Society: The Iraq War, Abu Ghraib, and the Moral Failure of the Secular* (2013).

Reconstructing Sociology

The Critical Realist Approach

DOUGLAS V. PORPORA
Professor of Sociology
Drexel University

CAMBRIDGE
UNIVERSITY PRESS

CAMBRIDGE
UNIVERSITY PRESS

University Printing House, Cambridge CB2 8BS, United Kingdom

Cambridge University Press is part of the University of Cambridge.

It furthers the University's mission by disseminating knowledge in the pursuit of education, learning and research at the highest international levels of excellence.

www.cambridge.org
Information on this title: www.cambridge.org/9781107514713

© Douglas V. Porpora 2015

First published 2015

Printed in the United Kingdom by Clays, St Ives plc

A catalogue record for this publication is available from the British Library

Library of Congress Cataloguing in Publication data
Porpora, Douglas V.
Reconstructing sociology : the critical realist approach / Douglas V. Porpora.
    pages cm
Includes bibliographical references and index.
ISBN 978-1-107-10737-3 (Hardback : alk. paper) – ISBN 978-1-107-51471-3 (Paperback : alk. paper)
1. Sociology. 2. Critical theory. I. Title.
HM585.P666 2016
301–dc23   2015013727

ISBN 978-1-107-10737-3 Hardback
ISBN 978-1-107-51471-3 Paperback

To my wife, Lynne, with love

Contents

Acknowledgments

I would especially like to thank Margaret Archer and Christian Smith, who have long been distinctly supportive of my work in this area. My debt also goes to Roy Bhaskar and Andrew Collier, who just passed as I write. Aside from being originators of critical realism, they were, even in adversity, always cheerful and empathic souls, so kind to all they encountered. I join many others in saying I will miss their friendship dearly.

This particular book was made possible and actively encouraged by a grant from the John Templeton Foundation, which is seeking to encourage consideration of critical realism in American sociology. My thanks to Kimon Sargeant at the foundation for shepherding the whole effort. My thanks as well to the others involved in the project and for their feedback on earlier drafts. In addition to Roy, Maggie, and Chris, these include Philip Gorski, Ruth Groff, Mervyn Hartwig, Margarita Mooney, Alan Norrie, Tim Rutzou, George Steinmetz, and Frédéric Vandenberghe.

The ideas contained herein reflect conversations going back sometimes for decades. I am grateful in that regard to all the members of the International Association of Critical Realism (IACR), which, along with Peter Manicas, Paul Secord, and Charles Smith, first welcomed me to this body of ideas. For their support and feedback along the way, I would also like to thank Ismael Al-Amoudi, Jack Barbalet, Michael Blim, Kathleen Coughey, Charles Crothus, Hans Despain, Pierpaolo Donati, Donald Eckard, Daniel Finn, Andreas Glaeser, Mervyn Hartwig, Jonathan Joseph, Gary Klein, Kyriakos Kontopoulos, David Kutzik, Hugh Lacey, Magali Sarfatti Larson, John Latsis, Tony Lawson, Andrea Maccarini, John Levi Martin, Jamie Morgan, Caroline New, Joseph Romero, Rachel Sharp, Hal Shanis, Wesley Shumar, Sean Vertigan, and Colin Wight.

I am grateful to all my students, those who have become professors themselves, those who have gone on to other pursuits, and those I still have. I cannot express all they have added to my life. Discussions with them are also reflected in this book.

My appreciation also for all the technical help provided by Diana Dang and, for that matter, all the support of the office staff at Drexel University: Caroline Chmielewski, David Corbin, Gregory Lang, Mica Storer, and Sharon Wallace. My thanks as well to two anonymous reviewers, to my editors at Cambridge University Press, John Haslam, Bronte Rawlings, and Carrie Parkinson, and to the whole Cambridge staff.

Lastly and mostly, I thank my wife, Lynne, whose generosity knows no bounds and to whom this book is dedicated.

1 | *Seven myths of American sociology*

What is critical realism (CR) and who needs it?
Let us take the second question first. Sociology, particularly American sociology, needs CR. In the United Kingdom (UK) and elsewhere, it is already known. You might need CR as well. Are you unconvinced that a regression equation constitutes an explanation but do not quite know what does? Are you equally incredulous that ethnography and historical narrative do not explain? Maybe you hold the heretical view that not all reality is socially constructed but wonder how to formulate this counter case. Are you perhaps troubled by what various perspectives in sociology do with human personhood – decentering it, dissolving it into discourse, or otherwise deconstructing it? Perhaps you harbor doubts about the posture of value freedom that is supposed to characterize science. If these and other such disquieting thoughts about sociology fail to trouble you, carry on: You do not need CR. Otherwise, you do – at least a discussion about it.

This book is about CR and the contribution it can make to sociology. It is a book for those devoted to sociology who, nevertheless, are troubled by its current guiding assumptions. And sociology does have current guiding assumptions. All intellectual endeavors do. We may not notice them, but they are there. They exist at the level of presuppositions.

Sociologists are good at calling on others to recognize their presuppositions. Presuppositions are important, we tell them, because our presuppositions underlie and shape everything we do. Presuppositions determine what we think about our country and ourselves. They underlie and shape what we think is normal or deviant. Presuppositions shape how we think about criminality and poverty and religion.

Presuppositions are thus crucial to our current behavior and to the most radical changes we can make for the better – in ourselves, in our society, in the world. The word *radical* comes from the Latin, meaning root. So a radical shift or change is one that begins at the roots.

1

A radical change is thus deeper, more thoroughgoing than one that affects life only farther up the stem. And under the surface, the roots of our thinking are our presuppositions.

So we sociologists urge others to examine their presuppositions. We call this activity critical thinking, and when accrediting agencies come by to ask what it is we do and what value we offer society, it is the development of critical thinking we often tell them we provide. And in truth, we do get our students to think critically about their lives.

Critical thinking is a form of reflexivity, of thinking about ourselves. As sociologists, we assuredly do reflect on our collective lives more than most people. Reflection on our collective lives is our profession. What we do not do much of is critical reflection on our critical reflection. If that was one critical reflection too many, let me put it another way. For all our talk about critical thinking, we sociologists as a body do not tend to think very critically about our practice of sociology.

Admittedly, there is some, scattered, reflection on our discipline. There have been calls now for a "historical turn" to sociology, and historically framed pieces now show up in our top journals. Likewise, we now see isolated calls for newer thinking on causality or structure.[1] Such reflection, however, remains scattered and desultory.[2]

In the main, we rather repress critical reflection on sociology. It is a feature that distinguishes American sociology from, say, British. Think of the status that theory holds as a sub-discipline within American sociology. It is not one of the areas for which one sees many calls in the employment bulletin. The general assumption is that theory requires no specialized knowledge and that just about anyone can teach it.

That assumption, which itself is a disciplinary presupposition, follows from the function we expect theory to serve in the discipline.

---

[1] See, for example, Charles Tilly (2007) "Three Visions of History," *History and Theory* 46: 299–307; David Diehl and Daniel McFarland (2010) "Toward a Historical Sociology of Historical Situations," *American Journal of Sociology* 115 (6): 1713–1752; and Andrew Gelman (2011) "Causality and Statistical Learning," *American Journal of Sociology* 117 (3): 955–966. Likewise, see the 1998 "Symposium on Historical Sociology and Rational Choice Theory" in *American Journal of Sociology* 104 (3).

[2] See George Steinmetz (2005) *The Politics of Method in the Human Sciences: Positivism and Its Epistemological Others (Politics, History, and Culture)* (Durham, NC: Duke University Press). Steinmetz makes the further point that at the top departments in the discipline, positivist assumptions go largely unquestioned.

We run our doctoral students through one or two courses in socio-logical theory to ensure they are grounded in the work of the three major founders of sociology – Karl Marx, Emile Durkheim, and Max Weber – and to ensure that they are sufficiently familiar with the different paradigms current in sociology that they will be able to pick the one in which they will be most comfortable working.

Quickly, though, students are urged to leave behind the big questions that divide the paradigms and settle on some concrete, empirical project within one. In other words, students are urged in the direction of what Thomas Kuhn called *normal science*.[3] Normal science is science within a paradigm. Such science does not question the para-digm's basic premises – or if you will, its presuppositions. On the contrary, normal science is devoted to what Kuhn called *puzzle solving*. In normal science, the paradigmatic presuppositions are taken for granted and deployed to explain within their terms why something happens or is what it is. To the extent that the explanation is success-ful, then from the paradigm's perspective the puzzle has been solved. It is then onto the next puzzle.

Is that not what scientists are supposed to do and is sociology not supposed to be a science? There are a number of presuppositions in these questions that themselves generally go unquestioned in sociology. Coming from those so insistent on critical thought, the twin "suppo-seds" are particularly ironic. Who says that normal science is what scientists are supposed to do? Well, of course, Kuhn for one, but does sociology take its marching orders from Kuhn?

Interestingly, Kuhn himself did not say scientists necessarily should pursue normal science or pursue it exclusively. He said that in mature sciences, normal science is what scientists typically do. What did Kuhn consider to be a mature science? One where after considerable, pre-scientific debate, a single paradigm has won out over all others. That paradigm thus becomes the established way of approaching things in that science. The paradigm is the established way of approaching things because the scientists in that discipline have managed to reach consen-sus – at least for the time being – on fundamental reality in their field.

Kuhn's prime model of a mature science was physics and, as is well known, it was a social physics that was Auguste Comte's aspiration for

[3] Thomas Kuhn (2012) *The Structure of Scientific Revolutions* (Chicago, IL: University of Chicago Press).

sociology. Technically, however, in Kuhnian terms, physics might not be so mature after all. Physics, it turns out, is not governed by a single overarching paradigm but by two: Einstein's theory of relativity and quantum mechanics. One governs the physics of the large and very fast and one governs the physics of the very small.

Each of these paradigms, physicists tell us, is very highly corroborated. Neither has failed any empirical test to which it has ever been submitted. The credentials of these paradigms are thus enviably strong. Certainly, we have nothing like them in sociology and, likely, never will.[4]

Still, physicists know there is something wrong with each of these two governing paradigms. How do they know? Because, for one thing, the two paradigms are conceptually incompatible with each other. Thus, as currently formulated, at least one must be wrong. Physicists strongly suspect the problem lies with both.

Now, if physicists were sociologists, they would receive something like the following counsel: We are scientists, not philosophers. Don't spend too much time worrying about conceptual issues, and, for the love of God, please don't distract yourselves with endless debate over them. Doing so holds us up from our real job. Which is? Normal science: processing data. Thus, just settle on one of these two paradigms and get onto productive work.

Is physics following such advice? Well, certainly, most physicists do go on with normal science within one of the two paradigms, and I am hardly disparaging normal science as an activity. Scientific paradigms avail nothing if they are not applied to concrete questions in the form of normal science.

But where paradigms are incompatible, some very big questions – in fact, the biggest questions – remain. And physicists do not ignore them. In fact, in physics the biggest questions, the theoretical questions, attract the biggest names: Stephen Hawking, Stephen Weinberg, Brian Greene, Paul Steinhardt, and so on. So-called *theories of everything* (TOES) are, among other things, ways of reconciling relativity and quantum mechanics.

---

[4] Although I would argue that what philosophers of mind call "folk psychology" is every bit as predictive and successful. See Ian Ravenscroft (2010) "Folk Psychology as a Theory," *Stanford Encyclopedia of Philosophy Online.* http://plato.stanford.edu/entries/folkpsych-theory/.

Interestingly, at the edges of physics, where physicists debate matters like string theory or cosmic inflation or even multiple universes, theoretical development exceeds knock-down empirical evidence or even any current empirical evidence at all. At that point, physics finds itself in the position of sociology, where theory is largely underdetermined by data and where all physicists have is inference to the best explanation. Some physicists decry theorizing in this situation and call for a return to considering only those questions that data can answer.[5] Still, the theorizing at the edges goes on, and it goes on a lot. It is where the big questions lie.

Let us now return to sociology. Our field is much farther than is physics from any consensus on paradigms. Whereas physics has only two governing paradigms, both very successful, we have many, none of which can be described as very successful. Some cannot even be described as good.

If big questions about paradigm choice remain in physics, many more remain in sociology. In fact, in contrast with physics, sociology cannot at all be described as a mature science. In Kuhnian terms, sociology is not even a science. It is instead what Kuhn called pre-science. The appropriate activity in pre-science, Kuhn suggested, was not normal science but continued work toward paradigmatic consensus.

American sociologists do not want to work toward paradigmatic consensus. That prospect sounds too much like endless debate. It sounds too much like philosophy. It does not sound like science. American sociologists want to do normal science.

So what do we do? We christen ourselves a *multiple paradigm science*.[6] And voilà! With that designation, all our problems appear to disappear. We have no need to arrive at consensus, no need to address those big questions that divide us. We can each do normal science within our own chosen paradigm. All that is further necessary is to erect a mutual non-aggression pact. We will not attack anyone else's silly paradigmatic presuppositions if they will not attack ours.

---

[5] John Horgan (1997) *The End of Science: Facing the Limits of Knowledge in the Twilight of the Scientific Age* (New York: Broadway Books).
[6] George Ritzer (1975) *Sociology: A Multiple Paradigm Science* (New York: Allyn & Bacon). Ritzer himself, it must be said, at least tried to make the case for meta-theorizing. That case was much less well received than his designation of the discipline.

None of us need reflect on our presuppositions. Doing so would not be normal science. Doing so would not be science.

If we were social constructionists studying sociology as a tribe, we would know what to do. We would notice how the tribe constructs itself as a science by barring certain kinds of questions and by *othering* certain outsiders like psychologists and philosophers.[7] But then social constructionists rarely turn social constructionism on themselves. Doing so would raise all kinds of embarrassing questions: Are social constructionists' constructions just social constructions? If so, what epistemic weight do sociological constructions bear that warrants anyone's heeding them? Generally, social constructionists, too, do not want to consider such philosophical questions but rather pursue their own brand of normal science within their own paradigm.[8]

I began this book with two questions: What is CR and who needs it? From there, I went on to speak of sociology's presuppositions and of its reluctance to confront them. My point was that sociology does have underlying presuppositions that shape what we do.

Basically, the sum total of our presuppositions about science constitute a philosophy of science. And CR is a philosophy of science. That is what CR is. As such, CR is not a theory that directly explains anything, but a metatheory that establishes the boundaries between good and bad theorizing. It does so by advancing basic ontological and epistemological assumptions.

---

[7] Philosophers generally repay the compliment. Although the philosophy of science is a very important area of disciplinary philosophy, philosophy of social science is not. When disciplinary philosophers think of science, they think characteristically of physics, particularly in the philosophy of mind, which charmingly refers to all else, including sociology, as "special sciences," meaning fated ultimately for reduction to physics. For a critique of this orientation in the philosophy of mind, see Steven Horst (1996) *Symbols, Computation, and Intentionality: A Critique of the Computational Theory of Mind* (Berkeley, CA: University of California Press). For a notable exception in the philosophy of science, see Daniel Little's (2012) *Varieties of Social Explanation*, Amazon Digital Services. It is a book with which I often disagree but which shares with the present volume a similar (although less confrontational) sensibility and coverage of topics.

[8] The most reflective practitioners of the approach recognize the problem. See the debate on this point that pitted Steve Woolgar against Harry Collins and Steven Yearley in Andrew Pickering (ed.) (1992) *Science as Practice and Culture* (Chicago, IL: University of Chicago Press).

Do we need a philosophy of science or metatheory? Well, yes. The fact is you already have one. The question is whether you have the right one.

In Chapter 7, we will talk more about philosophies of science, finally putting together everything we discuss. There, we will exhaustively compare and contrast CR with other philosophical presuppositions on offer:

- positivism;
- postmodernism, poststructuralism, and discourse theory;
- social constructionism;
- analytical sociology;
- pragmatism;
- Marxism/Frankfurt School;
- symbolic interactionism and Verstehen sociology;
- actor–network theory (ANT);
- practice theory;
- relational sociology; and
- Bourdieusian thought.

We will end up with a chart, marking all the different positions of each perspective on a range of important questions. Here, let it suffice for me to say a few things. First, why do I say you already have a philosophy of science? Well, look at what I said a philosophy of science is: a body of presuppositions about science. Certainly, if you are practicing science, your activity rests on some presuppositions about what you are doing. Ipso facto, you are operating with a philosophy of science.

Second, as indicated above, prevailing in sociology is not one, but multiple different philosophies of science. In fact, as suggested, many of the different sociological paradigms listed come with their own philosophy of science. These philosophical or metatheoretical differences are what make inter-paradigm dialogue and adjudication so difficult. Our disputes concern not only the data but which data, what to do with them, and what to make of them. Many of our sociological paradigms differ in all these regards.

Historically and still today, the philosophy of science dominant in sociology has been positivism. Many sociologists today do not consider themselves positivists because they do not believe in running statistical regressions mindlessly, but no positivist ever really believed in doing that. The truth is that positivism is the philosophy of science behind empiricism, and most sociologists today remain empiricists in deep ways they do not even realize. Positivism is a philosophy of science for those who do not want to think about philosophy, and not wanting to think about philosophy is a salient characteristic of empiricism.[9]

As the term positivism or positive philosophy was coined by our own Auguste Comte, this philosophy of science aligns closely with sociology's founding myth. The founding myth is Comte's *Law of Three Stages*.

The *Law of three Stages* is a putative law about history, according to which human collective consciousness advanced in three stages. The first stage was religious consciousness, in which human beings derived their truths, their sense of reality from religion and religious authority. Stage two was the stage of speculative philosophy. It was a stage in which religion and other verities were challenged on philosophical grounds. As critique was prominent in this stage, there was a certain negative aspect to collective thought. The French *philosophes*, for example, were always coming down on this or that human practice or belief system.[10]

The modern period began, according to Comte, with a new, more positive way of thinking. That way was science. Whereas in the second stage of human consciousness, people thought through matters conceptually, in this new third stage, empirical inquiry becomes paramount. The search now was for the actual laws through which all of reality operates, and that search had to be empirical, that is, based on observation.

It was not just the laws governing nature that were to be empirically uncovered. For Comte in particular, it was also the laws of society and human behavior that the third stage of human thought was after. Hence, Comte's vision of sociology as social physics. Just as physicists were to find the laws of nature, sociologists were to find the laws of society.

---

[9] According to Steinmetz, *The Politics of Method*, at the top departments many positivist sociologists have actually adopted different ways of disguising their own positivism from themselves.

[10] See Irving Zeitlin (2009) *Ideology and the Development of Sociological Theory* (New York: Prentice Hall).

What was the point of all this law-finding? The answer comes in Comte's famous quip: Explanation in order to predict; prediction in order to control. In other words, empirical work (i.e., observation) was necessary to find the laws operating in a domain, say society. Laws, in turn, were necessary for explanation (a premise that CR in particular will strongly contest). And finally, the point of explanation was the ability to predict and control.

Prediction and control were in turn important because the ultimate point was to fix society for the better. Hence the positive element in positivism, the element of scientific optimism. Sociology was to be in the service of social progress, and the inevitability of progress was part and parcel of sociology's founding myth.

I use the word myth here in the way it is often used by religion scholars – not to designate a belief that is necessarily mistaken but a belief filled with larger significance for some group, a belief that tells the group members who they are, where they came from, and where they are going. The postmodernists – when they were still around – referred to these founding beliefs or myths as *meta-narratives*.[11]

A group's meta-narrative may well be historically false. I don't think, for example, that Rome really was founded by a pair of twins raised by wolves. At the same time, a group's founding myth or meta-narrative need not be false. Whether or not myths are false needs to be examined case by case. For all the criticism associated with Comte's sentiments, especially the connotations that prediction and control carry of failed social engineering, I do think there is something right about it. We do want to understand how the social world works and in part we want to do so in order to create a better world. Why else are we in this field? For all the criticism lodged against it, I also think something remains of the idea of human progress.

So I am not totally dismissive at least of the sentiment behind the positivist philosophy of science. It should be acknowledged, furthermore, that positivism has never been owned solely by sociology. On the contrary, Comte and Durkheim after him were part of a wider intellectual wave. For a long time – up, basically, through Kuhn in the late 1960s, positivism was the single, paradigmatic way of

[11] Jean-François Lyotard (1984) *The Postmodern Condition: A Report on Knowledge* (Minneapolis, MN: University of Minnesota Press). Now, everyone claims never to have been a postmodernist, just a poststructuralist. The postmodernist phase must have been a collective dream.

understanding science philosophically, so that anyone doing science in any field understood what he or she was doing in positivist terms. Sociology in fact is now much less positivist than economics and psychology, which even more stubbornly refuse to look at their founding presuppositions.[12]

There is also more to positivism than I have so far identified and developed. And, here, I do want to switch to a more colloquial understanding of the word myth, that is, myth as a false idea. After Kuhn and the post-positivist thought that ensued in the philosophy of science, we now know – to the extent that we know anything – that many of the tenets of positivism are wrong. Empirically and conceptually, they are untenable.

The problem is that various of those false positivist tenets live on comfortably in sociology as myths – strongly felt but demonstrably wrong ideas. What is worse, we will see, is that the positivist account of science is accepted even by many who oppose a sociology built on positivist principles. What positivism's sociological opponents often end up opposing is thus not just a faulty account of what it means for sociology to be scientific, but rather all scientific aspirations for sociology. In the process, the anti-positivists – the humanists, the post-Wittgensteinians, the postmodernists, and social constructionists – all end up endorsing counter-myths, strongly felt but equally wrong ideas. The problem is that with an empiricist-inspired, disciplinary repression of philosophy, we do not thoroughly think through these matters. Instead, we go with our instincts. We pick a paradigm in which we feel comfortable and prepare to conduct normal science for the rest of our lives.

The big questions remain unaddressed. In the process, the worst thing is, as Christian Smith points out, that sociology comes out with images of ourselves that we know cannot be true, images that we ourselves hardly carry with us into ordinary life, images of ourselves as structurally or culturally determined automata or as deconstructed congeries of subject positions. Like the economists with their fabled *homo economicus*, we are often content with the pretend people our theories offer instead of the real persons that as non-professionals we know we are.[13]

---

[12] See Steinmetz, *The Politics of Method.*
[13] Christian Smith (2011) *What Is a Person? Rethinking Humanity, Social Life, and the Moral Good from the Ground Up* (Chicago, IL: University of Chicago Press).

There is a problem here to which we ought to attend. Insofar as the problem arises with our basic philosophies of science, it is to the root of things we must go. The solution accordingly must be radical. In this book, CR will be offered as that radical solution, the most comprehensive – and tenable – philosophy of science for sociology.

In the remainder of this introduction, however, we will canvass the more surface problems caused by faulty philosophies of science, problems that CR is best able to address. Those problems surface as myths, myths again in the colloquial meaning of false beliefs. These false beliefs in sociology are propagated either by a positivist philosophy of science or by counter-philosophies of science that over-react to it, usually by sharing some of positivism's basic mistakes. Although the specific myths enumerated are somewhat arbitrarily identified, the terrain they mark out is not. It is not only critical realists who disbelieve some of these myths, but it is largely CR that as a coherent philosophy of science comprehensively disbelieves all.

Seven myths of American sociology

Myth 1: Ethnography and historical narrative too are only exploratory or descriptive. They are not explanatory. One of the ironies of American sociology is its ambivalence about ethnography. Ethnographies number among our favorite books and are certainly the favorites among our students. Ethnographies are also the books that most gain sociology its popular audience. Nevertheless, many counsel their graduate students against ethnographic study. Although today ethnography is becoming hotter, it continues to be disparaged, so much so that the ethnographers among us ended up forming their own subculture. So arises one line of fragmentation within our discipline.

If ethnography is still not entirely embraced by the discipline, it is because ethnography is considered less than scientific. Interestingly, ethnographers themselves often share this same assessment, viewing their craft more as an art than a science – as if the two were so easily distinguished – and what they produce as only description.

It follows that when ethnography is undertaken within our discipline, there is often a felt need to defend it as exploratory or by idiosyncratic appeals to "grounded theory."[14] The basis of the disparagement is the covering law model of causality, which identifies causality with the operation of universal laws. If laws must be universal, then they must hold generally over some domain of phenomena. If causality requires generality, then we need more than a single case. We need, in particular, some kind of statistical analysis. Hence the disposition in the discipline toward quantitative methods, what Herbert Blumer called *variable analysis*, the reduction of everything to covariation.[15]

Variable analysis is *nomothetic* or lawlike, and causal explanation in such terms is often called nomothetic-deductive. The alternative – explanation that makes no appeal to general laws but only to the particularities of a specific case – is called *idiographic*. Considered merely descriptive rather than explanatory in any causal sense, idiographic explanation includes both ethnographic analysis and historical narrative.

The fact is, however, that the non-causal nature of the idiographic is a myth. It relies, as I said, on the covering law model of causal explanation, and that model is simply and clearly untenable. It is untenable not just in the social domain, but actually in the physical domain as well.[16]

Critical realists are not the only ones to oppose the covering law model, but we are the ones who have given it the most sustained critique.[17] A clear demolition of the covering law model will occupy

[14] For the original, see Barney Glaser (1967) *The Discovery of Grounded Theory: Strategies for Qualitative Research* (Piscataway, NJ: Transaction). Grounded theory has subsequently become much more sophisticated. See Kathy Charmaz (2006) *Constructing Grounded Theory: A Practical Guide to Qualitative Analysis* (Thousand Oaks, CA: Sage).

[15] Herbert Blumer (1956) "Sociological Analysis and the Variable," *American Sociological Review* 21 (6): 683–690. Iddo Tavory and Stephen Timmermans helpfully make a case for how ethnography can be explanatory. Although they do not mention CR, their embrace of a mechanism's account of causality moves in a similar direction. They root themselves in pragmatism but, again, helpfully declaim pragmatism's overemphasis on habit. From a CR perspective, however, they remain too tied to a regularity view of the operation of causal mechanisms. See Iddo Tavory and Stephen Timmermans (2013) "A Pragmatist Approach to Causality in Ethnography," *American Journal of Sociology* 119 (3): 682–714.

[16] Nancy Cartwright (1983) *How the Laws of Physics Lie* (New York: Oxford).

[17] See Roy Bhaskar (2008) *A Realist Theory of Science* (New York: Routledge); Rom Harré and Edward Madden (1975) *Causal Powers: Theory of Natural Necessity* (New York: Blackwell); and Douglas Porpora (1983) "On the Prospects for a Nomothetic Theory of Social Structure," *Journal for the Theory of Social Behaviour* 13: 243–264. Most recently, see Philip Gorski (2004) "The Poverty of Deductivism: A Constructive Realist Model of Sociological Explanation," *Sociological Methodology* 34 (1): 1–33.

us in the first part of Chapter 2. From there, Chapter 2 will proceed to the alternative CR model of causality, which, like ANT, takes causal agency out of laws and puts it back into the things of the world. (Of course, CR will differ in important ways from ANT as well.)[18]

We already know in our hearts that the covering law model is a fake. It requires deterministic laws that are nowhere on offer, most notably in the social domain. There, we say, we are after something less binding than deterministic laws. We seek, we say, merely statistical laws. But, actually, as we will see in Chapter 2, we likewise don't have any of those. Instead, we are always just on the road to finding them.

As we will see, that road will never end because the needed statistical laws are not there to be found. Their existence is a myth. It is a myth we embrace because of our faith commitment to a positivist conception of science.

This faith commitment is a peculiar one. It leads us to declare of the entire volume of Immanuel Wallerstein's *The Modern World System* that it is just a description. It must be just a description because in the end, what does it offer? An N of one! Where are the laws? Where the hypotheses?[19]

There is a problem here, but it is not with *The Modern World System*. The problem resides with an understanding of causality that sees no explanation in that great work and that fragments the discipline into the variable analysts, the ethnographers, and now the historians. It is an understanding of causality we need to overcome.[20]

---

[18] For a recent treatment of CR causality, see Philip Gorski (2009) "Social 'Mechanisms' and Comparative Historical Sociology: A Critical Realist Proposal," pp. 147–196 in Peter Hedstrom and Born Wittrock (eds.), *Frontiers of Sociology* (Boston, MA: Brill).

[19] See discussion by Roland Wulbert (1975) "Had by the Positive Integers," *American Sociologist* 10 (4): 242–243. In his introduction to *The Modern World System*, Wallerstein himself feels bound to counter the same concern, suggesting that perhaps we might think of world systems as a variable applying to different planets. The oddity of the argument is symptomatic of our causal confusion. See Wallerstein (2011) *The Modern World System: Capitalist Agriculture and the Origins of the European World Economy in the Sixteenth Century* (Berkeley, CA: University of California).

[20] Many sociologists today think they have abandoned the covering law view by adopting a counterfactual account, as developed, for example, by Woodward. See James Woodward (2005) *Making Things Happen: A Theory of Causal Explanation* (New York: Oxford). We will revisit the point in Chapter 2.

Myth 2: The appropriate posture in scientific social research is value neutrality. We still think this way in the twenty-first century? Yes; although there have been continuous calls against this posture, its advocacy remains strong in the discipline.[21]

I have a personal story in this connection. A colleague and I wrote an article, since reprinted in the *Handbook on War and Society* edited by Morton Ender and Steve Carlton-Ford. The article was titled "Talking War: How Elite U.S. Newspaper Op-Eds Debated the Attack on Iraq." Before the piece was accepted for the special issue of *Sociological Focus* in which it was originally published, one reviewer chastised my co-author and me for using the word "Attack" in our title. It was, this reviewer maintained, pejorative.

I actually did not think the word attack was pejorative, but suppose it was? If not attack, what had the United States done? The reviewer counseled a more neutral designation for our visit to Iraq. The reviewer suggested "Operation Iraqi Freedom."

You see the point. Maybe not. The point is not that the reviewer also failed at finding an objective description of what happened. Nor actually is the point that there is no objective description.

What there is not is a value-free description. Owing again to our positivist legacy, we tend to confuse objectivity with neutrality. The equation of objectivity with neutrality is another myth. To see the point another way, consider a counter-example cited by Roy Bhaskar.[22] Which of the following is the most objective statement about the Holocaust:

(1) In World War II, six million Jews lost their lives.
(2) In World War II, six million Jews were killed.
(3) In World War II, six million Jews were systematically murdered.

---

[21] The classic attacks in sociology of course are Robert Lynd (1939) *Knowledge for What? The Place of Social Science in American Culture* (Princeton, NJ: Princeton University Press); and Alvin Gouldner (1961) "Anti-Minotaur: The Myth of a Value-Free Sociology," *Social Problems* 9 (2): 199–213. The more recent literature includes Andrew Collier (2007) *In Defense of Objectivity* (New York: Routledge); Hugh Lacey (1999) *Is Science Value-Free? Values and Scientific Understanding* (New York: Routledge); Hilary Putnam (2002) *The Collapse of the Fact/Value Dichotomy* (Cambridge, MA: Harvard University Press); and Harold Kincaid, John Dupré, and Alison Wylie (eds.) (2007) *Value-Free Science? Ideals and Illusions* (New York: Oxford).

[22] See Roy Bhaskar (1998) *The Possibility of Naturalism: A Philosophical Critique of the Contemporary Human Sciences* (New York: Routledge).

Ask this question of your undergraduate students. Ask it of almost anyone, and you will get a surprise. Many respondents will insist the correct answer is (1).

Why? People choose (1) because they mistakenly equate objectivity with neutrality and with the absence of moral evaluation, assuming the latter signifies something subjective, entirely in our head and not inherent in the object of evaluation itself.

Surely, however, it is statement (3), the least neutral of the three, that is most true and most objective. As Andrew Collier argues, to be objective is not to be neutral but true to the object of consideration.[23] When the object of consideration is the Holocaust, the truest account is that six million Jews were systematically murdered. The two more neutral accounts are not objective. Instead, their posture of neutrality actually misleads us about what happened. They convey impressions short of the full truth. Did six million Jews just die? Of what, car accidents? In their sleep? Nor is it enough even to say they were killed. They did not, after all, die in battle. They were murdered and murdered systematically. Here, it is neutrality rather than partisanship that distorts.

There is then no escape from value judgment. Neutrality, too, is a value judgment and not always the most objective one. Sometimes, as above, it is neutrality that represents bias.

An absolute fact-value distinction is a myth. In truth, many of our descriptive terms – like murder, rape, and genocide – have values already built into them.[24] It is silly to pretend otherwise, to say, for example, Seinfeld-fashion that, yes, I study genocide – not that there is anything wrong with that. Even worse is to use other descriptors so that it no longer is evident what you are even talking about or what moral significance it holds.

Instead, we need to come clean and admit that in many cases we are dealing with thick descriptions and moral facts, hybrids of fact and value. What we are examining may be something that is highly value-laden, like rape, but whether or not it occurred on any given occasion is an empirical matter.[25] We need a philosophy of science that helps us better navigate this terrain. We need CR.

---

[23] Collier, *In Defense of Objectivity*.

[24] See Kwame Anthony Appiah (2010) *Experiments in Ethics* (Cambridge, MA: Harvard University Press).

[25] John Searle refers to such phenomena as "institutional facts." See Searle (1995) *The Construction of Social Reality* (New York: Free Press).

Myth 3: There is no truth. Everything is socially constructed. All is relative. This myth represents the interpretivist or postmodernist overreaction to the previous myth. In Chapter 3, I will argue that at least one pragmatist position on truth is likewise problematic.

I say that this myth is an overreaction to the previous one. The logic here is that if facts and values cannot be separated, then nothing is fully objective. It must then follow that all judgments are ultimately subjective. Since we are sociologists, we tie that subjectivity to the social and declare everything – everything! – a social construction. That determination in turn implies that there is no such thing as absolute truth. Instead, all judgments are relative to the culture in which they are made. This doctrine we then teach to our students in an effort to make them more tolerant. We must not say anyone is wrong. That would be intolerant. It would be totalizing. We thus arrive at the mythology of multicultural postmodernism.

There are multiple confusions here, which we will unpack more fully in Chapter 3. For now, let us focus on one: confusion over ontology and epistemology. Confusion over ontology and epistemology sets in when we inquire about something's objectivity.

The problem is that objectivity plays a role in both ontology and epistemology. When we ask about something's ontological objectivity, we are asking about its existence independent of us. Are there, as Marx and even Bourdieu (sometimes) proposes, objective social structures that exist independent of our consciousness? No, a favored answer is today, because there is nothing objective.

That response, however, confuses epistemological and ontological objectivity. The lack of epistemological objectivity does not preclude ontological objectivity. We may not be able to know anything in a value- or theory-neutral way, but it hardly follows that there is nothing ontologically objective to be known. We may understand global warming only via our own concepts, but, surely, if it is happening, global warming is an ontologically objective fact independent of how or even if we conceptualize it. Our understanding may be socially constructed but not the ontological reality itself. If it is really happening, global warming will not cease by our merely ceasing to think about it. The same I will argue for social structure.

Confusing the two senses of objectivity, the reduction of all questions of being to questions of knowledge, is to commit what CR calls the *epistemic fallacy*.[26] The fallacy is a hallmark of positivism. We thus find a glaring example of the epistemic fallacy in earlier editions of Earl Babbie's effective but positivist text on research methods. Assign it to your class (as I do regularly), and Babbie earlier would have informed your students that there actually is no such thing as prejudice. There are such things as nasty remarks about minority groups, thinking women should stay in their place, and so on. We can observe all those phenomena. Conversely, we cannot observe prejudice. So it does not exist. In his companion volume for students in communication, he similarly told them that love does not exist.[27]

Of course, on this reasoning, causality does not exist either, and it then becomes rather a mystery why such observables as holding hands, kissing and so forth all tend to co-occur. Missing from Babbie's argument is CR's *causal criterion of existence*. According to the causal criterion, if something has observable effects, then it exists, whether we can observe it directly or not. With the causal criterion, ontology reasserts itself against epistemology.[28]

Now, by the 14th edition of *The Practice of Social Research*, Babbie has discovered CR and the objection. Now, he writes, "critical realism suggests that we define 'reality' as that which can be seen to have an effect. Since prejudice clearly has an observable effect on our lives, it must be real according to this point of view."[29] Not quite a ringing endorsement and the last we hear from Babbie about CR, but it is something.

The epistemic fallacy has multiple manifestations, but in all cases questions of being are reduced to questions of knowledge. Thus, as noted, the poststructuralist line takes the same positivist reasoning in a different direction. If there is no epistemically objective way to determine what exists, the poststructuralist conclusion is that nothing possesses ontologically objective existence, that there is no world separate from human conceptualization. And since human conceptions differ

---

[26] See Roy Bhaskar (2009) *Scientific Realism and Human Emancipation* (New York: Routledge).

[27] Earl Babbie (2011) *The Practice of Social Research* (Independence, KY: Wadsworth), p. 125. The companion volume for communication is Leslie A. Baxter and Earl Babbie (2003) *The Basics of Communication Research* (Independence, KY: Wadsworth).

[28] Bhaskar, *The Possibility of Naturalism*, p. 13.

[29] Earl Babbie (2013) *The Practice of Social Research* (Belmont, CA: Wadsworth), p. 42.

from culture to culture, we must say that each constructs its own truth
and its own reality. Truth, then, and reality, to the extent that we keep
these concepts at all, become relative.[30]

CR refuses this relativist understanding of truth for, in the end, it is
incoherent, i.e., self-contradictory. Actually, it is not only incoherent
but also detrimental to the critical stance in the service of which it is
often invoked.

To illustrate, I have another story. As I work on political communication, I frequently attend meetings of communication associations.
On one such occasion, I was attending a session on bias. It seemed to
me that the speakers were evaluating bias just in terms of comparative
representation in the press.

I, however, thought in terms of the considerations about value neutrality we discussed in relation to Myth 2. As in the example above about
the Holocaust, I reasoned that some perspectives might receive more
hearing not because of bias but because they are in fact more cogent.
So, during the question period, I said I thought it difficult to make
assessments of bias without some corresponding judgment about what
is objectively true.[31]

Immediately, a woman a few rows ahead of me turned around to
assert indignantly that truth is a classification that has been used
historically to subjugate women, people of color, and all others whose
cause we social scientists would normally champion.

---

[30] At points Bourdieu seems to say the same thing. See, for example, Pierre
Bourdieu and Loïc Wacquant (1992) *An Invitation to Reflexive Sociology*
(Chicago, IL: University of Chicago Press), pp. 20–21. Whereas Reflexive
Sociology nevertheless resists relativism (see pp. 47–48), its grounds for doing so
are not well articulated. Because, as Wacquant suggests, Reflexive Sociology is
more a posture and method in practice than a theoretical system, inconsistencies
and incoherencies remain. In spirit, Reflexive Sociology shares much with CR,
and CR could actually help make a number of Reflexive Sociology's
commitments stronger. Although, for example, Bourdieu accuses other anti-
positivist approaches of retaining elements of positivism (see Bourdieu and
Wacquant above, p. 73), Bourdieu himself retains some traces of positivism
himself. A stronger statement of his position would jettison them.

[31] As it turns out, others in communication share my reservation. See, for example,
the series of papers by David Niven (2004) "A Fair Test of Media Bias: Party,
Race, and Gender in Coverage of the 1992 House Banking Scandal," *Polity* 36
(4): 637–650; (2003) "Objective Evidence on Media Bias: Newspaper Coverage
of Professional Party Switchers," *Journalism and Mass Communication
Quarterly* 80 (2): 311–326; and (1999) "Partisan Bias in the Media? A New
Test" *Social Science Quarterly* 80 (4): 847–857.

I looked back at her and retorted, "That's true."

Well, okay, I actually did not make that retort. Not truly. I thought it but reasoned that I was deep in enemy territory and had exhausted my license to speak.

I do think what the woman said about truth is true, but what of it? Our conclusion certainly cannot be that we can dispense with the concept of truth. The woman's point on behalf of the oppressed carries moral weight only to the extent that it is true. Nor is that all. As Jürgen Habermas has pointed out, assertions like the woman's carry implicit validity claims. We take the woman to be saying *sincerely* that the concept of truth has *truly* been used in the ways she says. If we do not take the woman to be asserting a truth about the way truth has been used ("It is true that truth has been used historically..."), her utterance is entirely unintelligible.

The denial of truth is what both Jürgen Habermas and CR, both following Karl Apel, call a *performative contradiction*.[32] As in the case of the woman's comment above, the denial of truth is not a speech act that can be coherently performed. The reason is that the very intelligibility of the denial rests on an appeal to the concept of truth denied.

What sociology does need – and badly – is a tenable understanding of truth.[33] The problem is that both positivists and anti-positivists (including even Habermas) have understood truth epistemically, equating it with a foundational knowledge process that yields certainty. To the extent that positivists believe *mistakenly* that an epistemically *foundational* road to certainty is possible, so too do they believe, as it turns out *correctly*, that we can arrive at truth. For their part, anti-positivist postmodernists believed *correctly* that epistemic foundationalism fails. Their mistake was to conclude *mistakenly* that this failure implies the inaccessibility of reality and of anything we can call truth.

The way out of the impasse is to jettison the entire epistemic account of truth, shared by both positivists and anti-positivists, and to adopt in its place an *alethic* account that is more ontological. As we will see in Chapter 3, the ontological direction is the way followed by CR.

---

[32] Karl Otto Apel (2003) *The Response of Discourse Ethics to the Moral Challenge of the Human Situation as Such and Especially Today* (Belgium: Peeters), p. 43.

[33] Again, a commitment to some non-relativist notion of truth is one that Bourdieu seems to share, but sharing it and philosophically grounding it are two different things. See Bourdieu and Wacquant, *An Invitation to Reflexive Sociology*, pp. 47–48.

Sociologists like to speak about theoretical turns. Thus, in social theory, we have had the so-called "linguistic turn," the "rhetorical turn," the "cultural turn," the "historical turn" and now most recently the "practice turn."[34] In such terms, we might think of CR as representing an *ontological turn*.[35]

Myth 4: The most important scientific questions are empirical. Empirical questions are questions that require observation to answer. What is the distribution of wealth in the United States? Do religious people tend to be politically conservative? Does poverty lead to crime? These questions are all empirical. To answer them, we must observe. We must collect quantitative or qualitative data and analyze them.

Sociologists, particularly American sociologists, like empirical questions. They differentiate us from philosophers. Philosophers just sit on their butts and think. We are scientists. We get up, go outdoors, and look. This vigorous, macho image appeals to our Protestant work ethic and mantles us with scientific authority. We like that.

We like it too much. Our impatience with and disparagement of conceptual questions and conceptual work is exactly what makes us empiricists. The posture goes back to Comte, and it is a mistake. A deeply consequential mistake.

Conceptual questions are questions that take reason or logic to answer. Although reference to empirical cases is always necessary too, resolving conceptual questions does not require the collection of yet more data. Required instead is the analysis of ideas. Conceptual questions concern the meaning of what we are talking about.

Although American sociology privileges empirical questions, the fact is that conceptual matters are prior and more important. For sociologists – or at least American sociologists – this heretical declaration may be the most disturbing thing I have said so far. Implied is a need to change the whole balance of discussion in sociology. That sounds drastic. And yet it is true.

---

[34] Theodore Shatzki, Karin Knorr Cetina and Eric von Savigny (eds.) (2001) *The Practice Turn in Contemporary Theory* (New York: Routledge).

[35] See Gorski, "Social 'Mechanisms'." Gorski does not actually use that phrase but aptly identifies ontology as CR's orientation. For emphasis, see George Steinmetz (1998) "Critical Realism and Historical Sociology: A Review Article," *Comparative Studies in Society and History* 40: 170–186, p. 172.

Why do I say that conceptual questions are prior to empirical questions? First, because all empirical questions need to be conceptualized. They rest on conceptual distinctions. Without concepts, we have no questions. Look back at all the empirical questions with which we began this section. Take the second question, for example: Do religious people tend to be more conservative politically? Well, what does it mean to be religious? That question is conceptual rather than empirical. It is not answered by collecting more data. Yet, if we get it wrong, our empirical research goes wrong. Ditto for what it means to be politically conservative. We may successfully collect gobs of data, but if our concepts are awry, our data may be meaningless.

There is a second reason why conceptual questions are more important than empirical questions. This second reason follows from the first. The concepts we use to formulate our empirical questions embody various presuppositions, and, as we have discussed, those presuppositions are themselves open to critique.

Thus, depending on the presuppositions built into our concepts, our empirical research may be dubious from the start. As we will see, such conceptual dubiousness has dogged and continues to dog a good many sociological research programs: functionalism; reductive Marxism; rational choice theory; poststructuralist discourse theory; radical social constructionism; the practice turn, and on and on.

Such dubiousness also characterized the work of Durkheim, sociology's founding figure who most pointed us in the positivist direction. Leave aside for the moment Durkheim's famous second rule of the sociological method: *Explain social facts only in terms of other social facts and not at all in terms of individual consciousness.* Before moving on, however, first ask yourself why we no longer accept this total exclusion of individual agency: Was it because of incoming empirical data or because of new ways of conceptualizing the relation between structure and agency?

Suicide allows us to see the point more quickly. In *Suicide*, Durkheim makes two grave conceptual errors. The first is an error at least from the CR point of view. We will see presently that, on the contrary, Bourdieusian practice perspectives would actually commend Durkheim's lead. As it happens, however, Durkheim's second error cancels it out.

From the CR perspective, the first conceptual mistake Durkheim makes is to reject the conventional definition of suicide as *intentional self-homicide*. We should not define suicide in terms of intention,

Durkheim argues, because (1) intentions are not what cause people's actions, and (2) because even if they were, intentions are too difficult to observe. Thus, Durkheim opts for a theoretical definition of suicide that makes no distinction between intended and unintended death.[36]

Reason 2 for rejecting consideration of actors' intentions is a non-starter. If intentions do cause actors' behavior, then it is no use arguing, as Durkheim does, that intentions are too difficult to find. Then Durkheim would be advising sociology to act like the drunk who looks for his house keys not at the door where he dropped them but under the lamp post on the street because the light there is better. If intentions are causally central to action, then, however difficult to identify, we must try.

And, the fact is, we cannot explain or even identify individual action without appeal to actors' intentions. Post-Wittgensteinians and ethno-methodologists might argue that intentions are not causes, a claim we will contest in Chapter 2, but not even they would say we can dispense with intentions. Quite the opposite. For them, intentions are the very way we identify which act an actor has performed.[37]

With such conceptual confusion, the danger for Durkheim was that even if successful, what he might have ended up explaining empirically was not suicide but a mélange of intended and unintended consequences, not comprising any one action, which we would need to call something different, perhaps *durkicide*.

Fortunately for his project, Durkheim makes a second conceptual mistake that completely cancels out this first one: To study suicide rates, Durkheim relies on official statistics. Now, as we know, that decision introduced famous methodological problems that led Durkheim astray, but what we overlook is how this operationalization also completely corrected for Durkheim's otherwise disastrous theoretical definition. Governments were not using Durkheim's theoretical definition to identify suicide, but rather the conventional definition Durkheim rejected. Thus, fortunately for Durkheim, whatever his methodological mistakes, he was after all telling us about suicide and not some totally bizarre and uninteresting *durkicide*.

[36] Emile Durkheim (1951) *Suicide* (New York: Free Press), p. 43.
[37] See David Rubinstein (1977) "The Concept of Action in Sociology," *Journal for the Theory of Social Behaviour* 7 (2): 209–236; and Alan Blum and Peter McHugh (1971) "The Social Ascription of Motives," *American Journal of Sociology* 36: 98–109.

Conceptual confusion then can completely vitiate all our painstaking empirical research. That danger applies not just to our individual research projects but to entire research programs or paradigms. Thus, conceptual matters assume much greater importance than empiricists acknowledge. In fact, I just before alluded to one important conceptual flaw that, from a CR perspective, undermines the so-called practice perspectives: Their confusion about and consequent denigration of actors' intentions. That issue brings us to our next myth.

Myth 5: Sociology can and should dispense with the Cartesian cogito. The Cartesian cogito refers to the centered consciousness we associate with the ordinary Joe's understanding of human personhood. CR does not accept the radical mind–body dualism of Descartes. Still, with the ordinary Joe, CR stands for human beings as coherent selves, centers of consciousness and feeling, as thou's to whom we must always relate as thou's. In this respect, as Jean Paul Sartre said of existentialism, CR is a humanism.[38]

Louis Althusser, in contrast, declared structuralist Marxism an anti-humanism. Michele Foucault likewise expressly claimed to be following an anti-humanist line. Indeed, French theorists have been trying to kill off centered consciousness since their debates with Sartre and their therapy sessions with Jacques Lacan.[39] Deconstruction and discourse theory have tried to dissolve personhood into language. Thus, instead of coherent persons we are left with subject positions. Margaret Archer will go on to call such moves *upward conflation*, the upward reduction of the person to the social (in contrast with the downward reduction of the person to the biological).[40]

The Bourdieusian perspectives – reflexive sociology, structuration theory, and practice theory – are not anti-humanist in the sense of French poststructuralism, but do sometimes categorize themselves as post-humanist, likewise dismissing the conscious intentionality of the human actor. Practice and *habitus* stand in its place.

---

[38] Jean-Paul Sartre (2007) *Existentialism is a Humanism* (New Brunswick: Yale University Press).

[39] See Mark Poster (1977) *Existential Marxism in Post-War France* (Princeton, NJ: Princeton University Press).

[40] Margaret Archer (1995) *Realist Social Theory: The Morphogenetic Approach* (Cambridge: Cambridge University Press); and, more directly here, (2001) *Being Human: The Problem of Agency* (Cambridge: Cambridge University Press).

Practice and habitus are valuable concepts, but in contemporary sociology they overreach. Humans are more than just performances and practices and their doings frequently entail more than just a "feel for the game." One cannot care for performances and practices and subjectivities. It is for whole persons we seek justice and well-being. As Margaret Archer argues in *Being Human* and Christian Smith in *What is a Person*, we need CR to re-secure the humanism that sociology seems desirous of abandoning.[41]

Myth 6: There is no difference between structure and culture or structure and action. All is practice. This central myth of sociology will occupy us in Chapter 4. It is a very contemporary myth. There was a time in sociology when structure, culture, and action were analytically distinct. Structure and culture particularly were very distinct in 1965 when Daniel Patrick Moynihan, then US Assistant Secretary of Labor, issued his famous report, *The Negro Family*, which blamed urban black poverty on an African-American subculture.

Everyone could agree that racist economic structures had initially given rise to a culture of poverty among urban blacks. What Moynihan argued, along the lines of Oscar Lewis, was that this culture of poverty had become self-perpetuating, so that poverty remained even after the originating racist economic structures had subsequently been removed.

There ensued a historic debate over the comparative influence of culture and structure. In this opposition, culture represented the intersubjective, those things that people mentally share: values, beliefs, and norms or rules. It was the realm of ideas, what today we would call the *discursive*. Structure, particularly in this case the so-called opportunity structure, referred to social relations – objective social relations that were material or independent of people's thoughts. They were what we today would call *extra-discursive*.

The debate went on for a long time. Conservatives and even liberals like Moynihan favored some version of the culture of poverty theory. The voices then considered radical insisted instead on the continuing structural determinants of urban, black poverty. They accused the culture of poverty theory of being one step removed from blaming the victim. Their most compelling study was Elliot Liebow's *Tally's Corner*,

---

[41] Archer, *Realist Social Theory*; *Being Human*. Smith, *What is a Person?*.

which I mention because it was an ethnography and thus illustrates how ethnography can be powerfully explanatory.[42] *Tally's Corner* explained by depicting – or at least by seeming to depict in a compelling way – the underlying structural *mechanism* through which continuing economic disadvantages produced behavior that looked as if it were following subcultural rules and values. As we will see in Chapter 2, in so describing causal mechanisms, ethnography, according to CR, performs a vital scientific task.[43]

The culture of poverty debate abated during the administration of President William Jefferson Clinton, when with welfare reform and economic prosperity the welfare roles actually shrank. Now, after the 2008 financial collapse, poverty rates have again been increasing.

In this present context, culture-of-poverty theory has returned.[44] This time, however, sociology has no robust conception of social structure to counter it.[45]

Where is our conception of social structure? It got eaten by culture. Admittedly, at the time of the Moynihan report, sociology tilted excessively in the direction of social structure. Structural analysis was considered part of what distinguished sociology from anthropology, which did focus on culture. I remember being told in my graduate student days that culture was just a residual category, to be brought in only after structure had explained all it could. The tendency thus was toward *structural reductionism*.

Since then, first with the so-called Cultural Turn, the tendency has reversed. Now structure has disappeared, replaced by *cultural reductionism*. In part, the problem ensued from the confusion over

---

[42] Eliot Liebow (2003) *Tally's Corner: A Study of Negro Streetcorner Men* (New York: Rowman & Littlefield).

[43] As Tavory and Timmermans note, depicting the "unfolding moments of action" particularly as they related to distant causes is something ethnography is singularly capable of doing. See Tavory and Timmermans, "A Pragmatist Approach," p. 683.

[44] See, for example, Patricia Cohen (2010) "'Culture of Poverty' Makes a Comeback" *New York Times*. March 26. www.nytimes.com/2006/03/26/opinion/26patterson.html?pagewanted=all

[45] See the renewed discussion of the culture of poverty debate in the 2010 *Annals of the American Academy of Political and Social Science*, where, seemingly alone, William Julius Wilson struggles to reintroduce the structural contribution to poverty. Wilson (2010) "Why Both Structure and Culture Both Matter to a Holistic Analysis of Poverty," pp. 200–219 in *Annals of the American Academy of Political and Social Science* (Thousand Oaks, CA: Sage).

epistemology and ontology previously noted: If there is no epistemic objectivity, then there is no ontological objectivity either. Thus, there is no extra-discursive social structure, nothing outside of culture – or as Jacques Derrida would put it, "nothing outside the text."

In a highly influential series of works, which represented one Anglophone translation of Bourdieu, Anthony Giddens dismissed social relations as epiphenomena and identified structure with rules and resources. Structure was thereby amalgamated into culture.[46] That move, however, was not enough for the cultural sociologists. In another highly influential work, William Sewell said that in addition to rules, structure also had to include cultural schema.[47] Structure was thus further enveloped within culture.

Of course, culture itself was eventually to be swallowed by practice. For where does culture reside? At one time we would have said in the realm of the inter-subjective, that is in the collective heads of actors. But with actors de-centered, the only place left was their behavior, i.e., their performances or practices.

Whither ontologically objective, extra-discursive social relations? In much of sociology today, they are gone, forgotten along with Marx. Social relations remain, of course, in Relational Sociology; there it is actors that disappear. Social relations also remain in Bourdieu, the contemporary stand-in for Marx, as part of the concept of *field*. Even there, however, as we will see, the presence of any extra-discursive structure is insecure and, in America, ever in danger of complete collapse into habitus and practice. To avoid such collapse, which Archer considers another conflation, we need the metatheoretical underpinnings of CR, for as CR has developed historically, it stands not just for full-bodied agency but also for an analytically distinct, extra-discursive conception of social structure.[48]

---

[46] See, for example, Anthony Giddens (1979) *Central Problems in Social Theory* (Berkeley, CA: University of California Press).

[47] William Sewell (1992) "A Theory of Structure: Duality, Agency, and Transformation," *American Journal of Sociology* 98: 1–29.

[48] See Archer, *Realist Social Theory*. Also see Archer (1982) "Morphogenesis Versus Structuration: On Combining Structure and Action," *British Journal of Sociology* 33 (4): 455–483; and (1988) *Culture and Agency: The Place of Culture in Social Theory* (Cambridge: Cambridge University Press). Likewise, Douglas Porpora (1985) "The Role of Agency in History: The Althusser–Thompson–Anderson Debate," in Scott McNall (ed.), *Current Perspectives in Social Theory*, Vol. 6, (Oxford: JAI Press); (1989) "Four Concepts of Social

Myth 7: We can dismiss statistical analysis as the distinct methodology of positivism. There are some in CR who support this stance. In his influential book on CR methods, for example, Andrew Sayer dismisses statistical regression and kindred statistical analysis as "a poor form of explanation."[49] Today, I would say, the dominant line in CR is the opposite.

The first paper I ever presented at a meeting of the International Association of Critical Realism (IACR) was titled, like Chapter 2, "Do Realists Run Regressions?"[50] At the time, I considered my point banal. Yet, I arrived to a crowded room – not my usual reception – presided over by Tony Lawson, the Cambridge CR economist featured in George Steinmetz's *The Politics of Method*.

I disagreed with Sayer that regression is a poor form of explanation. Instead, I countered, regression is not a form of explanation at all. Its elevation to such was a positivist mistake. Correctly understood and used, like other statistical techniques, regression is not an explanation but a fallible form of evidence for and against explanations. For CR to reject the use of analytical statistics, I further argued, would be to erect a new foundationalism in place of that of positivism. Instead, CR must uphold a Feyerabendian methodological anarchy.[51]

The crowded room, filled, I was to learn, with CR economists, was aghast, but the few sociologists in the audience agreed with me. Since then, I would say, among CR sociologists and political scientists this view is now dominant, and there is now a CR literature supporting it. Thus, now, even Bhaskar would say the "holy trinity" of interdisciplinary research is metatheoretical unity, theoretical pluralism, and methodological specificity to the question asked – some questions, being quantitative, appropriately calling for statistics.[52]

Structure," *Journal for the Theory of Social Behaviour* 19: 195–212; and (1993) "Cultural Rules and Material Relations" *Sociological Theory* 11: 212–229.

[49] Andrew Sayer (2010) *Method in Social Science: A Realist Approach*. (New York: Routledge).

[50] Subsequently published with that title in Jose Lopez and Garry Potter (eds.) (2005) *After Postmodernism: An Introduction to Critical Realism* (New York: Continuum).

[51] Paul Feyerabend (2010) *Against Method* (New York: Verso).

[52] Roy Bhaskar (2010) "Contexts of Interdisciplinarity," pp. 1–25 in Roy Bhaskar, Cheryl Frank, Karl Georg Hayer, and Peter Naess, *Interdisciplinarity and*

In Chapter 2 I will go one step further. Not only, I will argue, does CR stand surprisingly with Feyerabendian methodological anarchy. In its rejection of epistemic foundationalism and embrace of fallibilism, CR actually aligns with what has been called the "rhetorical turn" in social science. Of course, the rhetoric CR embraces is that of Aristotle and not that, picked up by the postmodernists, which in Plato is associated with the Sophists.

The origins of critical realism

Around roughly the same time, the designation critical realism was introduced independently within two separate dialogues by two different sets of interlocutors. The interesting thing is that not only was the designation the same, but that both dialogues meant something similar by it. One set of interlocutors was examining relations between science and religion.[53] Since my mission here is to present CR in brief to sociologists, we will say no more about this highly interesting group. We should just know they are there.

The other group to develop CR was a circle of largely progressive philosophers and social scientists in the UK. *Causal Powers* by Rom Harré and Edward H. Madden made an important beginning on a non-positivist understanding of causality.[54] In my opinion, it is still one of the best, clearest accounts. CR became more widely known, however, when Harré's student, Roy Bhaskar, published two seminal books: *The Realist Theory of Science* and *The Possibility of Naturalism*. The latter particularly applied CR to the social realm, an extension Harré, a post-Wittgensteinian social constructionist, has always resisted.

Bhaskar consequently became something of a leader within the circle of critical realists concerned with the social. Bhaskar, however, was hardly alone. Indeed, being a philosopher rather than a sociologist,

---

Climate Change: Transforming Knowledge and Practice for Our Global Future (New York: Routledge), p. 20.

[53] Ian Barbour (1971) *Issues in Science and Religion* (New York: HarperCollins). Andrew Wright at Kings College continues to write in this tradition, although he is now linked to the sociological CR community as well. See, for example, Wright (2014) *Christianity and Critical Realism: Ambiguity, Truth, and Theological Literacy* (New York: Routledge).

[54] Harré and Madden, *Causal Powers*.

The Possibility of Naturalism could itself be criticized from a more mature CR perspective. In particular, the *Transformational Model of Social Action* (TMSA) that Bhaskar initially presented was hardly distinguishable from Giddens's structuration theory. It took conversations with Margaret Archer and her *Realist Social Theory: The Morphogenetic Approach* for Bhaskar to come around to what many of us would consider a more analytically robust conception of social structure.

Besides Bhaskar and Archer, there were many others in that first generation. In philosophy there was Andrew Collier, also featured in Steinmetz's *The Politics of Method in the Human Sciences*, and Peter Manicas and Christopher Norris.[55] Among sociologists there were Andrew Sayer, already mentioned, Bob Jessop, and Ted Benton, known for his *Philosophy of Social Science*.[56] William Outhewaite, known for his work on critical theory, was also associated with the movement, as were for a time, Russell Keat and John Urry.[57] In economics there was the group at Cambridge centered around Tony Lawson.[58] In Law, Alan Norrie.[59]

Subsequently, the movement expanded, making inroads throughout the world and in such disciplines as International Relations (IR).[60]

---

[55] Steinmetz "Critical Realism and Historical Sociology."

[56] Ted Benton (2010) *Philosophy of Social Science: The Philosophical Foundations of Social Thought* (New York: Palgrave Macmillan). See Peter Manicas (2006) *A Realist Philosophy of Social Science: Explanation and Understanding* (Cambridge: Cambridge University Press).

[57] See R. William Outhewaite (2010) *Critical Theory and Contemporary Europe* (New York: Continuum); Russell Keat and John Urry (2012) *Social Theory as Science* (New York: Routledge).

[58] Tony Lawson (2003) *Reorienting Economics* (New York: Routledge).

[59] See Alan Norrie (2014) *Crime, Reason, and History: A Critical Introduction to Criminal Law* (New York: Cambridge University Press).

[60] Coming out of Italy, see, for example, Pierpaolo Donati (2012) *Relational Sociology: A New Paradigm for the Social Sciences* (New York: Routledge); and Andrea Maccarini, Emmanuele Morandi, and Riccardo Prandini (2011) *Sociological Realism* (New York: Routledge). From Sweden, see Berth Danermark, Mats Ekstrom, Liselotte Jakobsen, and Jan ch. Karlsson (2005) *Explaining Society: An Introduction to Critical Realism in the Social Sciences* (New York: Routledge). From Belgium by way now of Brazil, see Frédéric Vandenberghe (2013) *What's Critical about Critical Realism* (New York: Routledge). In IR see, for example, Jonathan Joseph and Colin Wight (eds.) (2010) *Scientific Realism and International Relations* (New York: Palgrave Macmillan); Jonathan Joseph (2012) *The Social in the Global: Social Theory, Governmentality and Global Politics*, (Cambridge: Cambridge University Press);

Under its former editor, sociologist Charlie Smith, *The Journal for the Theory of Social Behaviour (JTSB)*, which I now co-edit, has long been hospitable to CR – as it is to structuration theory, social positioning theory, constructionism, and other alternatives to positivist thought. Today, with its own journal, *The Journal of Critical Realism*, the IACR meets annually, alternating between the UK and other countries, particularly the Global South.

and Colin Wight (2006) *Agents, Structures and International Relations: Politics as Ontology* (Cambridge: Cambridge University Press) and Heikki Patomaki (2001) *After International Relations: Critical Realism and the Reconstruction of World Politics* (New York: Routledge).

2 | *Do realists run regressions?*

The question posed by the title of this chapter has already been answered briefly in the introduction. Yes, critical realists do run regressions – and other analytical statistics – but not with the same understanding or point as positivists. The reason is that CR has a completely different understanding of causality and causal explanation. In this chapter we will take things slowly. We will begin by seeing why the positivist understanding of causality is completely untenable and why, if we replace it, there is no reason to deny causality in the human sphere as do the post-Wittgensteinians and their interpretivist followers in sociology.

The CR conception of sociology is associated with mechanisms and with emergence. In this book, I will speak sparingly of emergence. Although I believe in emergence and, as we will soon see, it is sometimes key, we can understand much of CR without raising the complications associated with it.

Mechanisms, on the other hand, are central. As Philip Gorski observes, mechanisms are now trendy, increasingly spoken of also by Symbolic Interactionists, historical sociologists, and rational choice theorists.[1] Thus, one thing we will need to do is differentiate the CR conception from these others. Doing so will to some extent anticipate our discussion in Chapter 4, because the differences also involve differences in the ways we think of structure and agency.

Mechanisms, however, do not exhaust the CR approach to causality or its implications for plurality in research methods. According to CR, causal analysis proceeds at three different levels. First is the identification and description of causal mechanisms and causal powers; second is the invocation of those causal mechanisms and causal powers in

---

[1] Philip Gorski (2009) "'Social Mechanisms' and Comparative-Historical Sociology: A Critical Realist Proposal," pp. 147–196 in Peter Hedström and Björn Wittock (eds.), *Frontiers of Sociology* (Boston, MA: Brill).

narrative accounts of contingent, causal conjunctures. Narrative, not regression equations, is, according to CR, the canonical form of causal explanation – not just in the social sciences but in all open systems, including physics.

The final level at which causal analysis proceeds is the methodological adjudication among rival explanations and narratives. Just because we offer an explanation or narrative does not mean it is the right one. There may be better explanations or narratives. At this level, recapturing a fractured unity, CR embraces methodological pluralism. Thus, by the end of this chapter, we will see that according to CR, ethnographic description, statistical correlations, and narrative explanation all are equally important but different aspects of a scientific approach to a causally open world. CR, we will thus see, offers sociology the chance to unify quantitative and qualitative research approaches all on an equal footing.

Actualism in sociology

Reading George Steinmetz's argument for CR in historical sociology, I think I now understand better a global feature of American sociology that long puzzled me. I allude to this feature in the introduction, but let me be more specific here. The relation between structure and agency has long been regarded as one of the central issues in sociology, but much of American sociology seems intent on doing away with either structures or agents or both. Rational choice theory and Symbolic Interactionism have actors and interactions but no strong sense of relational structure. American relational sociology, on the other hand, does have relations but, strangely, no agents related by them, only some kind of free-floating agency.[2] Practice theory finally displaces both agents and relational structures.

What is going on? Why such attraction to both anti-humanism and anti-structural sociology? There are likely several reasons, but one, I now think, is an *actualist* tendency in the discipline fostered by positivism. Let us begin with Steinmetz:

---

[2] I refer to American relational sociology to distinguish it from the Italian form advanced by Pierpaolo Donati, which is closely aligned with CR. See Pierpaolo Donati (2012) *Relational Sociology: A New Paradigm for the Social Sciences* (New York: Routledge).

Positivism is closely related but not reducible to empiricism, an ontological position which rejects the positing of theoretical or invisible entities. This mistrust of invisible entities might seem paradoxical in fields like sociology, whose master signifier, society or "social relations," is hardly an immediately visible object (see Frisby and Sayer 1986). This empiricism is expressed less in Humean terms than in a vaguer "actualism" – that philosophy which "denies the existence of underlying structures which determine . . . events and instead locates the succession of cause and effect at the level of events" (Collier 1994: 7). The untheorized presentation of empirical regularities is preferred to so-called "metatheory."[3]

We already observed in Chapter 1 Earl Babbie's aversion to unobservable theoretical entities. We saw too that this aversion makes much of the world inexplicable and ultimately deprives us even of the very concept of causality. And, indeed, since Hume, some empiricists have thought that as something unobservable, causality too is a concept we should junk.

What Steinmetz is saying in the passage above is that what results from sociology's aversion to unobservables is less any formally articulated doctrine than an actualist tendency that privileges events. Because neither agents nor structures are events, contemporary American sociology is uncomfortable with them. In contrast, practices, habits, routines, and interactions are, as *doings*, all events and so attractive to sociology. They are events that can be linked to other events. Events can also take on values of variables, making them even further attractive. In American sociology, events are welcomed; entities and relations not.

Empiricism narrows the range of science even more. For empiricism, the purview of science is observable events. Observable events are clearly just a subset of all extent events. CR, by contrast, expands the range of science. For CR, the real includes not just observable events and for that matter not just events, observable or otherwise. For CR, the real also includes entities and relations along with their causal properties (see Figure 2.1).

Consider social power. With the combined influence of Michel Foucault and Pierre Bourdieu, sociologists today have become obsessed with power, as if it were the only social property that commends study.

---

[3] George Steinmetz (1998) "Critical Realism and Historical Sociology: A Review Article," *Comparative Studies in Society and History* 40: 170–186, p. 172.

	Domain of Real	Domain of Actual	Domain of Empirical
Mechanisms	X		
Events	X	X	
Experiences	X	X	X

Figure 2.1 Bhaskar's depth realism.
(*A Realist Theory of Science*, p. 13, reprinted with permission of Taylor and Francis)

But what is social power? It is not itself an event, but rather something unobservable that lies behind and explains events. Foucauldeans sometimes talk of power as an effect, but that is not the most helpful way to speak. If power is an effect, of what is it an effect? Power is better conceived as a capacity, a capacity to exert certain effects. For Foucault, actually, power is a capacity that inheres in discourses or certain microtechnologies like the confessional or Panopticon. For Foucault, power is the capacity among other things to mold our subjectivity.

For Bourdieu, in contrast, power refers to capacities that accrue to the incumbents of different social positions. Think, for example, of the capacity of a high-school principal to expel students from classes. One crucial point for CR is that causal properties like power can exist and exist consequentially even if they go unexercised. Thus, the principal retains the power to expel students even while he or she does not exercise it. Put otherwise, as a capacity, the power to expel is not reducible to the observable event of its exercise. As an ever present threat, even unexercised, the power to expel reigns like a shadow over the interaction between students and principal. The principal's power to expel thus becomes *power over* students and as *power over* not just an atomic capacity but a social relation. Insofar as the principal's relational power over students shapes the entire interaction between principal and students, the interaction cannot be fully understood apart from that power and the capacity in which it inheres.

These points are – or should be – pedestrian. Yet they cannot be accommodated at all by an actualist philosophical orientation. To appreciate them, they require ontological realism about entities, capacities, and relations and thus movement in the direction of CR. Thus, if we ask about the purchase of CR as a philosophy of science, we already here receive one strong response. Something like CR is required for a full, sociological understanding of power and kindred capacities. But we've only just begun.

The covering law model of explanation

Consistent with actualism is the so-called covering law model of causal explanation, which remains the dominant understanding of causal explanation in sociology – among both its positivist proponents and its anti-positivist opponents. A central component of positivism, the covering law model is a framework that understands causality as relations among events, relations that Bhaskar terms event-regularities.[4]

Specifically, the covering law model conceives of causal explanation as a species of deductive argument in which the explanandum (that which is to be explained) is logically deduced from the explanans (that which does the explaining). According to the covering law model, the key part of the explanans is a covering law, which relates two types of events: an antecedent event (A) – which may be a compound event – and a consequent event (B). Taking the form "If A, then B," the covering law simply stipulates that if an event of type A occurs, then an event of type B will occur. To explain any particular event B, the full explanans consists of the covering law "If A, then B" and the observation that an event of the antecedent type A has in fact occurred. Event B follows as a logical deduction as according to the following scheme:

If A, then B.
A.
——————
Therefore, B.

The covering law simply links events: If one thing happens, then another thing happens. Thus, all that remains of causality is a conceptually thin empirical regularity, Hume's constant conjunction.

Such a meager understanding of causality is ideal if the objective is a thorough-going, actualist empiricism. There are no structures. There are no entities. There are no capacities. All there is are events, observable events.

An extra benefit is that causality can now be fully expressed mathematically. That mathematical formulation is the ideal expression of sociological theory was the central idea behind Hubert Blalock's

---

[4] Roy Bhaskar (2005) *A Realist Theory of Science* (New York: Routledge).

highly influential *Theory Construction: From Verbal to Mathematical Formulation*. Consistent with that idea, sociology came to elevate statistics from technique to theoretical language. In other words, statistical formulations – regression equations, for example – became not just a way of determining which explanations are correct but the explanations themselves.

What gets distorted when causality is so thinned out for mathematical formulation is not just causality, but theory as well. Theory on this view is a series of logically connected one-liners, each of which can be tested as an empirical hypothesis. Thus, does Blalock describe theory circa 1969:

> It has been noted that theories do not consist entirely of conceptual schemes or typologies but must contain lawlike propositions that interrelate concepts of variables two or more at a time. Furthermore these propositions must themselves be interrelated. For example, if one proposition relates variables A and B, a second C and D, and a third E and F, then there must be additional propositions enabling one to make deductive statements connecting these three propositions. Ideally, one might hope to achieve a completely closed deductive theoretical system in which there would be a minimal set of propositions taken as axioms, from which all other propositions could be deduced by purely mathematical or logical reasoning. More realistically, we might take the model of the completely closed deductive system as an ideal which in practice can only be approximated.[5]

Around the same time, Peter Blau described theory almost identically. Three features of the description are worthy of note. First is the call for "lawlike" propositions that can fit the covering law model. Second is the equation of theory with an interrelated set of such propositions. Finally, there is the ideal of theory as a completely closed deductive or "axiomatic" system.[6]

This positivist understanding of theory and causality privileges a narrow range of empirical research. In fact, empirical research becomes equated with quantitative, statistical research. If causal explanation

---

[5] Hubert Blalock (1969) *Theory Construction from Verbal to Mathematical Formulations* (Upper Saddle River, NJ: Prentice-Hall), p. 2.

[6] Peter Blau (1977) *Inequality and Heterogeneity: A Primitive Theory of Social Structure* (New York: Free Press). For more extended analyses of this trend in sociology, see Douglas V. Porpora (1979) *The Concept of Social Structure* (Westwood, CT: Greenwood Press); and George Steinmetz (2005) *The Politics of Method in the Human Sciences: Positivism and Its Epistemological Others (Politics, History, and Culture)* (Durham, NC: Duke University Press).

must follow the covering law model, then all causal explanation must be nomothetic or general. Statistical generalizability and random sampling become the sine qua non of causal attribution. Unless a cause can be shown to be generally operative, it is not a cause at all. In contrast, idiographic explanation, which does not invoke general laws but rather the particularities of an individual case, does not count at all as causal explanation. It is considered instead mere description. Thus marginalized is all qualitative research that adopts historical or ethnographic methods.

Counterfactuals?

Today, many empiricists in sociology will deny that they are searching for laws. Instead of nomothetic laws, they will say, they think of causality in terms of counterfactuals along the lines of James Woodward and Judea Pearl.[7] A counterfactual statement is one that denies that a given event would have occurred had not some prior event (or events) occurred. Discussing counterfactuals, Jaegwon Kim provides the following example:

(C) If this match had not been struck, it would not have lighted.[8]

It first should be said that there is nothing special about counterfactuals. Everyone agrees that in addition to subjunctive conditionals, causal claims are supposed to support counterfactuals, and conventional nomothetic laws certainly do. Second, like nomothetic laws, an understanding of causality exclusively in terms of counterfactuals equally goes back to Hume, and on its own equally declines to speak of the mechanism through which some putative cause produces its effects. An exclusively counterfactual approach is in that sense equally actualist. True, in the kind of structural equation models produced by Stephen Morgan and Christopher Winship, intervening variables provide something of a mechanism, but, there again, what it is about

[7] James Woodward (2005) *Making Things Happen: A Theory of Causal Explanation* (New York: Oxford); Judea Pearl (2000) *Causality, Models, Reasoning, and Inference* (Cambridge: Cambridge University Press).

[8] Jaegwon Kim (2007) "Causation and Mental Causation," pp. 227–242 in Brian McLaughlin and Jonathan Cohen (eds.), *Contemporary Debates in the Philosophy of Mind* (New York: Basil Blackwell), http://colbud.hu/bloewer/Kim_Causation_and_Mental_Causation_-_Debates-1.pdf.

the intervening variables that has such effect lies beyond mere actualist, counterfactual connectivity.[9]

In relation to our discussion, however, the main thing to be said is that equating causality exhaustively with counterfactual relations implicitly trades on nomothetic laws.[10] As Kim observes, "dry matches struck in the presence of oxygen usually and reliably ignite, and ... it is our knowledge of this regularity, or ceteris paribus law, combined with knowledge of the actual circumstances in which the match was struck (e.g., it was dry, oxygen was present, etc.), that accounts for our knowledge of (C)."[11] Thus, Kim concludes, "it is difficult to see how evaluations of conditionals like (C) could avoid adverting to laws and regularities."[12] And, whether or not empiricist sociologists choose to acknowledge it, with the return to laws, we return as well to the covering law model.

The further hegemony of the covering law model

The covering law model of causality exerts its hegemony in sociology not only among its positivist supporters but also even among those

---

[9] Steven L. Morgan and Christopher Winship (2007) *Counterfactuals and Causal Inference* (Cambridge: Cambridge University Press). Morgan and Christopher (p. 237) dismiss what they call CR's transcendentalism. Although there are references to transcendence in CR, some of which I have employed myself and some of which are admittedly obscure, none seems to have anything to do with the substance of Morgan and Winship's twofold complaint about CR: (1) that it upholds irreducible layers of reality; and (2) its putative affirmation that "the validity of a mechanism cannot be undermined by its inability to explain anything in particular" (p. 235). As they present the first complaint, Morgan and Winship seem to think that CR somehow upholds sociological holism, which it does not – although it also opposes the methodological individualism that Morgan and Winship seem to consider the only alternative. See Chapters 4 and 6 of this volume for the actual alternative CR offers. The second complaint as stated is ambiguous. Certainly, if CR held that mechanisms can *never* explain *anything*, the CR position would be ludicrous. CR hardly holds that position. Does CR hold that a mechanism may sometimes operate without producing its characteristic effects? Yes, certainly, when it is counteracted. Counteraction is frequent. It is unclear why Morgan and Winship should find so scandalous the existence of what are generally known as suppressor variables.

[10] Significantly, Morgan and Winship do not rest with an exclusively counterfactual account; rather, they themselves speak of mechanisms. See Morgan and Winship, *Counterfactuals and Causal Inference*, pp. 237ff.

[11] Kim "Causation and Mental Causation," p. 11.

[12] Ibid. The other possible alternative is to move beyond actualist connectionism to mechanisms or causal powers.

who oppose positivism. Positivism's major opposition in sociology is *Interpretivism*.[13] *Interpretivism* is perhaps a suitable label for a whole range of sociological approaches that emphasize interpretive or hermeneutic methods. These approaches range from Symbolic Inter-actionism and phenomenology to ethnomethodology and even deconstruction.

Those we might classify as *interpretivists* do not share all the same assumptions, but one assumption they widely share is a distinction between *understanding* and *explanation*. This distinction goes back to Wilhem Dilthey and, of course, was picked up by Weber with whom the concept of *Verstehen* is most associated.

To understand this distinction, keep in mind that in origin, positiv-ism roughly coincided with the "unity of science movement," which advanced common postulates of science across the disciplines. Disciplines seeking to partake of scientific status adopted those postulates, including the covering law model of explanation. Economics, political science, and psychology all adopted the postulates assiduously, as did sociology.

Interpretivists also accept the conception of causality entailed by the covering law model. They accept, that is, that causality involves universal laws and that such laws imply determinism – i.e., necessary connections among events. Interpretivists simply deny that causality reigns in the human sphere. Rather, for interpretivists, the covering law model of explanation is confined to the natural sphere.

Thus, in opposition to any unitary scientific methodology, Dilthey posed his famous distinction between the *Natur* and *Geistes Wis-senschaften*, that is, the natural and the human (literally spiritual) sciences. What the distinction marks is a fundamental difference in governing principle. Whereas the natural order is governed by the principle of causality and causal relations, the human order is governed by reason. Thus, whereas the natural order is a domain of determin-ism, the human order is a domain of freedom. Thus, as well, whereas the natural order can be studied objectively from the outside, the human order must be studied subjectively from within. In general,

---

[13] See Piergiorgio Corbetta (2003) *Social Research: Theory, Methods and Techniques* (Thousand Oaks, CA: Sage). The following treatment follows Douglas Porpora (2011) "Recovering Causality," pp. 149–166 in Andrea Maccarini, Emmanuele Morandi, and Riccardo Prandini (eds.), *Sociological Realism* (New York: Routledge).

acceptance of these distinctions marks the point of view variously called Interpretivism or the Verstehen school.

Interpretivists were among the early opponents of reductionism. For them, the irreducible hallmark of the human sphere was *Intentionality* or the quality of "aboutness."[14] Humans, in other words, distinctively have thoughts and feelings *about* things, quite apart from the qualities of the things themselves. The things themselves – like unicorns and witches – may not even exist. As interpretivists observed, this distinct human dimension of aboutness has no counterpart in the physical domain of the natural sciences and cannot be ignored.

As noted, according to interpretivists, the human quality of aboutness means that what operates within the human sphere is reason, not causality. This distinction the post-Wittgensteinian philosophers made even more pronounced. Followers of the later Ludwig Wittgenstein, the so-called post-Wittgensteinians (G. E. M. Anscombe, A. I. Melden, R. S. Peters, and Peter Winch), distinguished between explanations in terms of causes and understanding in terms of reasons.[15] Consider, for example, one of Durkheim's explanations of suicide: If social cohesion declines, then the suicide rate will increase. Such an *if–then* proposition putatively *explains* in a causal way why people commit suicide.

Durkheim's causal explanation does not, however, at all help us *understand* the specific thinking that leads individual people to kill

---

[14] Franz Brentano (1973) Psychology from an *Empirical* Standpoint, transl. by A. C. Rancurello, D. B. Terrell, and L. McAlister (London: Routledge). Intentionality (ordinarily capitalized) referring to aboutness is a technical philosophical term not to be confused with its ordinary sense of purposiveness.

[15] G. E. M. Anscombe (1957) *Intention* (Oxford: Basil Blackwell); A. I. Melden (1961) *Free Action* (London: Routledge & Kegan Paul); R. S. Peters (1960) *The Concept of Motivation* (London: Routledge & Kegan Paul); and Peter Winch (1958) *The Idea of a Social Science* (London: Routledge & Kegan Paul). The post-Wittgensteinian approach differs from the more phenomenological in placing motives outside the actors in public rules. In sociology, the move was first picked up by ethnomethodologists like Peter Blum and Alan McHugh. See Blum and McHugh (1971) "The Social Ascription of Motives," *American Sociological Review* 36: 98–109. See also Jeff Coulter (1989) *Mind in Action* (Cambridge, MA: Polity Press); and David Rubinstein (1977) "The Concept of Action in the Social Sciences," *Journal for the Theory of Social Behaviour* 7: 209–236. For the extension of this approach to International Relations, see Martin Hollis and Steven Smith (1990) *Explaining and Understanding International Relations* (Oxford: Oxford University Press). In anthropology, the post-Wittgensteinian lines was picked up by Clifford Geertz (1977) *The Interpretation of Cultures* (New York: Basic Books).

themselves, the unfolding meaning-making, which Tavory and Timmermans say is uniquely uncovered by ethnography.[16] To *understand* why any individual commits suicide, we need to comprehend that individual's specific reasons. In contrast with mechanical explanations in terms of causal laws, accounts in terms of reasons adopt a teleological language of motivation. Specifically, rational accounts involve reference to agents' goals, to their desires, and to their beliefs. When we want to *understand* why people commit suicide, we want to hear what they *believe* suicide will accomplish and why they *want* or *desire* to accomplish that goal. Perhaps, for example, suicide victims just *want* to escape a state of deep depression, and in that state, *believe* suicide is a way to accomplish that end.

Explanations in terms of reasons do not reference laws. If, for example, we say a particular woman committed suicide because she wanted to end an unhappy existence, we are not necessarily implying any lawlike connection between unhappiness and suicide. There are, after all, other ways to deal with unhappiness. One could wait out the unhappiness; talk it out with friends; consult a therapist; or try to change the specific source of unhappiness.

It may seem to follow from the irreducibly idiographic nature of human rationality that causality has no place in the human sciences. That was the conclusion advanced in Peter Winch's seminal *The Idea of a Social Science* (ISS).[17] Essentially, ISS dismissed the legitimacy of causal analysis in the social sphere, including specifically the kind of causal analysis modeled by Durkheim. ISS thus did more than just challenge the privileged position of statistics in social scientific methodology. According to the argument of ISS, statistical analysis in the social sciences was not even appropriate. Privileged by ISS instead were the hermeneutic methods associated with history and ethnography. Instead of laws, each of these methods explains through the construction of a narrative or story, over the course of which reasoned action unfolds in a contextualized way that makes it understandable.

As correct as interpretivists may be that human reasoning does not conform to laws, it goes too far to rule out causality completely from the human domain. In important respects, reasons seem to function

---

[16] See Iddo Tavory and Stephen Timmermans (2013) "A Pragmatist Approach to Causality in Ethnography," *American Journal of Sociology* 119 (3): 682–714.
[17] Winch, *The Idea of a Social Science*.

like causes. Like causes, reasons support both counterfactuals ("he would not have done so had he not been so motivated") and subjunctive conditionals ("had I possessed that reason, I would have...").[18] There seem, moreover, social forces like moral or social cohesion that do exert causal effects on us in however un-lawlike a manner. And, finally, the complete denial of causality in the human domain seems to preclude the influence beyond reasons of social structures. An entirely subjectivist or idealist account in other words is not the whole story of our lives.

Thus, the interpretivist denial of social causality comes at a high price. It is not a price, however, that we need to pay. We need only follow CR in rejecting the covering law model of causality to which both positivism and interpretivism jointly subscribe.[19]

The failure of the covering law model of causal explanation

There is a bit of a problem with the covering law model. It utterly fails to work. In *A Realist Theory of Science*, Bhaskar shows that the covering law model fails even in the natural sciences. Nancy Cartwright subsequently buttressed that argument in a more highly detailed way. Here, we may much more briefly see that the covering law model certainly fails in application to the social sciences.[20]

Recall that according to the covering law model, causal explanation takes the form of a deductive argument in which the event to be explained is logically deduced from a covering law and from the occurrence of a prior event or events to which the event to be explained is connected via the covering law. Look back in the previous section at the canonical form taken by the covering law model. Notice that in this

---

[18] See Joseph Margolis (1979) "Action and Causality," *Philosophical Forum* 11: 47–64. Also Douglas Porpora (1983) "On the Post-Wittgensteinian Critique of the Concept of Action in Sociology," *Journal for the Theory of Social Behaviour* 13 (2): 129–146; and Colin Campbell (1998) *The Myth of Social Action* (New York: Cambridge University Press).

[19] In the most recent edition of ISS, Winch concedes that if causality is understood more along CR lines (although he does not mention CR by name), then he would have no problem with understanding reasons to be causes.

[20] Nancy Cartwright (1983) *How the Laws of Physics Lie.* (New York: Oxford University Press). The argument here follows Porpora (1983) "On the Prospects for a Nomothetic Theory of Social Structure," *Journal for the Theory of Social Behaviour* 13: 243–264. A similar argument is made by Gorski in "Social Mechanisms" and by Steinmetz in "Critical Realism and Historical Sociology".

canonical form, a certain degree of determinism is required. Event B must follow from A with some degree of necessity. We can make that implicit determinism explicit as below.

If A, then (necessarily) B.

A.
_____
Therefore, B.

It is the absolute fixity of the connection between the antecedent and consequent events that permits the logical deduction that is the heart of scientific explanation according to the covering law model.

The problem is that no deterministic laws have ever been found to govern human affairs. Worse, nobody even expects deterministic laws to be found. To understand why, it is helpful to think in terms of a CR distinction between *open* and *closed* causal systems.[21] A *closed system* is one in which a single causal mechanism operates in isolation. Because in a closed system there are no other causal mechanisms interfering with the mechanism under observation, it might be possible to observe lawlike event-regularities. In such circumstances, without outside interference, the same input may lead regularly to the same output.

Closed systems, however, are generally the artificial construct of a laboratory. The real world beyond the laboratory is rarely closed but, more often, radically open. In an *open system*, an unlimited number of ever-changing causal processes operate simultaneously, interfering with each other in irregular ways. Hence, in an open system, it is very unlikely that the same input to any one process will lead to exactly the same output. The most we can expect in an open system is a rough statistical relation between two variables.

Clearly, as the social world studied by sociologists is an open system, we cannot expect to uncover any deterministic relationships there, and no one does. Again, look back in the previous section, this time at the passage quoted from Blalock. Note already the characteristic hedge. Departing from the canonical version of the covering law model, the propositions for which Blalock calls are not actually laws, but only lawlike.

How far from actual laws can propositions depart before the covering law model ceases to work? You often hear positivist sociologists

---

[21] See Bhaskar, *A Realist Theory.*

maintain that in the social realm, they seek not deterministic laws but only statistical laws. You can tell they are completely unprepared for the follow-up question: What are statistical laws?

If by a statistical law, the positivists mean a formulation like, "If C, then there is an invariant probability α that E," then statistical laws also will support a relaxed form of the covering law model as below:

If A, then there is an invariant probability α that B.
A.
—————————
Therefore, there is an invariant probability α that B.

In the case of statistical laws, what will be deducible from the explanans is not the actual occurrence of the explanandum but at least the invariant probability of its occurring. Unfortunately for positivism, no one has uncovered even any statistical laws of the above form, and nor, again, is anyone likely to. The reason is the same as before. In any open system, like the social world, conditions are unlikely to stay sufficiently fixed to yield unchanging probabilities of anything – particularly in a social system, subject to historical change. Any observed statistical relation between two social variables is subject to modification by changes in the ways humans think. Human thought is itself an intrinsically open system without limits on the new thoughts that can be entertained, which potentially might alter any previously observed relationship among social variables.[22] Such considerations preclude any statistical laws of the requisite fixity.

At most, what can be found are what are called "ceteris paribus" propositions, that is, propositions of the form, "ceteris paribus, if C, then E." The ceteris paribus clause stipulates that the following relationship holds only with "all things being equal."

Unfortunately, with ceteris paribus propositions, we have reached the point of sham. Although sophisticated-sounding, ceteris paribus propositions do not at all support explanations conforming to the covering law model. If the factors referenced by a ceteris paribus clause can be specified and it is clear what it means for them to be equal, then a ceteris paribus proposition poses no difficulty. In such a case, the

[22] I actually can offer something close to a mathematical proof that human thought is intrinsically open, that the thoughts we could possibly think comprise an infinite set. See Porpora (2013) "How Many Thoughts Are There? Or Why We Likely Have No *Tegmark Duplicates* $10^{10^{115}}$ Meters Away," *Philosophical Studies* 163: 133–149.

conditions referenced could in principle be explicitly enumerated in the proposition, which would thereby be converted into either a deterministic or statistical law. On the other hand, if the ceteris paribus clause references an indeterminate inventory of factors, and it is unclear what it means for those factors to be "equal," then the ceteris paribus clause renders vacuous the proposition it prefaces. To see this, consider that for any such "ceteris paribus" proposition formulated (e.g., "Ceteris paribus, if A then B"), a contrary ceteris paribus proposition could be formulated with equal validity (i.e., "Ceteris paribus, if A, then not-B"). It all depends on which factors are chosen for the baseline and which factors are relegated to the ceteris paribus clause. For this reason, if the factors referenced by the ceteris paribus clause are indeterminate and their condition of equality unspecified, the following deduction is utterly invalid:

Ceteris paribus, if A, then B.

C.
_____

Therefore, B.

Instead, in order to determine whether B had to follow A in any particular case, the particular nature of the case needs to be examined. But that – contrary to the whole point of the covering law model – is to explain B's occurrence in an *idiographic* rather than a *nomothetic* manner, that is, in terms of a case's unique context rather than in terms of a general law. If the facts associated with each individual case need to be examined idiographically to determine whether some general relationship holds, then the general relationship loses all value.

In short, positivist sociology's emperor has no clothes. The covering law model does not work, and without it, beyond supporting counterfactuals, most sociologists are at a complete loss to say what causality is. Behind all the mathematical glitter lies a void. There is a deep problem here that needs to be addressed.

The CR solution

As may be becoming clear by now, in many ways CR philosophically articulates common sense. It is just that with all the conceptual confusion in the discipline, common sense seems like high theory. Thus, as we go through the following technicalities, try to keep hold of how close the whole is to your own pre-sociological common sense.

In contrast with the covering law model, the CR conception of causality does not promote a search for event regularities, not even the impermanent, localized regularities of which Bourdieu speaks. CR does not search for regularities because CR does not conceptualize causality in terms of regularities nor even primarily in terms of events. Instead, on the one hand, CR conceptualizes causality as a relation between causal structures or *mechanisms* and *causal properties*. On the other hand, for CR, causality involves the operation of these mechanisms and properties in situated, conjunctural contexts. Admittedly, in such contexts, the operation of mechanisms and properties does entail events, but in the open world where multiple mechanisms always operate, the events produced will not likely be regular. In fact, as in our historical record, they will often be unique.

The above dense formulation needs to be unpacked. Let us begin with mechanisms. It is first of all a mistake to hear that word necessarily connoting something we would normally consider mechanistic or sub-organic.[23] Of course, in the natural world, the word mechanism might refer to something of that nature. We perhaps quickly think of the mechanism of a clock. Today, that mechanism is a solid-state configuration of transistors and micro-processors. In the past, it consisted of gears and springs and such. In both cases, the word mechanism refers to that which makes the clock work. In both cases, the mechanism is not best thought of as an event or even as a series of events. The mechanism is better thought of as a structure, a rather complex organization or relation of different elements.

When CR speaks of causal mechanisms, then, it speaks of what makes things work. Generally, what makes things work is some kind of causal structure. In biology, for example, we might speak of the structure of the DNA molecule, a very special "double helix." In physics, we might speak of the structure of the atom, which was first conceptualized as a point particle, then as a mini-solar system, and now as a kind of quantum cloud.

The first thing to notice is that the identification of such structures requires description, something discursive rather than an equation. Let us hear that again because this point is crucial. Atomic structure or the structure of DNA are more pictures that need to be painted than equations that need to be solved. Right away we realize that much of

---

[23] See also Gorski, "Social Mechanisms."

even natural science is descriptive and hence qualitative. Nor is this qualitative component to be disparaged. Nailing down atomic structure and the double helix of DNA were among the greatest of all scientific achievements.

One of the first things CR presses, as Christian Smith observes, is that we need "to learn better to value sheer description. The first thing realism always wants to know is: What actually exists? The foremost task, therefore is to describe what is."[24] Often, a key part of what we must do, even before explanation, as Isaac Reed observes, is to "establish the phenomenon" to be considered.[25]

Description is especially important when, in what Reed calls *resignification*, things are described in specialized language that brings to light their theoretical significance.[26] Think of Erving Goffman's revelation of impression management and strategic interaction, or of Elliot Liebow's ethnographic attack on culture of poverty theory, his demonstration of the operation of a social structural mechanism.[27]

Similarly, in the empirical research I conducted with my colleagues for our book, *Post-Ethical Society*, our main objective was just to describe a societal condition, what we went on to call America's *macro-moral disconnect*, the failure of secular public discourse in America to confront macro-moral matters in moral terms. True, we went on to offer some explanation for this condition and used statistics to delineate its contours, but we were not searching for general laws. The main work, even with our use of statistics, was to describe something

---

[24] Christian Smith (2010) *What Is a Person? Rethinking, Humanity, Social Life, and the Moral Good from the Person Up* (Chicago, IL: Chicago University Press), p. 305.

[25] Isaac Reed (2011) *Interpretation and Social Knowledge: On the Use of Theory in the Human Sciences* (Chicago: University of Chicago). Reed here is following Robert K. Merton's (1987) "Three Fragments from a Sociologist's Notebooks: Establishing the Phenomenon, Specified Ignorance, and Strategic Research Methods" *Annual Review of Sociology* 13.

[26] Reed, *Interpretation and Social Knowledge*.

[27] See Elliot Liebow (2003) *Tally's Corner: A Study of Negro Streetcorner Men* (New York: Rowman and Littlefield). Actually, Reed, *Interpretation and Social Knowledge*, is a most instructive, concrete meditation on abduction. Thinking of Liebow, we can also consider the more recent treatment in this line by Alice Goffman. See Goffman (2014) *On the Run: Fugitive Life in an American City* (Chicago, IL: University of Chicago Press).

to which sociology had previously been insufficiently attentive. What we had to do, as Reed put it, was establish the phenomenon.[28]

Although my colleagues and I employed content and discourse analysis toward an end that was actually descriptive, CR's validation of description applies even more strongly to ethnography. Ethnography likewise shows us what there is. Whereas discourse analysis involves a close reading of a text, ethnography involves a close reading of life. As such, it is kin to ethology, the descriptive study of animal behavior in its natural setting. Why would it not similarly be scientific to learn all that comprises human behavior in its natural setting? Even apart from any causal mechanism in play, when a sensitive ethnographer like Colin Jerolmack describes the I–Thou relation that arises between humans and pigeons in a public park, an important aspect of human being has been disclosed.[29]

Once the covering law model is abandoned, no more can ethnography be dismissed as just the anecdotal. The covering law model tied causality to generality, but CR separates the two. The existence of a mechanism or process is one thing, even if it only operates in one place and one time. How widespread or general that mechanism may be is a separate question altogether. Thus, although not necessarily in the same study, ethnography and statistics can work together. Ethnographic analysis describes mechanisms; statistical analysis does not. What statistical analysis can do is examine where and how generally such mechanisms operate.[30]

---

[28] Douglas Porpora, Alexander Nikolaev, Julia Hagemann, and Alexander Jenkens (2013) *Post-Ethical Society: The Iraq War, Abu Ghraib, and the Moral Failure of the Secular* (Chicago, IL: University of Chicago Press). Actually, although they did not call it such, some attention to a macro-moral disconnect was previously paid by Steven Hart (2001) *Cultural Dilemmas of Progressive Politics: Styles of Engagement among Grassroots Activists* (Chicago, IL: University of Chicago Press); and by Michèle Lamont (1992) *Money, Morals and Manners: The Culture of the French and the American Upper Middle Class* (Chicago, IL: University of Chicago Press). Still, the phenomenon as such needed to be further established.

[29] Colin Jerolmack (2013) *The Global Pigeon* (Chicago, IL: University of Chicago Press).

[30] I am told by my friends in anthropology that they think of ethnography differently from us. Whereas we see ethnography as a method, they see it as an orientation – an encounter with the other that can include statistical analysis. I am attracted to this position, especially as in these terms they consider me an ethnographer, but I continue to write here from a sociological perspective.

With such understanding, Adam Smith's *The Wealth of Nations* is better appreciated as the scientific accomplishment it is, for what Smith does in this work is describe the market mechanism. What Smith famously called "the invisible hand" is an effect of the competitive relations that govern production. Those competitive relations – a social structure – are collectively the mechanism through which market efficiencies are caused.[31]

Smith's description of the market is simultaneously a theory but not a theory in the positivist sense. Like Goffman's account of impression management, the theoretical description of the market mechanism is an elaboration, not a list of axiomatic propositions. Already evident, therefore, is how separate for CR causality is from anything nomothetic and how recovered by CR is the value of theoretical description.[32]

The same market relations, Marx argued, would produce other, destabilizing tendencies in capitalist systems, namely tendencies toward insufficient aggregate demand and a falling rate of profit. These putative tendencies too are causal properties, albeit detrimental ones, exhibited by capitalist systems – at least according to Marx. Whether or not Marx's analysis is correct, from a CR perspective, the descriptive derivation of these tendencies from a structure is, like Smith's effort, important scientific work.

Positivist critics of Marx always objected that neither of the tendencies he identified was causal because neither is lawlike. Like the invisible hand described by Smith, the tendencies Marx posited can be counteracted.

From a CR perspective, this positivist objection is misguided. It comes from thinking of causality in terms of deterministic event-regularities. Yet the tendencies of which Smith and Marx speak are not event-regularities. They do not even share the *if–then* form of event-regularities. The tendencies of which Smith and Marx speak are better conceptualized not as laws but as forces. Whereas laws imply

---

[31] Notice that I am speaking of competition as a relational condition in which capitalists are enmeshed, not as the behavior in which they engage, although certainly the former leads to the latter. The former, however, is what sociology's actualist tendency would have us overlook. Then capitalist behavior gets explained in a way that does not explain it as capitalists' habitus. It is their habitus to compete. Why is that?

[32] This, too, is a point made by Bhaskar in *A Realist Theory*.

determinism, forces are causal properties that can be countered. Consider the force of gravity, which also can be counteracted in various ways. There are no events gravity necessarily produces. Nevertheless, the frequent need to counteract gravity already means that gravity exists as a force requiring counteraction. The same applies to the kinds of forces to which Smith and Marx refer.

There is another point to notice. As in the case of the market mechanism, not all generative mechanisms – sometimes called "powerful particulars" – involve physical parts.[33] The efficacious element of the market mechanism is more the competitive relations among producers, relations being abstract objects rather than anything physical.

Another mechanism that involves no material parts is that which generates biological evolution: blind variations and selective retention. Neither of these processes is a physical part. Together, however, they comprise the mechanism that generated all life. It is not a mechanism incidentally that is at all deterministic. In fact, Stephen J. Gould argues that if the planet's history of biological evolution were to be re-run myriad times, it would be very unlikely to eventuate once again in human beings. Instead, according to Gould, our appearance depends on a long series of contingencies, unlikely to be repeated.[34] Mechanisms, then, even in the natural sphere, are often far from deterministic.

CR similarly understands human rationality as a generative mechanism without physical parts. In referring to rationality as a mechanism, CR means simply that humans operate rationally; rationality is the way human beings work. People behave according to reasons; they act on their wants and beliefs. It is people's wants and beliefs that cause their actions – although, to be sure, not in lawlike ways. Thus, it is to the coherent system through which mental states relate to each other and to action that CR refers when speaking of rationality as a mechanism. Yet, although wants and beliefs are states of an agent, they are not necessarily physical. Rationality again exemplifies a generative mechanism without physical parts.[35]

---

[33] The term "powerful particular" goes back to Rom Harré and Edward Madden (1975) *Causal Powers* (Totowa, NJ: Rowman & Littlefield).

[34] Stephen Jay Gould (1989) *Wonderful Life* (New York: Norton).

[35] Again, within our discipline, the very word rationality is loaded with confusion. As used here, rationality is not to be associated with rational choice theory's complete equation of rationality with utility maximization.

So much for what CR means by mechanisms. What about causal properties? What does CR mean by that designation? Actually, a broad range of things – from tendencies and dispositions to capacities and powers. Instead of the covering law model's colorless and unilinear understanding of causality, CR's powers view makes sense of our entire, rich vocabulary of *causative verbs*: pushing, pulling, attracting, repelling, corroding, insulting, killing, reproducing, exiling, deceiving. These verbs and so many others like them are the textured ways we speak of causal properties in concrete situations. Causality is a multi-form matter.[36]

CR does not completely rule out talk of events causing other events. In the event that a baseball, flying through the air, breaks a window, it could be said that the one event caused the other. But more fundamental than events are the ontological particulars involved – the baseball and the window – and their causal properties. It is the hardness of the ball, its projectability, and its momentum that gives it the power to break, and the brittleness of the window that disposes it to breaking.[37]

In each case, the causal powers of the particular derive from its essential properties, which in turn derive from its internal structure.[38] What makes glass brittle, for example, is the lack of long-range structure in its molecular make-up. Rom Harré and Edward Madden offer us a more extended example:

Consider the case of a suction pump. Let us say that the pressure of the air on the reservoir and the partial vacuum in the cylinder of the pump are the conditions the obtaining of which are jointly sufficient for raising the water up the pump and out of the spigot. Ordinarily we would say that the atmosphere has the power to push the water up the cylinder, which manifests itself when there is no counteracting pressure, and that the water has the liability, or disposition, to be pushed up the cylinder in the absence of air. This power or ability of the atmosphere, in turn, would be explained by referring to the nature of the atmosphere. The atmosphere is a blanket of air around the surface of the earth. Air has weight and so exerts pressure, and

---

[36] This is a point that has been repeatedly pressed by Nancy Cartwright. See, for example, Cartwright (1999) *The Dappled World: A Study of the Boundaries of Science* (New York: Cambridge University Press).

[37] The example is taken from Eric Marcus (2009) "Why There are No Token States," *Journal of Philosophical Research* 34: 215–241.

[38] See Stephen Mumford (2008) "Powers, *Dispositions*, Properties or a Causal Manifesto," pp. 139–151 in Ruth Groff (ed.), *Revitalizing Causality* (New York: Routledge).

the farther down in the blanket of air, the greater the weight of air above and so the greater the pressure, etc.[39]

In the above exposition, the power of air to move the water up the suction pump is explained as deriving from its essential qualities, its composition as discrete particles, each of which has mass and weight. Although Harré and Madden speak of joint causal sufficiency, the intent is not to point to a law but what obtains in a particular, closed causal context without counteracting forces.

Gorski's ECPRES model with amendment

We have covered a lot of abstract ground here, so much that it might be difficult to put everything together. Toward that end, Philip Gorski's ECPRES model is very useful.[40] It brings together and interrelates all the essential elements of the CR approach to causality. I think it provides a good rule of thumb, but offer two amendments.

According to Gorski, the various elements of the CR approach can be captured by the letters encompassed by the acronym ECPRES. E stands for emergence and CP for causal powers. RE and S stand for related elements of a system.

Gorski's basic idea is that RE and S together comprise what CR means by a causal mechanism. CR thinks of causal mechanisms primarily as systems of related elements. Again, the elements need not be physical, nor need they be parts. We have already observed that wants, beliefs, and intentions are all systematically related to each other but not necessarily physically.[41] Nor are these mental states properly thought of as parts of anything.

For CR, causal powers arise out of mechanisms. They *emerge* from them. Thus the initial E and CP. Emergence, as I have said, is properly

---

[39] Harré and *Madden, Causal Powers*, pp. 63–64.

[40] See Gorski, "Social Mechanisms."

[41] As Gorski points out in "Social Mechanisms," any physical interpretation of mental states depends on the vindication of physicalist reductionism. Although it is beyond the scope of this book to much address that topic, suffice it to say that physicalism has long been in trouble. See Daniel Stoljar (2009) "Physicalism," *The Stanford Encyclopedia of Philosophy (Fall Edition)*, Edward N. Zalta (ed.), http://plato.stanford.edu/archives/fall2009/entries/physicalism. See also David Chalmers (1996) *The Conscious Mind* (New York: Oxford University Press); and Joseph Margolis (1979) *Persons and Minds: The Prospects for a Non-reductive Materialism* (New York: Springer).

the topic of a long conversation. By emergence here and now, I just mean the appearance of a new causal property in the world that was not there previously, one that is a property of a mechanism as a whole by virtue of its organization and not a property of any of its constituent elements. Gorski cites the example of a clock. Telling time is a new causal property of the entire clock taken as a whole and not a property of any of its parts. Similarly, catching mice is a causal capacity of a mouse trap taken as a whole and not of any of its parts. The new causal properties come into being or emerge from the organization of the whole.

Now, for my two amendments. The ECPRES model represents the CR approach to causality at its most elaborate, but oftentimes things are much simpler. In many contexts, particularly narrative contexts, when we speak of the mechanism involved in a causal process, we refer not to an entire system but just to a single causal property. Consider again our principal. The mechanism we previously noted that shapes the principal's interaction with the students is a single relation, the principal's power over the students.

Perhaps it could be said, if we want, that this relation itself constitutes a mini-system because contra Mustafa Emirbayer's relational sociology, if there is a relation, then there must be relata, i.e., elements related by the relation.[42] In that case, we do have two social positions here, the principal and the student, related by power. Thus, we are back to the RE and S of the ECPRES model.

Okay, but let us move back a bit. What is the cause of the principal's power over the students? Remember we said it was the capacity or power the principal possesses to expel students (and to impose other disciplinary sanctions). So here the mechanism behind the power relation is not in fact an entire system but a single capacity. Hence, my first amendment: Often, the relevant mechanism is not an entire system but a single causal property.

Let us move back further still. From whence arises the principal's capacity to expel? Again, we might say it derives from an entire system of elements. A principal is a social position within an entire system of social positions that comprises an educational institution; a principal

---

[42] Mustafa Emirbayer (1997) "Manifesto for a Relational Sociology," *American Journal of Sociology* 103 (2): 281–317. Smith, *What Is a Person?* , pp. 230–234 also makes this very point.

has no meaning outside of that system. And within such system, an essential part of being the principal is to have the capacity to discipline students.

But what is the cause of this whole educational system? An educational institution is not a natural kind. Clearly, the educational system of relations was produced by a prior set of cultural rules that established the educational institution to begin with. So my second amendment: in the social world, causal properties like social relations often emerge not from some lower level set of elements but from rules. Rules, too, are an important causal mechanism.

Relations in turn, once they emerge from the cultural rules, have objective causal effects of their own that do not necessarily depend on anyone's notice or interpretation. As we have seen, the principal's capacity to discipline students, which derives from the rules, creates a power relationship that exists and exists objectively, i.e., independent of anyone's interpretation. Such emergently objective or material relations are routinely overlooked by the interpretivist bent in American sociology. As Neil Gross says, describing the pragmatist conception of causal mechanisms, "it is interpretation all the way down."[43] No, according to CR, it is not. Along with the discursive, there is also the extra-discursive, the two often intertwined. To forget the latter in an exclusive focus on the former is a reductionism of an idealist sort.

CR mechanisms and causal properties vs. alternate accounts

With the ground we have covered so far, we can now appreciate the distinctive move made by actor–network theory (ANT) to extend agency beyond humans to other *actants* operative in the world. We can both appreciate that move and see how it misleads.[44]

In a sense, the positivist covering law model sucks the causal agency out of the things of the world and relocates it in putative causal laws. The things of the world are thus left inert. Instead, it is the transcendental causal laws that possess the *umph* that makes things happen. The things of the world just supply initial conditions.

---

[43] Neil Gross (2009) "A Pragmatist Theory of Social Mechanisms," *American Sociological Review* 74: 358–379.

[44] See Bruno Latour (2007) *Reassembling the Social: An Introduction to Actor Network Theory* (New York: Oxford University Press).

ANT and the so-called "new materialism" are a reaction to this positivist picture, and from the CR perspective the reaction is warranted. If by agency, ANT and the new materialism mean causal agency, then from the CR perspective they are right to dispense with laws and to see the things of the world as alive with causal powers. Yes, from this perspective, many of the things in the world are *actants* besides people. We speak of the agent or active ingredient in a medicinal tablet. What we mean by active ingredient is that particular ingredient that possesses the causal force to accomplish whatever it is the tablet is designed to do. CR is perfectly behind this move.[45]

What is misleading about ANT terminology is that the word agency means something different in different contexts. In the case of human behavior, agency is normally meant to designate that subset of human behavior that we willfully direct and that is distinguished by its involvement in an intentional chain.[46]

Human persons are not the only beings that behave intentionally. Higher animals do as well. But not everything that ANT would term an actant does. A clock, for example. From the standpoint of this distinction, therefore, non-conscious actants are not intentional agents although they certainly are causal agents.

ANT seems to recognize this distinction. In contrast with Emirbayer's relational sociology, ANT acknowledges the divide between intentional and non-intentional agency; it just considers the distinction overplayed.[47] Here CR differs. The category of intentionality marks the realm of reasons, and there is a crucial analytical

---

[45] On the "New Materialisms," see Diana Coole and Samantha Frost (eds.) (2010) *New Materialisms: Ontology, Agency, and Politics* (Durham, NC: Duke University Press). It probably says something about core and periphery in academia and about academic non-listening that poststructuralists have now discovered on their own what critical realists have been saying to them for decades – that they had been promulgating a version of reductive idealism. Certainly that was at issue in the so-called "Sokal affair" of 1996 some 20 years ago. Nonetheless, the new materialism is a salutary development.

[46] See Donald Davidson (2001) "Agency," pp. 43–62 in Donald Davidson, *Essays on Actions and Events* (New York: Clarendon). Intentionality here (with a small i) denotes willful action as opposed to the "aboutness" of Intentionality (capital I). We will return to intentionality more frontally in Chapter 5.

[47] See Latour, *Reassembling the Social*, p. 71. In Chapter 5 we will centrally contest the account of agency provided by Mustafa Emirbayer and Ann Mische (1998) "What Is Agency," *American Journal of Sociology* 103 (4): 962–1023, which contains no mention of Donald Davidson's seminal article "Agency," or much talk of intentionality.

distinction, which CR upholds, between processes that are reasoned and processes that are not. Forgetting this analytical distinction is not required in order to acknowledge the causal powers of other actants.

Potentially a deeper problem with ANT is its notion of network. Latour defines a network as a series of actions, and some of the subsequent work in ANT seems to overstress performativity.[48] In both respects, ANT veers toward actualism. Not all causal properties take the form of actions – affordances, for example. Chairs afford sitting and words meaning, but neither affordance is an action. Other causal properties act without acting. Think again of the capacity for action that stands behind a threat. The problem here, however, need not be fatal. ANT might protect itself from actualism via a stronger grounding in CR.

Although ANT does not actually use the word mechanism, as noted, other perspectives do. Their various understandings of mechanisms are similar to each other's, but notably different from CR's. They are different from CR's in being more limited in several specific ways. In particular, they tend to be individualistic and actualistic; they thus fail to encompass the true range of causal mechanisms operative in the social world.

To see what I mean, let us run through a number of these alternative understandings of causal mechanisms. According to the late historical sociologist Charles Tilly, "Mechanisms are causes on the small scale: similar events that produce essentially the same immediate effects across a wide range of circumstances."[49] For Margaret Somers, a mechanism is "a meaningful connection between events."[50] For rational choice theorists like Jon Elster and Peter Hedström, mechanisms always refer to *microfoundations* of larger social processes, specifically actors and their actions. Whereas Hedström at least speaks of actors as entities, placing him closer to CR, Elster remains actualistic, saying a mechanism is a "recurring and intelligible pattern"

---

[48] Latour, *Reassembling the Social*, p. 128. See John Law (2009) "Actor Network Theory and Material Semiotics," pp. 141–158 in Bryan S. Turner (ed.) *The New Blackwell Companion to Social Theory* (New York: Wiley-Blackwell).

[49] See Charles Tilly (2003) *The Politics of Collective Violence* (New York: Cambridge University Press), p. 20.

[50] Margaret Somers (1998) "We're No Angel: Realism, Rational Choice, and Rationality in Social Science," *American Journal of Sociology* 104 (3): 722–784, p. 726.

or a "frequently occurring and easily recognizable causal pattern," in either case, something that occurs or recurs; in other words, events.[51]

Tilly and Elster's understandings above are actualist, defining mechanisms in terms of events. With the exception of the understanding contributed by Somers, all of those listed above privilege micro processes and especially individual actors.

According to Neil Gross, the pragmatists' understanding of mechanisms is close to Hedström's, not actualist but privileging actors. Specifically, according to Gross, pragmatists "view mechanisms as chains or aggregations of actors confronting problem situations and mobilizing more or less habitual responses."[52]

Leave aside for the moment pragmatism's penchant for habit, which we will examine – or, as postmodernists taught us to say, *interrogate* – in Chapter 5. It is unclear exactly what Gross means by "chains," but he also, like the others, seems to embrace some kind of aggregative model of social action whereby macro processes are all always built up from below.

The CR understanding of mechanisms differs from these alternative views in several major ways. First, in contrast with the actualist emphasis in the alternatives, which comes from positivism, CR, as noted, does not think of mechanisms exclusively or even primarily as events. Rather, it thinks of mechanisms primarily as things with their causal powers or as the structured relations that comprise them. Thus, even in the case of causal processes like corrosion, which take place over time and thus encompass events, CR would still include among the mechanisms involved the molecular structures of the interactants, which are not events.

Aside from their heavy actualist tendency, the alternative understandings of mechanisms are also quite narrow and individualistic. Essentially, aside from events and what can be considered events such as actions and interactions, the only things that count as mechanisms are actors. Consider Gross's pragmatist restriction of mechanisms to the entire complex of actors responding to problem situations. Do not

---

[51] Peter Hedström (2005) *Dissecting the Social: On the Principles of Analytical Sociology* (New York: Cambridge University Press). Jon Elster (1999) *Alchemies of the Mind: Rationality and the Emotions* (New York: Cambridge University Press), pp, ix, 1.

[52] Neil Gross (2009) "A Pragmatist Theory of Social Mechanisms," *American Sociological Review* 74: 358–379.

problem situations themselves embody some kinds of mechanisms quite apart from how actors respond to them? Gross's implied ontology – and that of the others – is too sparse.

In contrast, for CR, besides actors and actions, many things are mechanisms, and they need not be built up from lower level social processes. Language, for example, is a mechanism that affords all kinds of causal effects and which certainly acts on us causally in many ways. Rules, similarly, as we have seen, are mechanisms that yield causally efficacious relations and other causal properties. Bombs are mechanisms too.

Yet, contra Gross's pragmatist understanding, language, rules, bombs, and such are neither actors nor even chains of actors. Nor are they events or actions. The same for relations, which are most notably absent from all the alternative understandings of mechanism. As previously argued, power-over must be understood as a relation and as such a causally consequential mechanism governing interactions. But taken at their word, none of the alternative understandings of mechanism encompass it.

Nor, again, are either rules or relations things that always must get built up from something smaller. The rules of property ownership that govern capitalist relations are not micro; nor are they composed of anything more micro. Similarly for the class relations that ensue from those rules. They, too, are irreducibly macro in nature, not the aggregation or chaining together of anything smaller. While it is definitely true that everything social is produced by individual people acting together, individual people acting together can also produce macro-constructs with macro-effects acting back down on them without anything intermediary.

In the end, sociology needs to free itself from a very narrow, individualistic, and actualist causal ontology. Sociology, particularly American sociology, needs CR.

A brief note on the causal criterion of existence

I mentioned the causal criterion of existence in the previous chapter and should say a bit more here. As we saw in Figure 2.1, for CR, reality encompasses more than is manifested. For CR, causal mechanisms may exist even when they go untriggered and thus fail to produce any events.

Hedström appears to find the causal criterion of existence a mysterious doctrine. How, he asks, do we know a mechanism exists if it goes untriggered?[53] The mystery is that Hedström finds the causal criterion so mysterious. The explanatory causal mechanism behind that mystery must be the ideological hold of empiricism for the causal criterion again just codifies common sense.

I say empiricism because the problem here is a neglect of conceptual considerations. We do not require empirical evidence to know that a principal has the capacity to discipline students. It is not as if we must see with our own eyes the principal's actually doing so. It is enough to know that this capacity has been bestowed on the principal by the rules. Similarly, even before Congress impeached president Andrew Johnson in 1868, it was known that Congress had the causal power to do so (and, yes, to *impeach* is another socially causative verb). Indeed, Congress could not have done so without knowing it had the power to do so – somehow without empirical evidence. Any remaining mystery about this is a product of empiricist ideology.

From causality to causal explanation

So much for the CR approach to causality. What about causal explanation? As noted at the start of this chapter, from a CR point of view, causal analysis enters in three different ways at three different moments. At one moment, we try to explain why things have the particular causal powers they possess. The causal features of things are explained by the constitutive natures of those things, that is, by describing the mechanism that generates the causal feature. Being descriptive, that task is very conducive to ethnographic methodology or in-depth interviews. The distinction here, however, between description and explanation is a false one because what is being described is an explanatory mechanism.

In the second moment, we try to explain why in a particular case a contingent conjuncture of mechanisms, each having its own causal powers, all combine to cause a particular, perhaps non-repeatable event. In this moment, explanation will typically take the form of a narrative that utilizes theoretical language to weave together the simultaneous operation of multiple mechanisms. It is in fact only such a

---

[53] Hedström, *Dissecting the Social.*

historical account that can accommodate the causally open system constituted by the real world.

Historical narrative is found not just in the human sciences but in the natural sciences as well. Consider cosmology, with its account of an unfolding universe that begins with a big bang; then a period of "cosmic inflation"; followed by different phases of cool-down and formation of different elements; the formation of galaxies, and so on. Here, even in physics, we have a history. In geology, too, if we are to explain the current distribution of continents, we must do so via a narrative. Likewise in biology if we seek to explain the descent of *Homo sapiens*.

Because the social world is so causally open, because, as Heidegger tells us, humans are beings especially embedded in time, it should be no surprise that history becomes the paradigmatic form of explanation in the human sciences. Historical narratives not only capture the temporal dimension of human life, they are uniquely able to encompass the operation of multiple causal properties of all sorts. Indeed, because for CR causality is no longer deterministic, even the effects of social structure can be woven into a history without any implication that all is reducible to that one mechanism. Consider briefly the following famous passage from the 31st chapter of the first volume of *Capital*:

The discovery of gold and silver in America, the extirpation, enslavement and entombment in mines of the aboriginal population, the beginning of the conquest and looting of the East Indies, the turning of Africa into a warren for the commercial hunting of black-skins, signalized the rosy dawn of the era of capitalist production. These idyllic proceedings are the chief momenta of primitive accumulation.

George Steinmetz stresses the distinct ability of narrative to capture three key features of causality in open systems: conjuncture, contingency, and complexity.[54] All are evident in the brief passage above. Although the passage is clearly a description, it is not just a description or merely a description. It is meant to be an explanation and, despite

---

[54] George Steinmetz (2005) *The Politics of Method in the Human Sciences: Positivism and Its Epistemological Others* (Durham, NC: Duke University Press). For additional recent work on the philosophy of history that is very helpful to the social sciences, see Daniel Little (2010) *New Contributions to the Philosophy of History* (New York: Springer).

the passage's deceiving simplicity, a complex explanation of one of the prerequisites for capitalism.

Conjuncture refers to the simultaneous operation of multiple causal mechanisms in a particular case, each operation occurring contingently. Contingency refers to a lack of necessity. It was not inevitable, in other words, that any particular mechanisms be operative in any particular case. In fact, it could well be that those same multiple mechanisms will never simultaneously operate again. Thus, the events produced by their joint activity could well be unique and not just unique but, because the product of a contingent conjuncture, contingent themselves. The resulting complexity is something that narratives are distinctly capable of elucidating.

The passage from *Capital* is explanatory first in its use of theoretical language. Primitive accumulation is a technical Marxian term, appearing within a system of related concepts about capitalism.[55] Primitive accumulation refers to the initial capital needed for the very first round of capitalist investment. From whence did this initial capital arise and, moreover, get into the hands of the particular investors who came to deploy it? That matter is what the passage attempts to explain. It explains the requisite primitive accumulation as a conjuncture of three main mechanisms or processes involving mechanisms: (1) the discovery of riches in America, followed by various processes through which the Europeans expropriated them; (2) the conquest and looting of the East Indies; and (3) the erection of mechanisms in Africa that constituted the institutions associated with the slave trade. Described narratively, there is no implication that these three processes inevitably co-occurred. Their co-occurrence rather was a contingent conjuncture.

The spare language of the passage hides a tremendous amount of causal complexity. That complexity is captured by a second way in which the passage explains, namely by its invocation of causative verbs: discovering, looting, conquering, extirpation, enslavement, and entombment (all of which, incidentally, imply intentionality – rather than, say, habitus). Each of these verbs connotes a process and a process that itself involves multiple mechanisms. What, for example, is a conquest, and who conquers? A conquest first of all is a relation, a relation between two peoples qua people. Thus, we are already dealing

---

[55] Re-description in theoretical language is one way Bhaskar suggests that qualitative accounts explain. See Bhaskar, *A Realist Theory*.

with collective- rather than individual-level phenomena. And how is conquest effected? By armies, which are themselves complex institutions, and by administrative institutions (complex social mechanisms) of conquest that maintain and exploit the hold.

The causative verbs thus encapsulate and chunk many subsidiary processes, not necessarily expressible by any series of laws. By virtue of that encapsulation and chunking, we are able to move on seamlessly, even unnoticeably, to higher levels of complex causal interaction. Again, the analytical movement appears just common sense. It is common sense but common sense in desperate need of recovery. This common sense gets lost when we attempt to strip down causality to linear event-regularities, whether nomological or counterfactual.

Analytical statistics

We come, finally, to the matter of analytical statistics. Clearly, CR displaces statistical techniques from their current position of methodological privilege. As we noted, for positivism, a regression equation serves simultaneously as both an explanatory covering law and as the statistical evidence of its own existence. Because for CR causal explanation involves mechanisms rather than laws, for CR, evidence and explanation once again become distinct. For CR, an event-regularity, even in the rigorous form of a regression equation, cannot ever serve as an explanation. It is at most one, fallible piece of evidence for an explanation.

Demoting regression and other statistical techniques from explanation to evidence, CR has no reason to reject them as such. Of course, when critical realists use statistical techniques, they are not searching for invariant relationships independent of social context. Instead, the statistics are employed to indicate the contingent operation of a mechanism in a particular socio-historical situation.

Let me illustrate the point by the use of statistics in my own research. I mentioned earlier the work I did with some colleagues for *Post-Ethical Society*. More specifically we examined the debate that ensued in US newspapers and news magazines about America's eventual decision to attack Iraq. One large question that concerned us was how the moral dimensions of the issue (the justness of the war, its legality, and so forth) were effectively muted in favor of exclusively prudential concerns (e.g., the cost in American lives, the wisdom of acting alone, or the fear of becoming bogged down in a long war). To the extent that what we were asking here was a "how" question, what was required was a qualitative analysis, specifically a discourse analysis of the rhetorical maneuvers through which moral concerns were dampened or channeled out of discussion.

Other aspects of the question, however, were quantitative. Specifically, did some publications – say America's elite newspapers – practice such "moral muting" more than others? Did secular publications practice it more than religious publications? These sorts of questions – which ask not how but rather how much, which, or where – are also important. In contrast with "how" questions, questions about relative frequency are quantitative in nature, answerable only by comparative counts. Not only must there be some measure of comparative prevalence, but there also should be some measure discounting the likelihood that any differences found are due only to chance. In short, such quantitative questions call for analytical statistics. The statistics themselves will not explain the differences found, nor will they yield any kind of universal law. They will simply support a claim that in this particular case, for certain reasons, which themselves are the explanatory mechanisms, moral muting was practiced by some publications more than others.

In the end, there are no specifically CR methods of research. Unlike both positivism and Interpretivism, CR does not pose an opposition between qualitative and quantitative methods. It specifically does not just reverse what is included and excluded. To do so would erect a new methodological *foundationalism*. Instead, CR reunifies sociological methodology. From a CR perspective, there is a valid and important place for all of the methods sociologists have employed – although not necessarily in the way they have employed them.[56] Statistics, as mentioned, should function as a form of evidence for an explanation rather than as an explanation itself. Conversely, sociologists using qualitative methods ought to become bolder than they now are about asserting and pursuing the scientific contribution of their work as descriptive of mechanisms and conjunctures of mechanisms in natural settings.[57]

[56] See, again, Smith, *What Is a Person?* , pp. 277–316 for concurrence with and further elaboration of this position.

[57] Again, it should be observed that some critical realists such as Andrew Sayer hold a different opinion. See Sayer (2010) *Method in Social Science: A Realist Approach* (New York: Routledge).

In the end, CR reclaims the unity of science that positivism was always after. Positivism sought that unity in a misconceived determinism and a model of causality built on it. Interpretivists were correct to resist that drive, but the problem was not confined to the human realm as the intepretivists thought. The positivist doctrine did not even fit the natural realm; even there the covering law model of causality fails to apply.

With CR, the epistemology of the natural and human sciences once again coincides. True, we do not hang out with or interview atoms, and nor do we use colliders to study people. Specific methods will always differ across domains. Yet a common understanding of explanation is preserved. If the human sciences uniquely require hermeneutic methods, it is because hermeneutics is the way to access the distinct mechanism through which human actors behave. For CR, method is not something a priori but always appropriate to the research question and the object of study. And interpretation is not always the key issue in the human sciences. Sometimes at issue is an effect that is extra-discursive. The effect of a falling birth rate is one such example. We sociologists should be using all the methods available to us to confront such predicaments. As a non-foundationalist approach, CR philosophically justifies methodological pluralism.[58]

---

[58] Roy Bhaskar, Cheryl Frank, Karl Georg Hayer, and Peter Naess (2010) *Interdisciplinarity and Climate Change: Transforming Knowledge and Practice for Our Global Future* (New York: Routledge).

3 | *What is truth?*

The question posed by this chapter's title was, according to the *New Testament*, Pontius Pilot's retort to Jesus.[1] Jesus had just declared himself the truth, effectively assigning himself what Roy Bhaskar would call Alethic truth and others Truth (with a big T), the ultimate truth behind "life, the universe, and everything." Pilot, clearly a proto-postmodernist, was having none of it.[2]

Today, especially with what postmodernists termed the "end of meta-narratives," many liberal thinkers are hostile to any kind of Truth with a big T, religious or otherwise.[3] They see assertions of such Truth as "totalizing," as repressive of alternate ways of thinking and seeing. If they countenance at all the concept of truth, they prefer local, shifting truths, truth with a little t. One of my feminist comrades tells me that of course she believes in facts. It is only Truth with a big T she opposes. Others are phobic even to such modest talk of truth. They prefer truth-surrogates like robustness or, better yet, no overt reference to truth at all.

The twentieth century ended with a crisis of truth, and we are still in it. Witness the continued popularity of Jean Baudrillard. There is even an *International Journal of Baudrillard Studies*. According to Baudrillard, in our era, the possibility of truth has vanished. Baudrillard's argument is essentially a poststructuralist one: The very words we would use to speak of reality merely conjure other words, the whole a self-referential system that fails to make contact with wordless reality as it is in itself.[4] As Jacques Derrida likewise put it, "Il n'y a pas hors-texte."[5]

---

[1] John 18: 38.
[2] Bhaskar begins speaking of alethic truth in Bhaskar (2008) *Dialectic: The Pulse of Freedom* (New York: Routledge).
[3] Jean-François Lyotard (1979) *The Postmodern Condition: A Report on Knowledge* (Minneapolis, MN: University of Minnesota Press).
[4] Jean Baudrillard (1981) *Simulacra and Simulation* (Ann Arbor, MI: University of Michigan).
[5] Jacques Derrida (1997) *Of Grammatology* (Baltimore, MD: Johns Hopkins University Press), pp. 158–159, 163.

Of course, as we already saw in our introduction, there remains the problem of *performative contradiction*. As speech acts, assertions ineluctably carry with them their own validity claims, among them that what is asserted is true. Severed from that validity claim, any putative assertion becomes unintelligible. Derrida's claim, for example, is meta-textual and so itself beyond its own textual announcement. So it is with Baudrillard. If we are to make any sense of Baudrillard's assertion, we must take him to be asserting it true that in our era, access to reality has passed. But then does not Baudrillard's own assertion imply contact with at least one reality, the possibility of which the assertion denies?[6]

Like Derrida as well, Baudrillard appears guilty here of a performative contradiction. Yet we must bear in mind that the French do social science as poets.[7] Thus, we must always take into account their penchant for hyperbole. Marc Poster places Baudrillard in more defensible perspective:

Baudrillard is not disputing the trivial issue that reason remains operative in some actions, that if I want to arrive at the next block, for example, I can assume a Newtonian universe (common sense), plan a course of action (to walk straight for X meters, carry out the action, and finally fulfill my goal by arriving at the point in question). What is in doubt is that this sort of thinking enables a historically informed grasp of the present in general. According to Baudrillard, it does not. The concurrent spread of the hyperreal through the media and the collapse of liberal and Marxist politics as the master narratives, deprives the rational subject of its privileged access to truth. In an important sense individuals are no longer citizens, eager to maximise their civil rights, nor proletarians, anticipating the onset of communism. They are rather consumers, and hence the prey of objects as defined by the code.[8]

Alors. We can better understand Baudrillard via our distinction between big and little truth. As Poster explains, Baudrillard is not denying our access to little truths, the micro-truths we need to navigate our way through life. It is Truth with a big T to which Baudrillard

---

[6] The same point about Baudrillard is made by Christian Smith (2010) *What Is a Person? Rethinking Humanity, Social Life and the Moral Good from the Person Up* (Chicago, IL: University of Chicago), pp. 142–143.

[7] I owe this insight to my friend (and boss) in anthropology, Wesley Shumar.

[8] Mark Poster (2001) "Introduction," pp. 1–12 in Marc Poster (ed.), *Baudrillard: Selected Writings* (Stanford, CA: Stanford University Press), p. 7.

denies our contemporary access, the truth, for example, about our current macro-social situation.

This clarification helps. There is something Baudrillard is saying about what used to be called ideology that is quite interesting. Yet to appreciate Baudrillard's point, we still must read him like a poet. The reason is that, literally, Baudrillard still contradicts himself. According to Poster, Baudrillard is denying only the "possibility of an historically informed grasp of the present." Yet is not "an historically informed grasp of the present" precisely what Baudrillard himself is offering by denying that contemporary possibility?

Is not the reality of global warming yet another instance of "an historically informed grasp of the present"? Is that reality as well too big a truth for us to grasp? At what point does big T truth become small enough for us to access?

Ultimately, we cannot tenably make a distinction between big T and little t truth. In the end, there are only individual truths or facts, and they come in sizes both large and small. But what is truth? We are back to Pilot's question.

CR's Holy Trinity

Again, CR can help us find our way. To begin with, we have the distinctions Bhaskar introduces between *ontological realism*, *epistemic relativism*, and *judgmental rationality* – another triad that Bhaskar calls a "Holy Trinity" (he liked spiritual designations).[9]

Almost everyone now accepts ontological realism. *Ontological realism* is the acceptance of a single, ontologically objective reality, common to us all and independent of human thought. Ontological independence here means that the world is what it is, regardless of what we happen to think about it or if, indeed, we do think about it. It means, for example, that to the extent that it is a reality, something like global warming will not go away even if we all join the US Republican party in refusing its existence. For his part, Herbert Blumer quite definitely rooted Symbolic Interactionism in ontological realism:

[9] See Roy Bhaskar (2009) *Scientific Realism and Human Emancipation* (New York: Routledge); also Mervyn Hartwig (2008) "Introduction," pp. ix–xxvi in Roy Bhaskar, *A Realist Theory of Science* (London: Verso).

I shall begin with the redundant assertion that an empirical science presupposes the existence of an empirical world. Such an empirical world exists as something available for observation, study, and analysis. It stands over against the scientific observer, with a character that has to be dug out and established through observation, study, and analysis.[10]

Even postmodernists, when they still identified themselves as such, protested that they were ontological realists.[11] Although today few want to be caught actually denying ontological realism, there still are popular attempts to equivocate about it. Consider John Law's commentary on Annemarie Mol's book, *The Body Multiple*, which follows a material-semiotic approach to ANT:

Annemarie Mol's book, *The Body Multiple*, describes diagnostic and treatment practices for lower limb atherosclerosis. The condition turns up in different forms in different places: in the surgery it presents as pain on walking; in radiography as appears as an X-ray photo of narrowed or blocked blood vessels; in the ultrasound department it takes the form of Doppler readings which detect increases in blood speeds at narrowed sections of vessels; and in the operating theater it manifests itself as a white paste scraped out of blood vessels by the surgeon (Mol 2002). It is tempting to say that these are different perspectives on a single disease.[12]

Law's last line is that it is tempting to say that what Mol describes are different perspectives on a single disease. That common sense view would be entirely unproblematic. "This, however," Law tells us, "is precisely what Mol rejects."[13] He goes on:

In material-semiotic mode, she argues that each practice generates its own material reality. This means that for atherosclerosis there are four actor networks or realities rather than one. Then she says that how these relate

---

[10] Herbert Blumer (1969) "The Metholodological Position of Symbolic Interactionism," pp. 1–60 in Herbert Blumer (ed.), *Symbolic Interactionism: Perspective and Method* (Englewood Cliffs, NJ: Prentice Hall), p. 21.

[11] See, for example, Stanly Fish (2003) "Truth But No Consequences: Why Philosophy Doesn't Matter" *Critical Inquiry* 3 http://brandon.multics.org/library/Stanley%20Fish/fish2003truth.html. Fish, like Richard Rorty, espouses a neo-pragmatism closely aligned with the postmodern sentiment. See similarly, with more of an ultimate realism, Pickering (2012) "The World Since Kuhn," *Social Studies of Science* 42 (3): 467–473.

[12] John Law (2009) "Actor Network Theory and Material Semiotics," pp. 141–158 in Brian Turner (ed.), *The New Blackwell Companion to Social Theory* (New York: Wiley-Blackwell), pp. 151–152.

[13] Ibid., p. 152.

together, if they do so at all, is itself a practical matter. Sometimes, and for a time, they may be coordinated into a single reality, but often this does not happen. *So Mol's claim is simple but counterintuitive. In theory the body may be single but in practice it is multiple because there are many body practices and therefore many bodies.* (Italics added)[14]

All the above is fine until we get to the italicized lines, which seem to be an equivocation or a non-sequitur. It may well be that each practice generates a new reality in the form of a separate actor network. But it hardly follows from the reality of those separate actor networks that atherosclerosis itself and any individual body that suffers it are each anything other than single. Of course, Law hedges with his distinction between theory and practice, suggesting something either true but banal – that in their practices technicians don't think of a whole disease or body but only of those aspects that concern them – or exciting but mad – that in fact ontologically, given the separate practices, there is no single whole disease or body. But let us hear from Mol herself:

If practices are foregrounded there is no longer a single passive object in the middle, waiting to be seen from the point of view of seemingly endless series of perspectives. Instead, objects come into being – and disappear – with the practices in which they are multiplied. And since the object of manipulation tends to differ from one practice to another, reality multiplies. The body, the patient, the disease, the doctor, the technician, the technology: all of these are more than one. More than singular.[15]

There is an implicit equivocation here as well. Mol says that according to her material-semiotic foregrounding of practices, objects of the world lose their ontologically independent existence to become the creations of our practices. If Mol is making merely an epistemological observation about material-semiotic theory, the claim is unproblematic but philosophically uninteresting. The interesting philosophical question is, given such implications, whether material-semiotic theory is something we should accept. Since Mol goes on to write an entire book about it, presumably she, like Law, is encouraging acceptance. In that case, Mol is not just making an epistemological observation about material-semiotic theory, but by virtue of

---

[14] Ibid., p. 152.
[15] Annemarie Mol (2003) *The Body Multiple: Ontology in Medical Practice* (Durham, NC: Duke University Press).

its acceptance an ontological claim about the world: There really are no objects independent of our practices involving them.

Such a claim is philosophically interesting but carries the epistemic fallacy to the extreme of collective solipsism.[16] For a while, Law was thus always careful never quite explicitly to endorse it but only nevertheless to speak as if he did.[17] By 2012, however, Law is prepared to be blunt: "One lesson that has been well-rehearsed elsewhere is that realities – objects, animals or people – are multiple. In different practices they are done in different ways."[18] With an actualism that reduces now even inert objects to doings, all that is solid melts into enactments.

Alas, next to the legerdemain of material-semiotics, ontological realism, if philosophically more tenable, is much more tame. It coincides with one of the traditional pillars of Marxian materialism – with the claim, that is, that material reality precedes subjective consciousness – or human practice. The precedence is in the first place chronological. Presumably, we all accept that there was a universe before the appearance of human beings, before in fact the appearance of any embodied consciousness or its enactments. If so, then, at least as we conceptualize it, the existence of the material universe precedes subjective consciousness and human practice not only chronologically but also ontologically. The material universe does not require human subjective consciousness or human practice in order to exist. Thus, however we think of it epistemically, the world's existence is

---

[16] It is also partly what comes from treating ethnography as mere description of what actors do. Such empiricist approach to ethnography strives to be ontologically innocent, which, according to CR, is impossible. For further discussion along such lines, see James Malazita (2015) "Ontic Communities: Speculative Fiction, Ontology, and the Digital Design Community," PhD Dissertation, Drexel University.

[17] See, for example, John Law and John Urry (2005), "Enacting the Social," *Economy and Society* 33 (3): 390–410. I say Law (and with him now Urry) equivocates because there is nothing problematic – or terribly exciting – about the claim that our theories, via effects like the self-fulfilling prophecy, can *sometimes* create the reality they purport to describe. What makes the claim exciting but also problematic is its extension to everything. Here, however, Law was still careful not to take us that far but only to write as if he had.

[18] John Law and Marianne Lien (2012) "Slippery: Field Notes on Empirical Ontology," *Social Studies of Science*: 10. www.sv.uio.no/sai/english/research/projects/newcomers/publications/working-papers-web/Slippery%20revised%2013%20WP%20version.pdf.

ontologically independent of us.[19] Put otherwise and contrary to the material-semiotic view, the material things of the world – tables, chairs, atoms, etc. – are objective particulars, not human enactments.

Consciousness, on the other hand, as the phenomenologists would say, is always *consciousness of*, that is, consciousness of something.[20] The something must therefore precede consciousness. Nor are we the floating consciousness of angels or ghosts. We are embodied consciousness, and the consciousness we represent requires first the evolution of certain kinds of bodies. Put in the words of high philosophy, materialism means that being precedes consciousness.

Of course, things get a bit trickier when we move from the natural to the social world. When we turn our attention to the social world, would we still say that being precedes consciousness? Is not at least the social world a social construction?

In one sense, yes, of course, the social world is largely a social construction, but here again is an important place where we need carefully to disentangle our ontological and epistemological talk. To say that the social world is largely a social construction is to make an ontological claim, a claim about a property of the social world. Perhaps it will help to say somewhat facetiously that, ontologically, the social world in large part is *objectively subjective* or, more properly, inter-subjective. But the objectivity referenced here is ontological rather than epistemological. It speaks not to our ways of knowing anything about the object of knowledge – in this case, the social world – but to the nature of that object itself, quite apart from how we know it.[21]

How do we know that what we say is true? Now that question is separate and the one that is epistemological. Who is the *we* referred to? Not us as objects of knowledge or study. Rather, the we referred to is the we who are the subjects of knowledge or study, we who are acting

---

[19] Unless of course we buy into some quantum-inspired notion of participatory universe such as is espoused by physicist John Wheeler. See, for example, Paul Davies (2007) *The Cosmic Jackpot: Why Our Universe is Just Right for Life* (New York: Houghton-Mifflin). Even in that case, some arrangement remains ontologically objective. Since, however, this range of possibility is too far afield from sociological concern, I say no more about it.

[20] See, for example, Jean Paul Sartre (1993) *Being and Nothingness* (New York: Washington Square Press), p. 222.

[21] The issue here concerns ontological kinds of reality. For a fuller discussion of that issue, see Smith, *What Is a Person?*, pp. 149–157, 185–190; and also John Searle (1995) *The Construction of Social Reality* (New York: Free Press).

in the capacity of the scientific observers, those of whom Blumer spoke. That category includes both those who have conducted some body of research and those with whom the putative findings are being shared and thus drawn into conversation about it.

Epistemologically, we must distinguish between the subject of knowledge and the object of knowledge, the knower and the known. In addition, we must speak of the content of knowledge, what the knower comes to know or observe about the object, which is again separate from the object itself. With regard to this latter distinction, Bhaskar speaks of the *transitive* and *intransitive* dimensions of knowledge. Roughly, the *intransitive* dimension of knowledge refers to the unchanging object of knowledge itself, and the *transitive* to the content of knowledge, which may change across time or across different subjects of knowledge.[22]

Most sociologists today would agree that, apart from the quantum realm, the transitive and intransitive dimensions of knowledge are separate. Beyond the realm of quantum phenomena, observation need not alter the object of observation. Indeed, the occurrence of such alteration, which our methods texts call an instrument effect, is generally thought to compromise epistemologically objective observation. Even ethnographers must deal with this threat to internal validity.

Analytically, ontological realism leads to a separation of the content and object of knowledge. CR affirms that separation even when we ourselves are the objects of knowledge. Our ability to make ourselves the object of our own observation is a central aspect of what it means for us to be self-conscious. We could not be self-conscious if our self-observation invariably altered the self we observe – although it may sometimes do so and although it might result in our doing so. In the main, though, even when observing ourselves, the content of our knowledge (what we come to think of ourselves) remains something ontologically distinct from the object of our knowledge (who and what we actually are).

So much for ontological realism. *Epistemic relativism* refers to the initial situated-ness of all knowledge formation. When as subjects of knowledge we come to know or observe, we do so always from a

---

[22] Bhaskar, *A Realist Theory*, p. 54. Also Mervyn Hartwig (2007) *Dictionary of Critical Realism* (New York: Routledge).

particular place at a particular time with particular norms of knowing that reflect our socio-cultural situation.

Is not epistemic relativism a key contention of social constructionism? Yes. Here, against a simplistic positivism, CR does align with social constructionism. That is why, like social constructionism, CR expects that *what is considered knowledge* (i.e., knowledge's transitive dimension) will vary culturally.

The difference between CR and social constructionism concerns the conclusion drawn from epistemic relativism. For social constructionism, epistemic relativism is the end of the story. The social constructionists thus either infer from epistemic relativism an unbridgeable gulf between the content and object of knowledge or they simply equate the objects of knowledge with the differing contents of knowledge. Stated otherwise, although social constructionists differ among themselves, to varying degrees they all think (1) that we can never know the ontologically real object in and of itself but only our constructions of it, and (2) that because our constructions of reality differ culturally, truth itself is relative, and we all virtually inhabit different worlds that we ourselves construct.

In contrast with social constructionism, CR believes that despite epistemic relativism, the possibility remains of what CR calls *judgmental rationality*. *Judgmental rationality* refers to our ability to adjudicate among rival reality constructions. The postulation of such an ability implies that our various constructions of reality are not all equally warranted, that on the contrary, some constructions are epistemically superior to others. Again, this position is upheld by Blumer's understanding of Symbolic Interactionism:

The traditional position of idealism is that the "world of reality" exists only in human experience and that it appears only in the form in which human beings "see" that world. I think that this position is incontestable. ... Nothing is known to human beings except in the form of something that they may indicate or refer to. To indicate anything, human beings must see it from their perspective; they must depict it as it appears to them. ... However, this does not shift "reality" as so many conclude, from the empirical world to the realm of imagery and conception. ... Such a solipsistic position is untenable and would make empirical science impossible. The position is untenable because of the fact that the empirical world can "talk back" to our pictures of it or assertions about it – talk back in the sense of challenging and resisting, or not bending to, our images or conceptions of it. This resistance gives the empirical world an obdurate character that is the mark of reality. ... It is this obdurate character of the empirical world – its ability to resist and talk back – that calls for and justifies empirical science.[23]

Although it is not my point at the moment, it is beginning to look as if CR rather than a subjectivist strain of pragmatism might be the better philosophical grounding for Symbolic Interactionism – at least for Blumer's version of it.[24] Indeed, the Blumer passage above also again exemplifies the difference between epistemological and ontological talk of objectivity.

Let us look closely at what Blumer is saying. He grants that we can apprehend the world only in terms of our own concepts. There is thus no epistemic objectivity. But as Blumer goes on to say, we must epistemically conceptualize a reality that is ontologically independent of us. Thus, at play here are two senses of objectivity, one epistemic and the other ontological. The absence of one does not imply the absence of the other. To conclude otherwise, Blumer avers, leads to solipsism.

Blumer's position thus differs markedly from the kind of pragmatism that Dimitri Shalin tells us was historically the philosophical root of Symbolic Interactionism.[25] Kin to the material-semiotic version of ANT, Shalin's wing of pragmatism denies that subject and object are separable as CR claims, and maintains instead that the ontologically objective world is co-created by us as we impose our concepts on it, that there is no world we encounter not already laden with our concepts. Thus, according to this pragmatism, there is a dialectical relation between us and the ontologically objective world, a position once also upheld by Balkan *Praxis Theory*. Drawing on the work of Florian Witold Znaniecki and others – but not so much Blumer, Shalin traces the imprint of such pragmatism on Symbolic Interactionism.

As should now be clear, from the CR perspective, this particular pragmatist point of view again confuses epistemic and ontological

---

[23] Blumer, "The Metholodological Position," p. 22.

[24] Dimitri Shalin represents the more subjectivist strain of pragmatism. See Shalin (1986) "Pragmatism and Social Interactionism," *American Sociological Review* 51: 9–29; and (1991) "The Pragmatic Origins of Symbolic Interactionism," *Studies in Symbolic Interaction* 12: 223–251. I call it one strain of pragmatism or neo-pragmatism as I am not sure it speaks as well for John Dewey or John Sanders Peirce.

[25] Shalin, "Pragmatism and Social Interactionism"; "The Pragmatic Origins."

objectivity – and the transitive and intransitive dimensions of knowledge. Yes, in the *transitive* dimension, we only know the world via our
own concepts, but that content of knowledge does not alter the
intransitive, ontologically distinct object of knowledge. We do not
change the ontologically distinct world simply by interpreting it differently. It is not as if a convicted man in actuality suddenly becomes
innocent ontologically when after 20 years new DNA evidence epistemically exonerates him. It may have taken us 20 years to recognize
the truth, but certainly, ontologically, the truth was that he was innocent all along. It is this CR view of matters that Blumer's version of
Symbolic Interactionism appears to endorse. Although he goes on to
qualify it, sociologist of science theorist Andrew Pickering endorses
it as well:

One reading of Kuhn would be idealist: the structure of the world conforms
itself to human ideas about it – as if the sun and the earth changed places
somewhere along the way from Ptolemy to Newton. My understanding is
different. We all live in the same world, and if the human race ceased to exist
the world would remain otherwise unchanged.[26]

It is only the transitive content of knowledge that changes with altering
interpretations, not the intransitive object of knowledge itself. But let us
return to our main point. Blumer concurs at the end of his account that
there is an epistemic dialectic between us and the world. The word
dialectic comes from the Greek, meaning dialogue. The dialogue Blumer
suggests is not the one posited by the pragmatists wherein we change
the world by re-interpreting it. Blumer's dialogue instead coincides with
the one suggested by more sophisticated versions of grounded theory.[27]
In our CR terms, it is a dialogue between the transitive and intransitive
dimensions of knowledge.

Blumer's point is that although we begin to approach the world from
our own situated concepts and norms of knowledge, we are not locked
into those starting epistemic positions. We are not locked in because
the world "talks back" to us. It talks back by confirming or resisting
our frameworks. Sometimes the world disconfirms our theories

---

[26] Pickering, "The World Since Kuhn," p. 468. Actually, Pickering endorses it only
up to a point. He still wants to preserve talk of our occupying multiple worlds.
[27] See Gary Thomas and David James (2006) "Reinventing Grounded Theory:
Some Questions about Theory, Ground and Discovery," *British Research
Journal* 32 (6): 767–795.

outright or hands us results so outside our expectations that our frameworks fail even to address them. As we revise our frameworks in response, we arrive at epistemically better conceptions of the world, conceptions that are more in line with the world's back-talk. To the extent that some conceptions of the world are in this sense better than others, the possibility exists of judgmental rationality. It is this judgmental rationality that CR affirms.

Thus, the main point: Although we all may start from different, situated points of view, by research and by learning from each other's culturally limited perspectives and adjudicating among them, we can move from situated knowledge to what constructionists often deride as "a view from nowhere," a truth that transcends the limits of our socio-historical situatedness.

In fact, according to CR, it is precisely toward a view from nowhere that knowledge ultimately aims. Consider, for example, the charge of feminist scholars that ours is a society in which women continue to earn less than men for the same work. Is this claim advanced as just how some, particularly situated, feminist scholars see something that could just as validly be viewed differently by others who are differently situated? If so, the charge loses all bite. So understood, as Christian Smith observes, such charges reduce to "emotivistic assertions."[28] To have any purchase, the charge must command the intellectual assent even of those otherwise situated, and that capacity requires the charge to represent something beyond a view from just one, situated quarter. Rather, the claim must be one that against rival claims best describes how things are, regardless of what anyone might have originally thought.

As Donna Haraway put it, "Feminists have to insist on a better account of the world; it is not enough to show radical historical contingency and modes of construction for everything."[29] Like Haraway's feminist empiricism with which CR much coincides, our ability to recognize better accounts of the world is what CR's judgmental rationality affirms. As Blumer says above, it is indeed difficult to make sense of our own sociological research or our own academic debates if judgmental rationality is denied.

[28] Smith, *What Is a Person?*, p. 140.
[29] Donna J. Haraway (1991) *Simians, Cyborgs, and Women: The Reinvention of Nature* (New York: Routledge), p. 187. More recently, see Jim McGuigan (2006) *Modernity and Postmodern Culture* (New York: Open University Press).

But are not all accounts of the world value-laden? Yes. And, according to CR, the truth may be value-laden too. As Haraway goes on to suggest, the best account of things may come from the margins or the oppressed with all the values that account may imply. The world, according to CR, is not itself value-neutral.[30]

CR concedes that epistemic rationality is always fallible so that at any particular time and place, it may actually not yield the truth. Our judgments can go awry. They can sometimes lead us away from truth. Notice, however, that for knowledge to be described as fallible, there must be at least a presumptive truth against which it is so judged. For relativism, in contrast, there is no fallibility. Nothing can ever be wrong because nothing can ever be right. It is indeed comforting never to be wrong, but then as Blumer argues, there is little sense in conducting empirical research.

Against the CR perspective, social constructionists will continue to lodge two critical questions. First, against the thesis of judgmental rationality, social constructionists will ask, as they always do, Who is to say? Who is to say which is the best construction of reality? The second question is that if it is admitted that the process of adjudication is fallible, how can it ever lead to certainty? And if it cannot lead to certainty, then how can it lead to truth, which is knowledge of which we are certain?

The social constructionists consider these questions unanswerable, but they are not. From the CR point of view, both lines of questioning begin from the same faulty premise, a premise, ironically, that social constructionists share with positivists. From the CR point of view, in several ways, the social constructionists are not post-positivist enough.

Alethic versus *epistemic* conceptions of truth

The basic problem is that constructionists and positivists both share an *epistemic* as opposed to an *alethic* conception of truth. The distinction has to do with what philosophers call the *truth-maker*. What is it that makes a statement or belief true? According to the epistemic account, the truth-maker is an epistemic protocol or methodology that produces

---

[30] For a similar statement, see Andrew Collier (1999) *Being and Worth* (New York: Routledge). As Smith observes, moreover, even mere description inevitably includes value judgments. See Smith, *What Is a Person?*, pp. 396–399.

the epistemic state of certainty. This approach to knowledge is called *foundationalism*. The idea is that by building on firm methodological foundations, we arrive, virtually algorithmically, at certainty. The content of the certain knowledge attained is truth. Stated otherwise, truth, according to the epistemic conception, is knowledge content that is certain. As its name implies, for the epistemic account, truth is equated with ways of knowing: best knowledge on foundational criteria, and the certainty they yield. The truth-makers thus are epistemic. Hence the name of the approach.[31]

I say that both positivists and constructionists accept this epistemic account of truth. The positivists accept it and, believing certainty possible, likewise believe in truth. In contrast, constructionists, also accepting the epistemic account of truth but rejecting foundationalism, do not believe certainty possible and, hence, reject the possibility of truth.

It is not only positivism and constructionism that accept the epistemic account of truth. Outside of CR, almost all articulated accounts in the social sciences do. It is precisely an epistemic account of truth that Jürgen Habermas originally associated with his concept of the *ideal speech situation*.[32] According to Habermas, the ideal speech situation is a Weberian ideal type, a forum in which all interlocutors have equal rights to speak and be heard. No extra-discursive forces or constraints operate.

In such a situation, Habermas says in a famous comment, the only force operative in the long-run is "the unforced force of the better argument."[33] It is a great phrase that refers to the entirely benevolent causal power that accrues to a good argument, the causal power to persuade rationally. If the power of good argument is the only long-run force operating in the ideal speech situation, then, Habermas originally supposed, in the long-run, consensus will be achieved, and this consensus will constitute truth. But in equating truth with consensus, even with an idealized consensus of the long-run, Habermas's account of truth was epistemic. Consensus, after all, is an epistemic state, and the

---

[31] See William Alston (1997) *A Realist Conception of Truth* (Ithaca, NY: Cornell University Press).

[32] Jürgen Habermas (2001) *Moral Consciousness and Communicative Action* (Cambridge, MA: MIT Press).

[33] Jürgen Habermas (1998) *Between Facts and Norms* (Cambridge, MA: MIT Press), p. 306.

means of arriving at it – the ideal speech situation – is foundational.[34] Peirce likewise rooted truth in consensus.[35]

In contrast with the epistemic conception of truth shared by positivism, constructionism, Peirce, and originally Habermas, it is an *alethic* conception of truth that is held by CR – or at least by the strain of CR I am defending. It is a strain actually resisted by Bhaskar but also defended by other critical realists such as Christian Smith and Ruth Groff.[36] It is a conception of truth championed most strongly in philosophy by William Alston and Gerald Vision, who, although also realists, are, properly speaking, outside the specific CR fold.[37]

Upon reflection, Habermas as well switched over to the alethic account, *althea* being simply the Greek name for truth. What Habermas ultimately saw was that even within the context of an ideal speech situation, the results of dialogue are still fallible. If for no other reason than continued personal limitations, any consensus reached might still fail to correspond with the way the world actually is. Such failure, on the alethic view, would represent some departure from truth.[38]

Again, the distinction between an epistemic and an alethic conception of truth concerns the truth-maker, that is, what makes a belief or claim true or not. As we saw, for the epistemic view, what makes a belief or claim true is an epistemic property, namely the certainty achieved via some foundational protocol. The epistemic view more or less equates truth with certain knowledge.

In contrast, the *alethic* view detaches truth from both certainty and from our methodological algorithms. For the alethic view, it is not

---

[34] Peirce likewise rooted truth in some idealized consensus of *researchers*. See Charles Sanders Peirce (1878) *Popular Science Monthly* 12 (January): 286–302. www.peirce.org/writings/p119.html

[35] See Charles Sanders Peirce (1878) *Popular Science Monthly* 12 (January): 286–302. www.peirce.org/writings/p119.html.

[36] Roy Bhaskar (2009) *Plato, etc.: The Problems of Philosophy and Their Resolution* (New York: Routledge). See also R. Groff (2000) "The Truth of the Matter: Roy Bhaskar's Critical Realism and the Concept of Alethic Truth," *Philosophy of the Social Sciences* 30: 407–435; and Smith, *What Is a Person?*, pp. 207–219. Although they have not written on it, Margaret Archer and Colin Wight, among others, would also share this view.

[37] Alston, *A Realist Conception*. Also see Gerald Vision (2009) *Veritas: The Correspondence Theory and Its Critics* (Denver, CO: Bradford).

[38] Jürgen Habermas (2003) *Truth and Justification* (Cambridge, MA: MIT Press). See also James Bohman and William Rehg (2011) "Jürgen Habermas," *The Stanford Encyclopedia of Philosophy (Winter 2011 Edition)*, Edward N. Zalta (ed.) http://plato.stanford.edu/archives/win2011/entries/habermas/.

either of those, but the world that is the truth-maker. If the world actually is as a belief or claim holds it to be, then the belief or claim is true – however certain or uncertain about that belief or claim we might be. I may be uncertain that I left the keys in the car, but if the car is where the keys are, then, from the alethic point of view, my suspicions, however uncertain, were nonetheless true.

Likewise, the alethic view detaches truth from methodology. For the alethic point of view it does not matter how a belief or claim was arrived at. Even if we are just speaking of an unproven hypothesis, if the world is as expressed, the hypothesis is nonetheless true. Precisely because the alethic view detaches truth from both certainty and methodology, it is said to offer a non-epistemic account of truth. Rather than an epistemic account of truth, the alethic account is ontological insofar as it is the world itself that is the truth-maker rather than our belief states or methodological protocols.

Is the alethic view not simply the traditional correspondence theory of truth – the idea that a belief or claim is true if it corresponds to the way the world is? Yes, actually it is.

Has not the correspondence theory been proven untenable? No. In fact, among philosophers, the correspondence theory remains the most frequently held theory of truth.[39] Of course, it has competitors and, like most ideas, critics. Here, I confine myself to dismissing the most frequent reason cited in the social sciences for dismissing the correspondence theory. The reason is a Kantian one. The putative problem with the correspondence theory is that we have no access to the world independent of our own conceptions against which to match our claims or beliefs.

This putative problem might indeed threaten the correspondence theory if the correspondence theory were meant primarily as the criterion of truth, that is, the way we determine the truth. It is meant, however, less as the criterion of truth than as the meaning of truth. Per the correspondence theory, a claim or belief is true if it matches the world. That correspondence, according to the theory, is what it means for a claim or belief to be true. It is not, however, how we necessarily determine the truth.

Well, how, according to the correspondence theory, do we determine what is true? The correspondence theory itself does not say

---

[39] David Bourget and David J. Chalmers (2013) *What Do Philosophers Believe?* http://philpapers.org/archive/BOUWDP.

because, for the alethic view, that question is a separate matter. How we determine what matches the world is the separate question of epistemology. The correspondence theory analytically separates the meaning and determination of truth.

Having said that, at one, quotidian level, the correspondence theory does indeed suggest how to determine truth: simple inspection. As prosaic as the point may be, it nonetheless is fundamentally important. In our daily routine, we most directly determine the truth of things by looking. I say I left the keys in the ignition; you say I didn't. How do we determine the truth? By looking. In this case not only can we look, we can look together in a public way that can in principle include as well the observation of neutral, third parties with no skin in the game. "Yes," they can concur. "There are the keys. Les voilà."

As banal as the point may be, it is, as I say, fundamentally important. At the end of the day, much comes down to simple inspection. What persuades us that what some social researcher says about society is true? What persuades even the researcher himself or herself? His or her data. And how do we know what the data say? We look. We look at it in a way that is in principle public. Ultimately, without inspection, we have nothing. Not even our data.

For most of what we do in life, simple inspection is how we determine truth. Of course, most of what we do in life takes place within a common, shared scientific paradigm or cultural conceptual scheme. We may not agree on where I left the keys, but we agree that there are such things as we call keys, cars, and ignition. We likewise generally agree on the existence of statistical correlations.

Where things get interesting is where correspondence with reality cannot be determined so directly. That is where we are when between paradigms or conceptual schemes, when, for example, we are trying to adjudicate not where I left the keys but whether there are such things as keys, when, for example, we are between entire frameworks like Western science and Zande magic. There is where epistemological questions loom to the fore. It is toward those questions that we now move.

Epistemic fallibility

So where are we? I have been arguing that positivism and postmodern post-positivism both subscribe to an epistemic account of truth that equates truth with the certain or algorithmic results of foundational methodological protocols. Whereas positivism affirms the possibility of such certainty, postmodern post-positivism denies it and consequently truth. In contrast, the correspondence theory offers an alethic rather than an epistemic account of truth, where the truth-maker is the world rather than some foundational procedure or the epistemic state of certainty that results.

Because the correspondence theory separates truth from epistemology, it allows us to speak of less certain states of knowledge. Besides absolute certainty, we can speak as in a criminal court of certainty beyond a reasonable doubt – which does not exclude all doubt. At a lower level, as in a tort case, we might simply be asked to judge which assessment reflects the preponderance of evidence. At still a lower level of certainty, we might simply have a hunch. In all cases, according to the correspondence theory, the possession of truth is not determined by our certainty, and so we might well possess the truth even in its absence.

To put the point somewhat facetiously, the CR line here is that you can often know the truth; you just often cannot know that you know it. The implication is that CR epistemology is fallibilist. CR believes we can make epistemic mistakes, that some of our truth claims or beliefs are false. The problem is we do not know which. If what it means to believe something is to regard it as true, then, to some extent, we think all our beliefs are true. Otherwise we would not hold those beliefs. Of course, we may have greater faith in some than other of our beliefs. Nevertheless, to believe something is at least to proceed as if it were true.

What CR's fallibilism implies, as Christian Smith points out, is an ever-present call for epistemic humility.[40] Although to believe something is to regard it as true, to be fallibilist about our beliefs is to recognize that what we currently believe true may not be. And that possibility means that all our own beliefs and truth claims must remain in some sense always provisional, always open to further debate.[41] We must always be willing to entertain new arguments against what we happen to believe. Of course, in some cases – as about the roundness of the earth – there is such a preponderance of evidence in favor of our beliefs that we are certain of them beyond a reasonable doubt. In such cases, therefore, it may take some doing for someone with an opposing belief to get our attention. In many such cases, attending may not be

[40] Smith, *What Is a Person?*, pp. 304–311.   [41] Ibid., pp. 304–311.

worth our time. Whenever we refuse to listen, however, we should always understand that there remains some probability, however remote, that we will miss a chance to correct ourselves. That is what it means to be fallibilist about our beliefs. It means that in the end our truth claims rest on bets. True, the more certain we are, the more likely we are to win our bet; but even then, even when we are close to certain, some bets about the truth we are going to lose.

Epistemic rationality

So according to the correspondence theory, the truth of our beliefs or claims is determined by their match with the world. How, though, in the toughest cases, in the cases where we are between paradigms, can we determine what matches the world? How can it even make sense in such cases to speak of matching or correspondence?

Social constructionism – especially that variety historically associated with the Sociology of Scientific Knowledge (SSK) – derives its skepticism about truth from two main sources: the alleged incommensurability of rival paradigms; and the alleged under-determination of theory by data.[42] The claim that rival paradigms are incommensurable originates with Kuhn's *The Structure of Scientific Revolutions*.[43] The alleged under-determination of theory by data goes back to philosophers Pierre Duhem and W. V. O. Quine and, more recently, Mary Hesse.[44] There is merit to both ideas, but in the hands of the social constructionists, the ensuing claims have been overblown. Even Kuhn distanced himself from the more anti-realist conclusions of paradigm incommensurability – and as we will shortly see, so now have some of the prominent originators of SSK.[45]

---

[42] For continued importance of incommensurability although it's no longer leading to skepticism, see Harry Collins (2012) "Comment on Kuhn," *Social Studies of Science* 42 (3): 420–423, p. 422.

[43] Thomas Kuhn (1996) *The Structure of Scientific Revolutions* (Chicago, IL: University of Chicago Press).

[44] Pierre Duhem (1991) *The Aim and Structure of Physical Theory* (Princeton, NJ: Princeton University Press); W. V. Quine (1980) *From a Logical Point of View: Nine Logico-Philosophical Essays* (Cambridge, MA: Harvard University Press); Mary Hesse (1980) *Revolutions and Reconstructions in the Philosophy of Science* (Brighton: Harvester). See also Kyle Stanford (2013) "Underdetermination of Scientific Theory," *Stanford Encyclopedia of Philosophy*. http://plato.stanford.edu/entries/scientific-underdetermination/.

[45] See Thomas Kuhn (2000) "Reflections on My Critics," pp. 123–175 in J. Conant and J. Haugeland (eds.), *The Road Since Structure* (Chicago, IL:

Let us develop these ideas a bit more. First incommensurability. In *The Structure of Scientific Revolutions*, Kuhn famously argued that rival scientific paradigms – or cultural conceptual schemes – are incommensurable, which has been taken to mean that they resist or even defy direct comparison or adjudication. They fail to permit as it were CR's principle of judgmental rationality.

To appreciate Kuhn's point, consider that according to the naive realism associated with positivism, there is a clear separation between theory language and observation language. An element of this idea remains in our methodological talk of operational definitions. Operational definitions are supposed to supply the purely observational criteria associated with our theoretical constructs. With clear separation between theory and observation, positivism counts on observations alone to adjudicate among rival theories.

The problem with positivism's naive realism is that there are no un-interpreted observations – no observations, that is, that are theory-neutral. Instead, what is considered a fact by one theory may not be so considered by its rivals. I referred earlier, for example, to the Zande people of Central Africa, studied most famously by Edward Evan Evans-Pritchard and whose witchcraft has since figured prominently in discussions of cultural relativism.[46] According to the Azande, a cow's sudden demise might be considered an instance of witchcraft. Obviously, no such fact would be conceded by Western science. Closer to home, we can consider the disputes about American economic policy after the 2008 financial collapse. Conservatives considered the looming fact to be the increasing insolvency of the "entitlement state," whereas readers of Paul Krugman's more liberal *New York Times* columns were told that there was no such insolvency. What are the facts of the matter in these cases, and whose framework should be employed to discuss them?

As Bhaskar says as well, we can know the world only under one or another description.[47] If we can know the world only through our descriptions and if different theories, paradigms or conceptual schemes

University of Chicago Press). See also Eric Oberheim (2013) "The Incommensurability of Scientific Theories," *Stanford Encyclopedia Online.* http://plato.stanford.edu/entries/incommensurability/#KuhSubDevInc.
[46] See Edward E. Evans-Pritchard (1976) *Witchcraft, Oracles, and Magic Among the Azande* (New York: Oxford University Press).
[47] E.g., Roy Bhaskar (1989) *Reclaiming Reality* (New York: Verso), p. 152.

offer us different descriptions of the facts, then it seems we cannot straightforwardly adjudicate among those different views by comparing their consistency with the facts, which are themselves under dispute. Instead, the distinction between theory and observation language breaks down, with rival views offering us rival facts. They offer, in Kuhn's words, different worlds. Alternately, Michel Foucault might refer to Zande magic and Western science as different regimes of truth.

Speaking of Foucault, it has been of course not just those in SSK who have made much of breakdowns in naïve realism. Such aporias have also fueled the more Nietzschean pronouncements of Foucauldians that all is but discourse, with truth claims nothing beyond a will to power. Lest I bore, I leave it an exercise for the reader to return what should now be the familiar CR rejoinder to such Foucauldian speech acts. Before a fuller response to the incommensurability thesis, let us first develop more what is meant by the under-determination of theory by data.

The under-determination of theory by data manifests in two different forms. The first form, *holistic under-determination*, strikes against falsificationism or at least what might be called naive falsificationism, the kind of falsifcationism we routinely practice in our empirical journal articles. In our empirical journal articles, we identify discrete null hypotheses we set out to falsify. The problem, however, is that when results are contrary to null expectations, we cannot be sure it is the null hypothesis specifically that has been falsified. The problem is that our null hypothesis is tied to a host of other assumptions – that our apparatus and procedures were correct and that other considerations we take for granted are actually true. So when results turn out contrary to null expectations, something somewhere might be false in a whole corpus of expectations, but it can be difficult to single out which.

Contrastive under-determination concerns our choice of entire theories. The contention here is that the empirical data alone are never enough to favor one theory over another. Empirical tests do not determine truth algorithmically. Informal judgment always enters deliberation. SSK constructionists are wont to hail this element of informal judgment as proof that science is social. Well, of course it is. What else would it be? Even if interpretations followed algorithmically or logically from experiments, experiments, algorithms, and logic are all social too.

What SSK constructionists seem to be suggesting is that ultimately science deals in rhetoric rather than proof. That conclusion also seems warranted, but, as we will see, relativist implications do not necessarily follow from it. Instead, much depends on what we mean by rhetoric.

Now that we understand incommensurability and under-determination, let us address them directly. As mentioned, Kuhn himself denied that incommensurability meant utter lack of comparability or the ultimate non-rationality of science.[48] In the first place, even if different paradigms carve up the world differently, they are still capable of referring to the same thing in different ways.[49] Gravity certainly means something different in the theories of Einstein and Newton, but just as certainly the two theories are referring in common to the same causal power operative in the world. Were they not, we would not even be comparing them. We do not, for example, try to compare the relative merits of Einstein's theory of relativity against Darwin's theory of natural selection. The two theories are not even remotely addressing the same thing.

The issue of relativistic incommensurability only arises when two theories or worldviews are referencing the same thing. The point appears to be missed by David Bloor, one of the founders of the *Strong Program in the Sociology of Science*, long a champion of relativism. "Relativists," Bloor tells us, "deny that humans are in possession of any absolute truths."[50] "The only kind of counterexample that could refute relativism," Bloor says, "would be an example of absolute knowledge."[51]

Although it sounds as if Bloor is upholding an epistemic account of truth requiring certainty for vindication, actually by absolute knowledge, Bloor is referring not at all to certainty but to comprehensiveness. He explains that in World War II, RAF pilots learned to fly close to incoming German V-1 rockets so that the airflow behind their wings would destabilize the rockets and make them drop harmlessly to the

---

[48] Kuhn, "Reflections on My Critics." See *Stanford Encyclopedia* entry on incommensurability of scientific theory.

[49] Oberheim, "The Incommensurability of Scientific Theories." See also Alan Chalmers (1999) *What is this Thing Called Science?* (Indianapolis, IN: Hackett Publishing Company).

[50] David Bloor (2011) *The Enigma of the Air Foil: Rival Theories of Aerodynamics, 1909-1930* (Chicago, IL: University of Chicago Press), p. 441.

[51] Ibid., p. 430.

ground. In contrast, while the experts back in the lab had already known about trailing vortices behind wings, given their concerns, they had not regarded the effect as of any practical importance. Speaking of their two perspectives, Bloor says "In both cases their understanding was objective rather than subjective, but it was also to be seen as relative to their standpoints. In neither case did it have an absolute character."[52]

Given that Bloor is willing to acknowledge (if only within bounds) the objective truth of both judgments (and of objective truth in general), not much seems to hang on his highly idiosyncratic version of relativism. Leave aside that if the issue were whether the vortices had any utility *to anyone*, Bloor's example would show the experts to have been absolutely wrong and the pilots absolutely right. But since utility by its very nature is relative to intents and purposes, the experts' disinterest in the vortices does not conflict with the pilots' interest.

Our very ability to determine which theories are rival accounts of the same phenomena already signifies the partiality of any incommensurability and its coincidence always with substantial theoretical overlap. The rival worlds at issue are never utterly alien to one another. In the case of the V-1 rockets, either one party was absolutely wrong or the two parties were not addressing the same thing. Either way, it is hard to see insurmountable incommensurability in the case or how the case otherwise supports any non-anodyne notion of relativism.

Bloor's colleague, Harry Collins, likewise explains how he too now declines from the more exciting relativism of a philosophical sort:

Philosophical relativism takes it that there is no truth of the matter. I held this view, and for the reasons explained – mental boot camp – it was important for me to hold it at the beginning of my work in the sociology of scientific knowledge; I held the view from around 1972 to 1981. *Methodological relativism*, on the other hand, proposes whether there is a truth of the matter or not, the social analyst must act as if there is no truth if the work of studying the establishment of truth is to be done properly. I have held this view since 1981 to the present and expect to continue to hold to it.[53]

---

[52] Ibid., pp. 442, 443.

[53] Harry Collins (2011) *Gravity's Ghost and Big Dog: Scientific Discovery and Social Analysis in the Twenty-first Century* (Chicago, IL: University of Chicago Press), pp. 305–306.

The putative utility of methodological relativism is an entirely empirical matter. Absent, however, any continued claim to philosophical relativism, I am happy to say, the SSK approach represented by Bloor and Collins does not conflict with CR. In fact, CR may be a better metatheoretical foundation for it.

Incommensurability is not only always partial. It also is usually resolvable by stepping back an epistemological level. SSK itself has been researching this phenomenon, drawing on the concept of "trading zones" introduced by Paul Galison.[54] There may be no single object language neutral to all theories, but between any two theoretical paradigms we can generally find ground neutral enough to both from which their assertions can be compared and adjudicated. Of course, at that level we are also often stepping back from the data to examine the tenability of underlying assumptions, which places us in the terrain of metatheory.

Metatheory – or reflection on theory – is the language of inter-paradigm communication. As such, it figures largely in any quest after the big questions. For that reason, it occupies a prominent place in CR.

Mainstream sociology, in contrast, absolutely shrinks from metatheory. The reasons are several. In the first place, dealing as metatheory does with paradigmatic presuppositions, metatheory eventually takes us outside the discipline to sociology's others: philosophy and psychology. Mainstream American sociology would rather halt our horses at the border and leave our ultimate presuppositions to faith.

Then, too, metatheoretical arguments tend to be more conceptual than empirical, appearing thus more kin to philosophy than to empiricists' conception of science. Completely overlooked by that conception is precisely what the SSK constructionists have decisively shown us: Scientific results rely on more than just empirical outcomes; they also rely firmly on informal judgments relating to conceptual criteria.[55] American sociologists, however, have very little patience with

---

[54] See Harry Collins, Robert Evans, and Mike Gorman (2007) "Trading Zones and Interactional Expertise," *Studies in History and Philosophy of Science Part A* 38 (4): 657–666; and Paul Galison (1997) *Image & Logic: A Material Culture of Microphysics* (Chicago, IL: University of Chicago Press).

[55] See, for example, Harry Collins (1992) *Changing Order: Replication and Induction in Scientific Practice* (Chicago, IL: University of Chicago Press); and Andrew Pickering (1999) *Constructing Quarks: A Sociological History of Particle Physics* (Chicago, IL: University of Chicago Press).

extended, conceptual debate, which they think holds us up from our real work: securing empirical outcomes. It is thus little wonder that no matter how many conceptual stakes are driven into their hearts, like the undead, rational choice theory and other theoretical vacuities keep haunting empirical sociology.

It is absolutely true, as the constructionists maintain, that if we confine ourselves to empirical findings alone, incommensurate differences seem irresolvable and, consequently, contradictory paradigms equally apt. But who says scientific discourse confines itself to the empirical findings? Only an entrenched empiricism. Thus, although SSK research clearly shows otherwise, the SSK researchers themselves had tended to miss their own point. Their previous relativist conclusions were more a reflection of the limits of empiricism than the actual accessibility of scientific truth.

The need to move beyond empirical data is implied as well by the under-determination of theory by data. In principle, more than one possible theory may fit any set of empirical findings. As noted, scientific truths do not emerge algorithmically from scientific experiments, let alone from empirical observation in general. Instead, even experimental results are subject to multiple interpretations. Remember, for example, the results of the cold fusion experiments. Indeed, when any point of serious contention is at stake, experimental results alone do not settle matters. As Andrew Pickering has pointed out, in high-energy physics, results from colliders are expressed against backgrounds of considerable noise, so that even with sophisticated programming, separating out the significant signals is an art, the success of which can always be contested.[56] Harry Collins likewise finds the same in the study of gravity waves. Lord knows our own sociological results are equally replete with noise.[57]

Constructionists in SSK again made much of theory's under-determination by data because of the epistemic conception of truth and knowledge they tended to share with positivism. According to that view, if there is no certainty, there is no truth or knowledge. And if theory does not follow algorithmically from data, then there is no certainty. Hence SSK's former relativist conclusions.

Once, however, per the alethic view, we separate truth from certainty, the relativist implications dissipate. On the alethic view, as we

[56] Pickering, *Constructing Quarks*. [57] Collins, *Changing Order*.

have seen, there are levels of knowledge below certainty, at all of which we may still be in possession of truth.

Science as rhetoric

It is again true as the constructionists suggest that once we concede the non-algorithmic nature of theory choice, we are in the terrain of rhetoric. But what do we mean by rhetoric?

As anyone who has studied rhetoric knows, there are at least two distinct views of it: the Platonic and the Aristotelian. The SSK constructionists, following a wider postmodernist sensibility, had followed the Platonic line.

Plato and his Socrates both were enemies of rhetoric. In their day, rhetoric was the art of oratory, taught for pay by itinerant teachers whom Plato identified as sophists. The sophists were the postmodernists of ancient Greece. Among them, Protagoras famously taught that "man is the measure of all things," which seems to suggest a social constructionist view of truth. Indeed, the sophists denied the existence of objective truth, Protagoras again arguing that in any dispute, a good rhetorician could always make the weaker case appear the stronger. Plato's Socrates derided rhetoric as an art of appearance rather than truth. It is from this Platonic view that rhetoric derives its bad name, as something used to mislead the intellectually unwary.

If, following a postmodernist sensibility, we identify science with rhetoric in the sophistic sense, then we seem to be saying that there is no objective truth and that all scientific determinations depend ultimately on social maneuverings or judgments that are equivalent to Sartrean choices without due reason. We thus reach Harry Collins's former contention that "if our beliefs about controversial features of the world are a consequence of the way the world is, this is not evident during passages of discovery and proof" and that, accordingly, we had best "treat the world as if it had no effect on what people believe about it."[58]

There is, however, an alternative view of rhetoric, the view of Plato's student, Aristotle. In his *Rhetoric*, Aristotle distinguishes epistemic contexts where formal proofs are available from epistemic contexts where we must rely instead on the best argument. Rhetoric, according

[58] Ibid., p. 185.

to Aristotle, is the discipline that helps us determine which in the latter contexts the best arguments are. So equipped, we perhaps will not allow ourselves to be persuaded unduly by the likes of Protagoras.

If, as CR would hold, it is in the Aristotelian sense that science is rhetorical, then although science may rely on fallible, informal judgments, it still remains in dialogue with the world. Thus, contrary to the position Collins had formerly maintained, in empirical research, as Blumer says, the world talks back. Of course, what the world says varies. Sometimes, as in the discovery of the Higgs particle, the world unequivocally answers to our descriptions of it. More often, the world speaks less decisively, as in the case of continental drift – or even the heliocentric view of the solar system – it can take decades for a preponderance of evidence to accumulate in one direction or another.

In short, the under-determination of theory by data cannot be pushed too far. Yes, in principle, it may be that multiple theories might fit any set of empirical findings. In practice, however, often only one alternative is eligible. The reason is that there are multiple conceptual criteria – like plausibility or fit with other, more established theories – that any eligible theory also must meet. As Collins himself reports, Joseph Weber's putative detections of gravity waves "are now universally disbelieved" by scientists because calculations showed they implied an energy dissipation "many orders of magnitude," beyond what could be generated by a universe that has lasted as long as ours.[59] Thus, a conceptual consideration here trumped data, a conceptual consideration, however, that reflects the way the world has told us it is. It is thus again by attending only to the empirical data and dismissing conceptual judgments that the world appears to make no difference to what people believe about it.

The restrictive filters of plausibility and other conceptual criteria are likewise clearly evident in Pickering's *Constructing Quarks*. Pickering says over and over that this or that set of empirical results not only confirmed one theory but also left physicists without any alternative. Actually, as Stephen Turner observes, were we to razor out Pickering's title and initial constructionist commentary, his book would stand as a most excellent exemplar of a realist history of science, which is how most scientists and philosophers now do read it.[60]

---

[59] Ibid., pp. 81–83.
[60] Stephen Turner (2012) "Whatever Happened to Knowledge?," *Social Studies of Science* 42 (3): 474–480, p. 477.

Finally, outside SSK, we find the same conclusion even among ethnographers. Commenting on the controversy in that field, Isaac Reed comments: "These maximal questions [of thick interpretation] can never be answered by the evidence alone, though they can never leave the evidence behind. Theory must be mobilized, and a fusion of theory and fact must be attempted by bringing together theoretical signifiers with evidential ones, in search of a new interpretation."[61]

Theory growth and decline

If, as CR would hold, science is rhetorical in the Aristotelian sense, then theory choice is likely to look very much like the sophisticated falsificationism alternately advanced by Imre Lakatos and Larry Laudan.[62] What makes such falsificationism sophisticated rather than naive is its fallibalism and long-term nature.

According to Lakatos and Laudan both, there is no algorithm for determining which research program or theoretical tradition is correct, not because the world fails to talk back to us or makes no difference but because the world talks back so slowly and in such multiform ways. At any given time, rival theories may offer us different arrays of scientific assets and deficits.

Predictive success is the most prized of scientific assets. It is an asset, however, that, although not absent, is comparatively weak in the social sciences. More directly important to the social sciences is what Lakatos called a research program's "positive heuristic," which has both vertical and horizontal dimensions. The vertical dimension of a positive heuristic refers to how an originally over-simplified model can be made more complex, how, for example, we might proceed from an ideal type to something more empirically realistic. An illustration would be the introduction of class fractions or contradictory class locations to Marx's original two-class model. Where it is clear how to correct an overly simple model, researchers know how to go on. The empirical

---

61 Isaac Reed (2011) *Interpretation and Social Knowledge: On the Use of Theory in the Human Sciences* (Chicago, IL: University of Chicago), p. 27.
62 Imre Lakatos (1970) "Falsification and the Methodology of Scientific Research Programmes," pp. 91–196 in Imre Lakatos and Alan Musgrave (eds.), *Criticism and the Growth of Knowledge* (New York: Cambridge University Press); and Larry Laudan (1978) *Progress and Its Problems: Towards a Theory of Scientific Growth* (Berkeley, CA: University of California Press).

work thus naturally flows, and the theoretical program garners excitement.

Along the horizontal dimension, a positive heuristic concerns the range and type of phenomena to which a theoretical tradition might be applied. With predictiveness weaker in the social sciences, it matters more whether a research program can even offer an account for certain phenomena. Along these lines, it counts in favor of Marxism and against, say, Symbolic Interactionism that the former can offer an account of the world system whereas the latter hardly has even an agenda for such an account. Conversely, it counts in favor of Symbolic Interactionism and against Marxism that the former can explicate the kinds of behavior detailed by Erving Goffman, whereas this time it is Marxism without any clear research agenda.

On the negative side, it certainly counts against a theory if its predictions appear to have been falsified – although such falsifications might be redeemed by new studies introducing new control variables. More commonly, as noted above, theories might fail even to address certain important phenomena, which remain for the theory what Laudan calls anomalies. As above, such anomalies are more detrimental to a theory when its rivals do address, explain, or even predict them.

In addition, theories might suffer a range of conceptual weaknesses, like incoherence, ill-fit with established theory, untenable assumptions, contradictory formulations, or, like rational choice theory, simple vacuity. As Laudan argues, because empirical problems are more isolated, less fundamental, and more readily solved than conceptual weaknesses, the latter are actually more damaging to a theory's epistemic status.

I have been saying theory, but Lakatos and Laudan both distinguish specific theories from larger theoretical traditions or research programs. In physical cosmology, the new inflationary scenario is in this sense a large theoretical tradition or research program. The program attempts to explain certain surprising peculiarities in our universe by advancing the hypothesis of a brief period of hyper-expansion called inflation during the early stages of the big bang.

Most cosmologists accept that there was some such kind of inflationary scenario, partly because of the theory's (questionable to me) predictive success but mostly because, aside from the hand of God, there currently is no alternative explanation for the peculiarities at issue. Nevertheless, physicists have had difficulty articulating a workable inflationary model. There are difficulties getting the process started and difficulties accounting for how it might turn off in ways that accord with the universe we see. Whereas a key prediction of initial formulations was a zero gravitational constant, it now appears that the gravitational constant of our universe is pretty clearly positive – resulting now in a universal expansion that is actually accelerating.[63]

What has been falsified are specific inflationary accounts but not inflation as a larger theoretical research tradition or program. Lakatos argues that although specific theories within research programs might be falsified, the larger program itself is secure against outright falsification by any number of auxiliary assumptions that might explain the falsification within the program's own terms. It is this resistance of a larger program to outright falsification that makes Lakatos's falsification sophisticated rather than naive. Instead of outright falsification, a research program simply stagnates – as the inflation program arguably is doing now. If some rival is conversely enjoying significant success, then the stagnating tradition will more likely be eclipsed rather than falsified. Even then, scientific decisions remain fallible as fortunes can change. A stagnating tradition might suddenly take off and even a previously abandoned tradition might experience new life.

If the inflationary scenario in cosmology seems far-removed, consider a research tradition closer to home: functionalism. After reigning supreme after World War II, functionalism was rather quickly abandoned in the period between 1968 and 1975. Why? Had functionalism been empirically falsified? Hardly. Its major weaknesses were conceptual: a tendency to derogate the lay actor as an "oversocialized" "cultural dupe" and, even more damaging, an "illicit teleology" at its core.[64]

But these features had always been with functionalism and, arguably, were not enough to sink it so suddenly and so quickly. It was true as well that functionalism enjoyed little predictive success, but as that is true generally in the social sciences, the lack of that asset likewise was not what lost functionalism its preeminent place.

---

[63] For more on inflation, see, for example, Alan Guth (1998) *The Inflationary Universe* (New York: Basic Books). For the current debate, see Paul Steinhardt (2011) "The Inflation Debate," *Scientific American* 37 (April): 37–43.

[64] Jonathan Turner and Alexandra Maryanski (1979) *Functionalism* (San Francisco, CA: Benjamin-Cummings).

What arguably did in functionalism was a deficiency in its positive heuristic, one that became salient around 1968. The deficiency was along the horizontal dimension. It was functionalism's failure to account for or even suitably to address social change. When the New Left generation entered the academy, that deficiency loomed large. Functionalism was not much use for addressing social inequality, civil rights struggles, and the Vietnam War.

Of course, after a brief flowering in the academy the New Left's own Marxian perspective was likewise quickly displaced for similar reasons. Those subsequently entering sociology represented more a cultural than an economic Left. Sociology's focus switched to the politics of identity, for the study of which Marxian theory had only a weak positive heuristic. Thus, among those not tied to persistent positivism, Marxian theory gave way to poststructuralism, Foucault, and postmodernism generally.

Now, with the turn of the century, postmodernism's positive heuristic likewise seems exhausted. Is it the turn of CR? Pickering's suggestion is that scientists are slaves to their practices so they will cling even to clearly flawed theoretical perspectives as long as those perspectives afford continued research opportunities along the same lines. For that reason, despite what came as close as possible to falsification, empiricist psychologists continued to practice behaviorism for decades. Behaviorism was finally abandoned not because it was falsified – that had been long true – but because it was finally eclipsed by a new fascination with the computer metaphor that coalesced into cognitive science.

Similarly, we should not expect empiricist sociologists to change. Their game is to apply the latest methodology to some data set, and as long as they can do so, they will so continue. What it all adds up to is not their concern. CR, furthermore, is a metatheory rather than a theory or research program; it is accordingly without a positive heuristic of its own. As a metatheory, CR grounds and justifies certain theoretical approaches and challenges others. Thus, whether or not CR catches on in sociology likely has less to do with its intellectual merits than with the attraction to the theoretical approaches CR serves to legitimate. Since from a CR perspective, those approaches would in fact serve an intellectually sounder sociology, one that is to boot more unified, we critical realists hope CR will catch on. A hope, however, is not a prediction.

4 | *Whatever happened to social structure?*

"'When I use a word,'" said Humpty Dumpty, 'it means just what I choose it to mean – neither more nor less.' 'The question is,' said Alice, 'whether you can make words mean so many different things.'"

When it comes to social structure, sociology has been like Humpty Dumpty. Over 20 years ago, in an article well-known among critical realists, I identified four different conceptions of social structure prevalent in sociology.[1] Today, those four conceptions are still very much with us, attesting to a definite stability in the discipline.

Does it matter what we individually call social structure, as long as we each know what we are talking about? Certainly, we cannot legislate meaning, and it is foolish to argue about mere semantics. But more than semantics is at stake. With different conceptions of social structure come different research agendas, emphasizing different aspects of social ontology. As William Sewell insightfully notes, "the term structure empowers what it designates."[2] Conversely, disempowered is what it ceases to designate.

Consider, as I have noted, that the American culture of poverty debate in the 1960s pitted culture against structure – specifically the opportunity structure – as rival explanations of chronic poverty with rival policy implications. As noted, that debate has recently returned, along with the rival policy implications.[3] But now that on one prominent view – the one in fact favored by Sewell – structure has virtually been devoured by culture or in Margaret Archer's terms conflated

---

[1] Douglas V. Porpora (1989) "Four Concepts of Social Structure," *Journal for the Theory of Social Behaviour* 19: 195–212.

[2] William H. Sewell (1992) "A Theory of Structure: Duality, Agency, and Transformation," *American Journal of Sociology* 98 (1): 1–29, p. 2.

[3] Patricia Cohen (2010) "'Culture of Poverty' Makes a Comeback," *New York Times*. www.nytimes.com/2010/10/18/us/18poverty.html?pagewanted=1&_r=2&hp&.

with it, how do we even formulate the former opposition?[4] Would-be advocates of a structural view are deprived even of the words with which to speak.

This chapter will revisit the four concepts of social structure I identified some 20 years ago. It will again state the case for the CR conception of social structure against its mainstream rivals.[5] Over the 20 years since that article, mainstream American sociology has not challenged but only ignored the CR view and the case for it. Such is the prerogative of epistemic dominance.

Today, however, the terms of debate are a bit different. New actors have entered the scene and one of the rival views has been amended – although not in a way that alters the CR critique. The critique now can also be put more sharply. Now better armed with a CR vocabulary, I can speak of rival views as both what Roy Bhaskar terms actualist and what Archer calls conflationary.[6] In the end, we will see, no matter what mainstream sociologists choose to call social structure, they cannot without analytical deficiency marginalize or ignore that which CR so labels. They can only ignore, as is the tendency now, the questions to which it speaks. Even so, as we will see, having denied its reality, what CR distinctly affirms continues without its name to creep back into mainstream accounts.

---

[4] Margaret S. Archer (1982) "Morphogenesis Versus Structuration: On Combining Structure and Action," *British Journal of Sociology* 33 (4): 455–483; and (1992) *Realist Social Theory: The Morphogenetic Approach* (Cambridge: Cambridge University Press). Dylan Riley argues that Sewell has since moved on from this conception of structure. I find Riley's argument convincing, but what Sewell has moved onto does not strike me as any more structural in the CR and Marxian sense. See Riley (2008) "The Historical Logics of Logics of History: Language and Labor in William H. Sewell Jr," *Social Science History* 32 (4): 555–565.

[5] I speak of "the CR position" on structure, but I mean the canonical form. There are dissenters from this view, notably Charles Varela, Rom Harré, and Dave Elder-Vass. See Varela and Harré (1996) "Conflicting Varieties of Realism: Causal Powers and the Problems of Social Structure," *Journal for the Theory of Social Behaviour* 26 (3): 313–325; and Elder-Vass (2011) *The Causal Power of Social Structures: Emergence, Structure, and Agency* (Cambridge: Cambridge University Press).

[6] Archer, "Morphogenesis Versus Structuration." Roy Bhaskar (1974) *The Possibility of Naturalism: A Philosophical Critique of the Contemporary Human Sciences* (New York: Routledge).

The four concepts of social structure

Let us begin, as 20 years ago, just by identifying the four concepts of social structure at issue with no more critical commentary than necessary to distinguish them. In subsequent sections, I will expand on the CR view and then use that expansion to critique more fully the other views. For now, we observe that social structure refers to one of the following:

(1) (Material) relations among social positions and social constructs.
(2) Lawlike regularities that govern the behavior of social facts.
(3) Stable patterns or regularities of behavior.
(4) Rules (or schemas) and resources that structure behavior.

Social structure as (material) relations among social positions and social constructs

The first conception listed above is the CR conception of social structure. After 20 years, I have introduced some refinements. Twenty years ago, I defined the CR conception of social structure as systems of relations among social positions. That statement, however, is a bit too narrow. First, the word system may be too restrictive. I am not sure what today it connotes for sociologists, but a society's social structure need not be a system in any strong sense. Its structure is the totality of social relations that characterize that society, although some of those relations may be more central and more definitive than others.

Second, the relations at issue are not exclusively relations among social positions but also relations of those positions to social constructs like resources. Thus, for example, within the Marxian framework, with which this conception of social structure is most closely associated, social classes are social positions, defined not just by their relation to each other but more fundamentally by their differential relationship to the means of production.

Finally, today, I have added parenthetically the adjective material to indicate the ontological objectivity of the social structural relations CR emphasizes. Both Christian Smith and Sewell observe that at one time at least, sociologists typically contrasted structure to culture, thinking of the former as something material and the latter as something subjective.[7] In contrast with the dominant trend in mainstream sociology today, CR continues to uphold this traditional view.[8]

As Gerry Cohen observes, the conception of social structure as social relations is consistent with the broader understanding of structure prevalent in common sense:

Consider some other cases: the structure of an argument and the structure of a bridge. The structure of an argument is given by the relations between its constituent statements, of a bridge by the relations between its constituent girders, spans, etc.[9]

In all cases, structure refers to a pattern of relations. *Wikipedia* likewise indexes a broader, common sense view of structure as configuration or arrangement of elements.

It is not only Marx who extends this common understanding to a view of specifically social structure as social relations. Network theorists do as well, although they emphasize only a single kind of relation, namely social ties. There are, however, many kinds of relation besides social ties. There are, for example, zero-sum relations, i.e., circumstances where one's gain comes only at another's loss. Further examples include exploitation, power, dependency, and inequality. The list goes on.[10]

It is important to be clear about terms here because American sociologists are peculiarly resistant to understanding relationality as an ontological category. Consistent with Symbolic Interactionism, contemporary American sociologists tend to understand relationality

---

[7] Sewell, "A Theory of Structure," p. 3. Christian Smith (2010) *What Is a Person?* (Chicago, IL: University of Chicago Press), pp. 317–318.

[8] Actually, I speak of the main sociological line within CR. In Economics, Tony Lawson would not speak of *material* social relations as I have. See Tony Lawson (1997) *Economics and Reality* (New York: Routledge).

[9] G. A. Cohen (2000) *Karl Marx's Theory of History* (Princeton: Princeton University Press), p. 36. This point is also made by Smith, *What Is a Person?*, p. 318 and by Omar Lizardo. See Lizardo (2010) "Beyond the Antimonies of Structure: Levi-Strauss, Giddens, Bourdieu, and Sewell," *Theory and Society* 39: 651–688, p. 652.

[10] Christian Smith points out to me that my list of relations seems all negative. Relations are not all negative, and, actually, aside from exploitation above, none of the relations listed is necessarily negative. Certainly, contrary to the image sociologists now have of it, power need not be negative. It depends, as in the case of benevolent parents or dissertation chairs, whether or not the subordinates' interests are being served. But then interests is another concept CR recovers from general disappearance in sociology.

only in an actualist way, in a way, that is, that manifests itself as events. In particular, per the third conception of structure above, American sociologists are wont to understand social relations only as interacting behavior and not also as the prior, objective, albeit invisible relational conditions that give rise to that behavior.

When American sociologists think of capitalist competition, for example, they typically think of capitalists competing. They think of competition, in other words, only as behavior, as if it were just the habitus or practice of capitalists to compete. Competition as just what capitalists do. What in contrast contemporary American sociologists seem unable or unwilling to cognize is the kind of relation represented by competition understood not as behavior but as the mutual threat (not itself a behavior) created by market economies and designated the invisible hand by Adam Smith that lies behind and motivates capitalist behavior. It is almost as if, long after its demise in psychology, American sociologists are intent on a form of neo-behaviorism. In contrast, the relations CR means by structure are the relational conditions underlying behavior.

Although he is not entirely consistent about it, the conception of social structure as relational conditions was also shared by Pierre Bourdieu. Not, of course, the Americanized Bourdieu who has been reduced to two concepts: *cultural capital* and *habitus*. Instead, CR's relational conception of social structure appears rather, as Mustafa Emirbayer and Victoria Johnson observe, in Bourdieu's more ramified concept of *field*, itself usually a condition of contest in which the contestants are unequally endowed:

An artistic field "is not reducible to ... the sum of individual agents linked by simple relations of *interaction* or, more precisely, of *cooperation*: what is lacking, among other things, from this purely descriptive and enumerative evocations are the *objective relations* which are constitutive of the structure of the field and which orient the struggles aiming to conserve or transform it." (italics in original)

Here, at least, Bourdieu clearly affirms the ontological objectivity of relations.[11] Likewise, in "The Principles of Economic Anthropology,"

---

[11] Mustafa Emirbayer and Victoria Johnson (2007) "Bourdieu and Organizational Analysis," *Theory and Society* 37: 1–44. http://link.springer.com.ezproxy2. library.drexel.edu/article/10.1007/s11186-007-9052-y/fulltext.html. Their citation is from Pierre Bourdieu (1996) *The Rules of Art* (Stanford, CA: Stanford University Press), p. 205. See also Pierre Bourdieu (1993) *The Field of Cultural*

Bourdieu castigates "the interactionist vision that, ignoring the structural constraint of the field, will (or can) acknowledge only the effect of the conscious and calculated anticipation each agent may have of the effects of its actions on the other agents."[12] Following Bourdieu, Emirbayer and Johnson call the American tendency the "interactionist fallacy."[13] Against such subjectivist interactionism, Bourdieu opposed the structural vision: "The structural vision takes account of effects that occur outside of any interaction: the structure of the field, defined by the unequal distribution of capital, that is, the specific weapons (or strengths), weighs quite apart from any intervention or manipulation, on all agents engaged in the field."[14]

However, beyond American sociology, all of what Bourdieu says above is consistent with CR. My CR complaint about Bourdieu is that such crisp statements of objective structure are just as continually effaced by the concept of habitus, which, as Loïc Wacquant tells us, is "based on a non-Cartesian social ontology that refuses to split object and subject, intention and cause, materiality and symbolic representation."[15] Bourdieu cannot have it both ways: if there really are ontologically objective social relations, then we do have at least two of the three Cartesian splits Wacquant says Bourdieu would rather overcome.[16]

Production (New York: Columbia University Press). Lizardo, "Beyond the Antinomies," makes a similar point as does Ivan Ermakoff (2013) "Rational Choice May Take Over," pp. 89–107 in Phil Gorski (ed.) *Bourdieu and Historical Analysis.* Durham, NC: Duke University Press, p. 90.

[12] Pierre Bourdieu (2005) "The *Principles* of Economic Anthropology," pp. 75–89 in Neil J. Smelser and Richard Swedberg (eds.), *The Handbook of Economic Sociology* (Princeton, NJ: Princeton University Press), pp. 77–78.

[13] See Emirbayer and Johnson, "Bourdieu and Organizational Analysis."

[14] Bourdieu, "The *Principles* of Economic Anthropology," p. 76. A survey of economic sociology shows it to be heavily disposed toward the interactionism Bourdieu criticizes. Thus, Richard Swedberg, one of the editors of the *Handbook of Economic Sociology*, observes that "using networks to analyze markets appears to be more popular than any other perspective in current economic sociology," but "it is unsatisfactory since it exclusively focuses on social interaction. Network analysis fails to consider the role of politics, the view of the actors, and what characterizes markets as social institutions." See Richard Swedberg (2005) "Markets in Society," pp. 233–253 in Neil J. Smelser and Richard Swedberg (eds.), *The Handbook of Economic Sociology* (Princeton, NJ: Princeton University Press).

[15] Pierre Bourdieu and Loïc Wacquant (1992) *An Invitation to a Reflexive Sociology* (Chicago, IL: University of Chicago Press), p. 5.

[16] In contrast with pragmatism, therefore, CR does affirm the subject–object dichotomy.

In *What Is a Person?* Smith suggests that many sociologists have difficulty believing in the objective reality of social relations because such relations are empirically unobservable. For an alternative sensibility, he points to the materialist tradition, and, as indicated, it is indeed from the tradition of historical materialism that I draw my own reference to materiality.[17] In that tradition, talk of materiality certainly does not convey any kind of physicalist reductionism, to which CR is quite opposed. Nor does it convey even what John Searle would refer to as "raw" natural facts.[18] As Smith says, "social structures ... always involve ideational, cognitive classifications and mental objects."[19] They may not, however, do so directly. Along these lines, although it may be impolitic to say today, in arguing against what he called "subjective sociology," an important distinction was made by Lenin, a distinction between what he called *ideological and material relations.* The difference, he explained, is that *ideological relations* are "such as, before taking shape, pass through man's consciousness," whereas *material social relations* are "those that take shape without passing through man's consciousness: when exchanging products men enter into production relations without even realizing that there is a social relation of production here."[20]

By *ideological relations* Lenin meant relations that are directly concept-dependent. The relation of marriage is an example. There is no marriage unless the parties to it understand what a marriage is and how it binds them. We thus say that marriage is constituted by internal relations.

Other relations, however, are external and not similarly concept-dependent. A relation may be exploitative, for example, without that being realized by the parties to the relation or even without the actors' having any concept of exploitation. It is not as if a relation becomes exploitative only when so named. CR expressly rejects

---

[17] Smith, *What Is a Person?*, p. 318. Smith, it should be said, however, worries some about the connotations of this terminology.

[18] John Searle (1995) *The Construction of Social Reality* (New York: Free Press).

[19] Smith, *What Is a Person?*, p. 324.

[20] V. I. Lenin (1970) *What the "Friends of the People Are" and How They Fight the Social Democrats* (Moscow: Progressive Publishers). www.marxists.org/archive/lenin/works/1894/friends/01.htm#v01zz99h-131-GUESS.

such absurdly extreme social constructionism. Were it so, we could end exploitation just by un-naming it.[21]

It is of course true that for a relation to be exploitative, the parties to the relation must be doing something they understand, engaging in some behavior that is concept-dependent. But it need not be the relation in question, in this case exploitation, that their behavior generates. The relation in such cases is an unintended and perhaps even unperceived consequence of what else the actors are doing. It is emergent but nevertheless ontologically objective, that is, existent whether or not the actors notice it. We thus speak of it as *emergently material* or objective.

Exploitation is not the only social relation to bear such ontologically objective character. Inequalities of various kinds do so as well. As in the case of exploitation, it is not as if economic inequality exists only to the extent that it is noticed. The same goes for power or dependency or threatening conditions. Along the lines that Smith suggests, cultural constructs like workers and jobs are both certainly concept-dependent, but the same is not true of the *ratio* of jobs to job seekers or of the match between the two profiles – which together once was called the economic opportunity structure. Instead, such economic opportunity structure again consists of relations ontologically independent of actors' notice or conceptualization. It is only, but importantly, such ontologically objective status that is being designated by the term material and primarily (although not exclusively) relations material in such way that CR considers social structure.

From whence do such material relations arise? CR does not claim they fall from the sky or exist as some raw natural fact. Social relations originate from multiple sources. Sometimes, as in the case of the ratio between jobs and job-seekers, they just emerge from whatever else actors happen to be doing. Other times they are imposed at the point of a gun or by the clutch of a fist. They can emerge, that is, from actors in struggle.

Alternately or conjointly, emergently objective relations may emerge from cultural rules. Not the *regulative* rules on which cultural sociologists focus, which establish procedures. It is rather what are called *constitutive rules* that give rise naturally to material relations. In

---

[21] This argument was also made by Ted Benton and Alex Callinicos. See Ted Benton (1981) "Some Comments on Roy Bhaskar's *The Possibility of Naturalism*," *Radical Philosophy* 27: 13–21; and Alex Callinicos (1985) "Anthony Giddens: A Contemporary Critique," *Theory and Society* 14: 133–166. Bhaskar came to harden his initial view of structure in *The Possibility of Naturalism* after conversations with Margaret Archer.

contrast with *regulative rules, constitutive rules* tell us not how to behave but what our behaviors signify. Languages, for example, are systems of constitutive rules stipulating the meanings attached to different behavioral utterances.[22]

Games similarly are built out of constitutive rules establishing what behaviors count as moves and how different outcomes are to be rewarded or punished. It is from the latter in particular that there may emerge relations that, though concept-dependent, exist, like Searle's institutional facts, independent of actors' notice. Thus, even while being concept-dependent, they nevertheless bear an element of objectivity or materiality. They may be said to be *emergently material.*

The constitutive rules of chess, for example, do not specify the strategic importance of the board's center. That importance is instead an objective, relational property of chess that arises from the rules. To be sure, the center's importance is relative to the concepts that constitute the game; it, and, say, a threat to a king, are not after all natural kinds. Given the rules of the game, however, such social relations and their game-relative affordances are, like natural kinds, ontologically objective in their independence of actors' notice. Some such features, like deep mathematical relations, await insightful discovery. Such after all is what chess theory is all about.

At a more socially consequential level, what Marx called class relations emerge from prior constitutive rules of property ownership. What counts as ownership and the prerogatives thereof create relations of unequal access to resources.[23]

CR distinctly affirms this Marxian and intermittently Bourdieusian sense of social structure as relational, material conditions that stand ontologically apart from both behavioral interaction and culture. It is a conception of structure, it should be noted, that also distinctly differs from the sociological holism of Durkheim, which conceives of structure as relations among social facts, residing over actors' heads. By contrast, in the CR view, social structure consists of human relations in the midst of actors that connects them to each other and to social things. As actors twist and turn and otherwise act within the structures that bind them, they modify those structures. We thus arrive at what

---

[22] The definitive work on constitutive rules is John Searle (1970) *Speech Acts: An Essay in the Philosophy of Language.* Cambridge: Cambridge University Press.
[23] For more on this topic, see Douglas V. Porpora (1993) "Cultural Rules and Material Relations," *Sociological Theory* 11 (2): 212–229.

Archer has called the *morphogenetic* approach to agency and structure, a fuller elaboration of which I leave for a later section.

As noted, the CR conception of social structure is something with which American sociology seems distinctly uncomfortable.[24] American sociology, consequently, we will see, variously tries to distance itself from it and to remain what Bourdieu calls interactionist. Nevertheless, as we will also see, the distancing is unsuccessful. Objective relational conditions continue to creep back into its accounts.

Social structure as lawlike regularities governing the behavior of social facts

The second conception of social structure listed above is the one familiar from what was once called Structural Sociology. Derived from a reading of Durkheim, it leads to an approach to the discipline that is positivist, quantitative, and sociologically holist. Subjective elements – whether individual or cultural – find no place within it. Instead, as noted above, structure floats above individual actors in an autonomous realm of social facts, governed by its own laws.

The putative laws conform to what Durkheim called relations of concomitant variation. That means that variations in one social fact, construed as a variable, are related to variations in other social facts, construed as variables. The approach that naturally suggests itself is what Herbert Blumer called "variable analysis," the quantitative, statistical analysis of covariations.[25]

Since variations in the values of variables are happenings or events, this positivist Durkheimian conception of structure is entirely actualist in nature. As George Steinmetz has argued at length, this positivist actualism continues to pervade the discipline.[26] Here, it is also closely tied to the positivist covering law model.

---

[24] In this regard again, the "new materialists" are a salutary development. See Diana Coole and Samantha Frost (eds.) (2010) *New Materialisms: Ontology, Agency, and Politics*. Durham, NC: Duke University Press. It has yet, however, been a force more in political theory than sociology.

[25] Herbert Blumer (1969) "Sociological Analysis and the 'Variable,'" pp. 127–139 in Herbert Blumer, *Symbolic Interactionism: Perspective and Method* (Englewood Cliffs, NJ: Prentice Hall).

[26] George Steinmetz (2005) *The Politics of Method in the Human Sciences: Positivism and Its Epistemological Others (Politics, History, and Culture)* (Durham, NC: Duke University Press).

As we have already seen, for the covering law model to really work, the covering laws must be sufficiently deterministic. Minimally, for the model to work, the laws must represent at least proper statistical laws, which specify invariant probabilities that some consequent event will follow from the antecedent events. The mere statistical generalizations quantitative sociologists typically offer will not work in the covering law model. In fact, laws with the requisite strictness have never been found in human affairs, and there are solid grounds bearing on human agency for supposing they never will be. The covering law model does not even seem to apply unproblematically to the natural realm.[27]

CR accordingly rejects the covering law model with its deterministic or, minimally, quasi-deterministic implications. As we now know, CR embraces instead a powers view of causality that is able to think of causality in terms of mechanisms and conjunctures and of reasoning too as involving a kind of non-deterministic, non-lawlike causality. Although the positivist Durkheimian conception of social structure continues to haunt American sociology's top journals – and its methods textbooks – it has been so thoroughly discredited that I will spend no more space on it in this chapter.

Social structure as stable patterns or regularities of behavior

If the previous conception of social structure was aligned with socio-logical holism, this one represents the methodological individualist end of the spectrum, what today is sometimes called the *micro-foundational* approach to sociology. Although this conception of social structure seems also embraced by rational choice theory, 20 years ago I associated it mostly with George Homans and Randall Collins.

---

[27] For more extended critiques, see Philip Gorski (2009) "'Mechanisms' and Comparative-Historical Sociology: A Critical Realist Proposal," pp. 147–196 in Peter Hedström and Björn Wittock (eds.) *Frontiers of Sociology* (Boston, MA: Brill); Douglas V. Porpora (1983) "On the Prospects for a Nomothetic Theory of Social Structure," *Journal for the Theory of Social Behaviour* 13: 243–264; George Steinmetz (1998) "Critical Realism and Historical Sociology: A Review Article," *Comparative Studies in Society and History* 40: 170–186, p. 172; and John Levi Martin (2011) *The Explanation of Social Action* (New York: Oxford University Press). For application of the same critique to the natural sciences, see Roy Bhaskar (2005) *A Realist Theory of Science* (New York: Routledge); and Nancy Cartwright (1983) *How the Laws of Physics Lie* (New York: Oxford University Press).

"As used by sociologists," says Homans, "structure seems to refer first to those aspects of social behavior that the investigator considers relatively enduring or persistent."[28] Collins is even more precise.

From a microviewpoint, what is the "social structure"? In microtranslation, it refers to people's repeated behavior in particular places, using particular objects, and communicating by using many of the same symbolic expressions repeatedly with certain other people.[29]

Articulated here is the Margaret Thatcher view of social structure. Thus, as Collins goes on to say, "Strictly speaking, there is no such thing as a 'state', an 'economy', a 'culture', a 'social class'. There are only collections of individual people acting in particular kinds of microsituations – collections which are characterized thus by a kind of shorthand." According to Collins, "The state exists by virtue of there being courtrooms where judges repeatedly sit, headquarters from which police repeatedly leave to ride in the same squad cars, barracks where troops are repeatedly housed and assembly halls where congresses of politicians repeatedly gather."[30]

Clearly, in focusing only on events – i.e., behavior, and repeated behavior at that – this understanding of structure is thoroughly actualist. It also reduces social structure entirely to an epiphenomenon, a dependent variable only with no causal effects. Collins says precisely that:

Social patterns, institutions, and organizations are only abstractions from the behavior of individuals and summaries of the distributions of different microbehaviors in time and space. These abstractions and summaries do not do anything; if they seem to indicate a continuous reality it is because the individuals that make them up repeat their microbehaviors many times, and if the "structures" change it is because the individuals who enact them change their behaviors.[31]

So for Collins, social structure is an abstraction, an enactment of individual behaviors. Thus, Collins's conception of structure is not only actualist in Bhaskar's sense and interactionist in Bourdieu's but

---

[28] George C. Homans (1975) "What do We Mean by Social Structure?," pp. 53–65 in Peter Blau (ed.), *Approaches to the Study of Social Structure* (New York: The Free Press).
[29] Randall Collins (1981) "On the Microfoundations of Macrosociology," *American Journal of Sociology* 86: 984–1014, p. 995.
[30] Ibid., p. 985.   [31] Ibid., p. 989.

also *conflationary* in the sense identified by Archer: Collins in effect has collapsed structure into agency. The result is a total loss of structure as an analytical category. As abstractions lack any causal powers, they can do nothing. Thus, as I said, for Collins, social structure is a dependent variable only, an epiphenomenon.

Collins's conception of social structure is still very much with us. It receives, for example, strong expression in John Levi Martin's *Social Structures*.[32] Like Collins, Martin suggests "that we begin by considering social structure simply as regular patterns of interaction." It turns out, however, that Martin has no intention of only beginning with behavior; he remains there: "Social structure is here considered to refer to recurring patterns of social interaction."[33] Martin's very words – his references to regularity and recurrence – again speak to the actualist (and interactionist) nature of this conception. And of course in equating structure with behavior, Martin's account also remains conflationary. On the surface at least, Martin, like Collins, also seems to consider relations epiphenomenal or at least nothing that can explain behavior patterns.

It becomes apparent that investigations of social structure have been derailed by the fantastic belief that social structure is something that *causes* regularities in action, when social structure is simply what we *call* regularities in action. As Barth (1981: 63) was to conclude, what we want then is not to examine the "effects" of such structures but rather how they "grow."[34]

Although Martin speaks of tendencies toward the emergence of structure, he does not speak in such contexts of the tendencies being caused by anything – possibly because his own first-person view of causality does not allow for it. Rather, according to the formal theory Martin seeks to articulate, in certain circumstances, certain behavioral regularities more or less spontaneously develop, crystallize into various forms like hierarchy and dominance, and thereby harden into what we call structure. As such, Martin says, "they then can confront actors as objective fact."[35]

Martin's careful wording is important here and key to the vulnerability of this conception of social structure. Notice that Martin does not speak of objective facts per se but only of what confronts actors as

---

[32] Martin (2009) *Social Structures* (Princeton, NJ: Princeton University Press).
[33] Ibid., p. 7.   [34] Ibid., pp. 7–8.   [35] Ibid., p. 20.

such. In the manner Bourdieu characterized as interactionist, Martin wants to remain entirely within the subjective realm of discourse and actors' experience.

Although unlike Collins, Martin recognizes relations as something concrete, they gain purchase in his formal theory only when as in a marriage, they are mutually recognized by those related, turning the relation into what Martin calls a relationship. Martin thus tends to understand social positions exclusively in terms of inter-subjective social roles.[36]

In the terms we have introduced, Martin's formal theory exclusively acknowledges only ideological or internal relations. The result is his conviction that "relations are not as important for the analysis of simple structures as is interaction."[37] We will see. We will see first that Martin's formal disregard of any material relations compromises his ability to make sense of fields. We will see further, ironically, that in Martin's *Social Structures*, the kind of material relations CR affirms reenter Martin's account to do precisely what Martin considers fantastic: Explain the behavioral regularities we see.[38]

Social structure as rules (or schemas) and resources that structure behavior

If the previous view of structure was both actualist and conflationary, then, at least on one construal, this one starts out as only conflationary. On initial construal, neither rules, nor resources, nor schemas are events. They are not behaviors. They are all at least something lying beyond. Of course, the beyond in which they lie is culture. Thus, even

---

[36] Martin formally rejects role theory as the kind of too cultural an account as represented by the third conception of structure we will consider (see Martin, *Social Structures*, p. 6). But if as Martin defines them, relationships are relations mutually acknowledged by the persons related with corresponding expectations, it amounts to the same thing.

[37] Martin, *Social Structures*, p. 11. Of course, the CR economist Tony Lawson would likewise limit social structure to discursively established relations, which is why he and I often argue. See *Economics and Reality*.

[38] I have to say that Martin has received my arguments most graciously, and we get on quite well – partly, I think, because he shares a wry, New York sense of humor similar to my own. In any case, we have continued to dialogue on these points. For anyone interested in following it further, I recommend his (2014) *Thinking Through Theory* (New York: Norton).

on this initial construal, the conception is conflationary: Structure is conflated with culture. Actually, structure is wholly swallowed by culture.

On a further construal, however, a second conflation operates. As Archer saw from the start, anticipating practice theory, if rules are held to exist only in their instantiation or enactment, then culture in turn gets swallowed by practice so that in a single, great conflation, like a collapsing black hole, culture, structure, and agency all become one. At that point, where only practice reigns, we are again back to an actualist behaviorism.[39]

But we get ahead of ourselves. This conception begins with Anthony Giddens, who famously defined social structure as rules and resources. The social relations that CR considers to be structure are classified by Giddens as social systems: "A distinction is made between structure and system. Social systems are composed of patterns of relations between actors or collectivities reproduced across time and space."[40]

According to Giddens, rules and resources "structure" (i.e., generate and reproduce) the systemic patterns of relations we see. He says, for example, that "structure" (i.e., rules and resources) refers to "structural property" or more exactly to "structuring property" that reproduces the social system. Thus the relations that define social structure on the CR account are an effect of rules and resources.[41]

From a CR perspective, as we have seen, it is fine to see relations as an emergent effect of rules. But for CR, those emergent relations have consequent causal powers of their own. Not according to Giddens. Like Martin, Giddens finds such relational conception of structure naive, observing that "Such conceptions are closely connected to the dualism of subject and social object: 'structure' here appears as 'external' to human action, as a source of constraint on the free initiative of the independently constituted subject."[42]

---

[39] See Archer, *Realist Social Theory*, particularly pp. 93–134.

[40] Anthony Giddens (1981) *A Contemporary Critique of Historical Materialism* (Berkeley, CA: University of California Press), p. 26.

[41] Anthony Giddens (1979) *Central Problems in Social Theory: Action, Structure, and Contradiction in Social Analysis* (Berkeley, CA: University of California Press), p. 64.

[42] Anthony Giddens (1984) *The Constitution of Society* (Berkeley, CA: University of California Press), p. 16. See also pp. xxiii, xxxi, and 17, in which Giddens, like Collins, depicts social relations as abstractions from repetitive behavior.

Thus, as with the third conception of social structure, for Giddens too, social relations are epiphenomenal.

Giddens's rules and resources require further explication. Resources, as Sewell notes, may be either material or subjective. Language or even money are resources that are culturally inter-subjective in nature. On the contrary, guns presumably are in some sense material. At least, people are not shot by pure ideas.

In either case, it is quite a departure from common understanding to consider resources a structure. Differential access to resources yes, but a differential is a relation. Just the resources themselves? Particulars are structure? The operative principle here seems to be that social structure is anything that structures social behavior. And, indeed, as seen above, in place of structure, Giddens prefers the phrase "structuring property." In that case, as Sewell suggests at one point, even one's physical prowess might then be considered structure.[43]

But surely what most matters structurally about resources – including physical prowess – is not the properties in themselves but their distribution (or the differentials associated with them) across social positions. And insofar as distribution is a relation – and an ontologically objective one at that – if distribution is what most matters in the case of resources, then what most matters is an objective or material relation. We see finally that reference to resources is a gloss that can be unpacked only by admitting the non-epiphenomenal status of relations. That admission, however, is one from which American sociology shrinks.

We are left with rules, which everyone seems to admit are cultural. That categorization still leaves us asking where rules reside. Giddens is characteristically murky here, saying rules have only a "virtual existence."[44] In some places, Giddens acknowledges that that existence might find occupancy inside actors' heads as "memory traces."[45] In other places, Giddens suggests that structural rules "exist in time-space only as moments recursively involved in the production of social systems."[46] On that construal, structure exists only when enacted in concrete behavior. That construal yields the actualist account where structure, reduced to culture, is finally reduced to action.

---

[43] Sewell, "A Theory of Structure," p. 9.
[44] Giddens, *The Constitution of Society*, p. 17. [45] Ibid., p. 25.
[46] Ibid., p. 26.

Sewell's influential article, "A Theory of Structure: Duality, Agency, and Transformation," which won the ASA's 1992 Culture prize, is described by Ann Swidler "as a kind of manifesto about culture and structure."[47] In it, Sewell amended Giddens so that structure would henceforth refer more broadly to schemas rather than rules. Borrowing what Giddens had said of rules, Sewell described schemas as "'generalizable or transposable procedures applied to the enactment of social life.'"[48] Among cultural sociologists, schemas have now come to include a wide variety of things, ranging from scenarios, frames, and repertoires to narratives, norms, and symbolic boundaries.[49]

In all cases, however, schemas remain culturally inter-subjective rather than anything relationally objective or material. As Sewell says, "structures consist of *intersubjectively* available procedures or schemas capable of being actualized or put into practice in a range of different circumstances" (italics added).[50] Although for Sewell, structure includes material *resources* as well, material *relations* still lose their structural designation and largely disappear from analytical attention. Structure has been swallowed by culture.

Yet however much a cultural manifesto Sewell's paper may have been, cultural sociologists seem partially to have misunderstood it. For Sewell, schemas do find subjective residence inside our heads. Sewell resists the practice turn that seems to have swept much of the ASA Culture Section.[51] Thus, while Swidler gets Sewell right when she says he "he wants to erase, or at least substantially reorganize the culture–social structure distinction," she less legitimately claims him for the practice turn when she says he conceives "of culture itself as a form of

[47] Sewell, "A Theory of Structure." Swidler (2001) "What Anchors Cultural Practices," pp. 74–92 in Theodore R. Shatzki, Karin Knorr Cetina, and Eike von Savigny (eds.), *The Practice Turn in Contemporary Theory* (New York: Routledge), p. 77–78.

[48] Ibid., p. 17.

[49] See Mario Luis Small, David J. Harding, and Michèle Lamont (2010) "Reconsidering Culture and Poverty," *Annals of American Academy of Political and Social Science* 629: 6–27. Note, however, Lamont's critique of cultural conflation also in her (1992) *Money, Morals and Manners: The Culture of the French and the American Upper Middle Class* (Chicago: University of Chicago Press), p. 16.

[50] Sewell, "A Theory of Structure," p. 8.

[51] William H. Sewell (1999) "The Concept(s) of Culture," pp. 35–61 in Victoria E. Bonnell and Lynn Hunt (eds.), *Beyond the Cultural Turn: New Directions in the Study of Society and Culture* (Berkeley, CA: University of California Press).

structured practice."[52] On the contrary, Sewell demurs from this entirely actualist account of culture. That is, he considers culture more than just what Swidler calls "culture in action."[53] Such, however, is how the sociologists of the practice turn conceive the whole of social life. Theodore Schatzki's statement is programmatic:

> In social theory, consequently, practice approaches promulgate a distinct social ontology: the social is a field of embodied, materially interwoven practices centrally organized around shared practical understandings. This conception contrasts with accounts that privilege individuals, (inter)actions, language, signifying systems, the life world, institutions/roles, structures, or systems in defining the social. These phenomena, say practice theorists, can only be analyzed via the field of practices. Actions, for instance, are embedded in practices, just as individuals are embedded within them. Language, moreover is a type of activity (discursive) and hence a practice phenomenon, whereas institutions and structures are effects of them.[54]

Shatzki allows that not all practice theorists accept all that is expressed above. No wonder. The number of categories Shatzki would collapse is breath-taking. Indeed, it is important to see that the actualist conflationism operative here means to do away with more than just the traditional notion of material structure upheld by CR. As Swidler makes clear, it also means to do away with culture understood "as some abstract stuff in people's heads which might or might not cause their action," and for that matter with people's heads as well:

> Theories of practice ... de-emphasized what was going on in the heads of actors, either individuals or collectivities. Instead, these theories emphasized "practices" understood as routine activities (rather than consciously chosen actions) notable for their unconscious, automatic, un-thought character.[55]

Whereas American sociology once worried about cultural dupes, it now embraces zombies. To be sure, practice theory's further reductions of both culture and agency to practice are analytically deleterious in

---

[52] Swidler, "What Anchors Cultural Practices," p. 78.

[53] See Sewell, "The Concept(s) of Culture." Ann Swidler (1986) "Culture in Action: Symbols and Strategies," *American Sociological Review* 51 (2): 273–286.

[54] Theodore R. Shatzki (2001) "Introduction: Practice Theory," pp. 1–14 in Theodore R. Shatzki, Karin Knorr Cetina, and Eike von Savigny (eds.) *The Practice Turn in Contemporary Theory* (New York: Routledge), p. 3.

[55] Swidler, "What Anchors Cultural Practices," p. 74.

their own right, and we will address those problems in the following chapters.[56] Our issue here is structure. We thus confine ourselves to the observation that this fourth conception clearly – even programmatically – conflates structure with culture and at the current extreme in practice theory conflates structure with behavior as well. At that point, the point of the great conflation – Hegel's "night in which all cows are black" – the third and fourth conceptions of structure fittingly meld together.

Why not relations?

Why does American sociology shrink from relations of other than an actualist, interactionist sort? In this section, I consider several possible reasons. We begin with medieval nominalism, which may still be with us.[57] In medieval times, granting relations objective ontological reality was resisted for two reasons. Perhaps the overarching reason was that relations appeared to be a species of abstract object not clearly localizable. If Socrates is taller than Plato, where does that relation reside? Without place, it does not appear to have concrete being.[58]

That first reason to resist the ontological reality of relations was reinforced by a second consideration, namely that in paradigmatic relations such as relative tallness, the relation appears to be supervenient on the relata taken monadically. What is there, for example, about Socrates's being taller than Plato than just Socrates's being the height he is and Plato the height he is? The comparative relation again appears not to be a third thing over and above these two monadic

---

[56] But also see Archer (2001), Being Human: The Problem of Agency (Cambridge: Cambridge University Press) and Christian Smith's forthcoming *To Flourish or Destruct: A Personalist Theory of Human Goods, Motivations, Failure and Evil* (Chicago, IL: University of Chicago Press).

[57] Indeed, Martin refers to it multiple times. See, for example, Martin (2013) "Personal Best," Contemporary Sociology 42 (1): 6–11, p. 6; and John Levi Martin (2013) "John Levi Martin's Response to Christian Smith," *Contemporary Sociology* 42 (1): 16–18, p. 17. Much of the discussion in Martin's "Personal Best" also addresses Western nominalism.

[58] Jeffrey Brower (2009) "Medieval Theories of Relations," *Stanford Encyclopedia of Philosophy*. http://plato.stanford.edu/entries/relations-medieval/. In international relations, Alexander Wendt is working on a new quantum theory of mind that will give special attention to such nonlocal causality. In International Relations, it should be noted, Alexander Wendt's new book, *Quantum Mind and Social Science* deals centrally with nonlocal causality.

relata. Such was the position of Abelard and William of Ockham. A kindred concern, harbored today by Charles Varela and Rom Harré, is that relations are not substantive things, substantive things, according to Varela and Harré, being the exclusive bearers of causal powers.[59]

It is unclear, however, that localizable, substantive things are the only possessors of causal powers. Much depends on what we consider ontologically basic. The natural attitude, which Varela and Harré follow, is to consider things bedrock reality. Yet, an equally compelling alternative is postulated by Wittgenstein in the *Tractatus*. The world, Wittgenstein famously says, does not consist of things but of everything that is the case. And what is the case (facts) are states of affairs. And constitutive of states of affairs are relations. In fact, in telling us that the world consists of facts in logical space, Wittgenstein virtually identifies states of affairs with relations. On this view, then, relations are ontologically basic.[60]

But can causal powers reside in relations? Arguably yes. Consider, for example, the so-called anthropic coincidences of physical cosmology. It is now generally agreed by physicists that the visible universe of ours is fantastically fine-tuned for life. Were any of countless physical parameters even minutely different, intelligent life as we know it could not have evolved. It is partly because of such considerations, in fact, that physicists, eschewing any implication of divine creation, now routinely posit myriad universes, among which, only in Goldilocks universes like our own can life appear.[61]

So the anthropic coincidences are causally necessary for life. And many of the anthropic coincidences are relational, ratios between different sorts of parameters – like the mass ratios of protons and electrons and protons and neutrons. Likewise, were all other constants

[59] Charles Varela and Rom Harré (1996) "Conflicting Varieties of Realism: Causal Powers and the Problems of Social Structure," *Journal for the Theory of Social Behaviour* 26 (3): 313–325.

[60] Ludwig Wittgenstein (1961) *Tractatus Logico-Philosophicus* (London: Routledge & Kegan Paul), p. 5. Even were they granted to be basic, relations are not, contrary to relational sociology, the only existent. We still need talk of particulars.

[61] See, for early well-known compendia, John D. Barrow and Frank J. Tipler (1988) *The Anthropic Cosmological Principle* (New York: Oxford University Press); or John Leslie (1996) *Universes* (New York: Routledge). There are since many others.

left unchanged and the strong nuclear force just 2% stronger, no hydrogen would exist, in which case, there would be no water and, hence, no life.

What causally matters with regard to the anthropic coincidences is not the monadic properties of any particular constant taken alone, but their relation to each other. Put otherwise, it is the relational state of affairs that matters, not the monadic properties of individual parameters.

The point can be put more prosaically. Suppose we place Socrates and Plato on opposite ends of a seesaw. Which way the seesaw tips depends not on the specific weights of Socrates and Plato considered separately. Their individual weights are not what matters. What matters is the difference between the two, the presence and direction of any discrepancy. What is causally efficacious is the relation.

It may be that the difference between the two weights is supervenient on the individual weights of Socrates and Plato. Supervenience, however, is not reduction.[62] There may still be a reason to posit the supervenient phenomenon over and above the base elements on which it rests. And from a CR perspective, there is such reason to do so in this case, namely the causal criterion of existence. To the extent that it is the relation and not the individual weights that is causally efficacious here, the relation exists not just as an abstraction but as something ontologically concrete. The concrete reality of relations, then, is manifested by their causal efficacy in time and space.

In the social sphere too, as I have suggested, relations can be causally consequential. In the school yard, one child dominates another because the first is bigger or more popular than the other. It is again not the properties in themselves that have the causal effect but the disparity, the relational difference. We will consider more examples later.

There are two further reasons why many American sociologists resist any reintroduction of specifically material relations. The first is voiced by Giddens above and also by Sewell.[63] It again reflects a positivist legacy. The worry is that talk of material effects on human behavior will re-enmesh human agents in a deterministic network

---

[62] See Daniel Stoljar, "Physicalism," *The Stanford Encyclopedia of Philosophy* (Fall 2009 Edition), Edward N. Zalta (ed.), http://plato.stanford.edu/archives/fall2009/entries/physicalism/, and also Jaegwon Kim (2006) "Emergence: Core Ideas and Issues," *Synthese* 151: 547–559.

[63] Sewell, "A Theory of Structure," p. 2. Lizardo, "Beyond the Antimonies" does as well.

of causal laws. It is the worry behind the post-Wittgensteinian demarcation between explanation and understanding.

Once, however, we adopt as CR does, a powers view of causality that rejects the positivist covering law model even as applied to physical phenomena, the specter of determinism disappears. What disappears along with it is any further need to distinguish strongly between understanding and explanation. Whatever causal effects material phenomena may exert, no laws govern the human, agential response, which will always exhibit degrees of creativity. Structurally material effects can therefore be admitted without any implication of structural reduction.

It is the positivist covering law model that lies behind the worry, and the positivist covering law model that continues to support the post-Wittgensteinian outlook that many cultural sociologists inherit from Clifford Geertz and Robert Wuthnow.[64] But the heyday of this post-Wittgensteinian view of agency was the middle of the last century; philosophers have long since found it untenable. Instead, as Bhaskar argues in *The Possibility of Naturalism*, philosophers have come to realize that reasons too are best considered causes, even if nondeterministic ones. Indeed, as previously noted, in the most recent edition of *The Idea of a Social Science*, even Peter Winch admits as much.[65] It is time for the cultural sociologists to do the same, but abandoning a cherished paradigm is difficult.

The second reason for resisting social relations that are even emergently objective, let alone completely objective, is the deep influence of pragmatism on American sociology, with its core denial of any separation between subject and object. As Martin says in response to Christian Smith's CR defense of ontologically objective reality, "It may seem to be splitting hairs, but it makes quite a difference whether we start with such a hypothesized reality or, like the pragmatists, begin with experience. The latter is directly empirical to persons, the former is not."[66] Actually, I do not at all consider it splitting hairs. I agree with Martin that

---

[64] Clifford Geertz (1977) *The Interpretation of Cultures* (New York: Basic Books). Robert Wuthnow (1989) *Meaning and Moral Order: Explorations in Cultural Analysis* (Berkeley, CA: University of California Press).

[65] Peter Winch (2010) *The Idea of a Social Science and Its Relation to Philosophy* (New York: Routledge), pp. xi–xii.

[66] John Levi Martin (2013) "John Levi Martin's Response to Christian Smith," *Conteporary Sociology* 42 (1): 16–18, p. 17. See also Christian Smith (2013) "Fellow Traveler in Theoretical Frontiers," *Contemporary Sociology* 42 (1): 12–16.

our differing views of reality make all the difference. Although, against Smith, Martin argues that pragmatism's constructionism is not extreme, it is extreme enough.[67] In its restriction of ontology to human empirical experience, pragmatism is notably of a piece with postivist actualism.[68]

Structure, agency, and culture (SAC) and the morphogenetic approach

The canonical CR treatment of social structure is what Archer formulated as the morphogenetic approach or perhaps better the morphogenetic/morphostatic (MM) approach.[69] The name, as Archer herself acknowledges, is less than pretty. Morphogenesis and morphostasis refer to changes in (genesis) or reproduction of (stasis) social systems.

While the name may be off-putting, the idea behind it is simple, even commonsensical, perhaps too much so for American sociology. The idea is the one famously expressed by Marx in his 18th Brumaire of Louis Napoleon: "Men make their history but not under circumstances of their own making."[70]

Described by Marx's dictum is a dialectical interplay of agency and circumstances. All human action originates from situated circumstances or context. Those circumstances are both cultural and structural. That is, people act from a social position related to other social positions and do so, although creatively, through the cultural milieu they inhabit. In the temporal process of acting, actors either reproduce or alter both or either the cultural and structural circumstances that originally bound them. The former case is what Archer means by *morphostasis* and the latter what she means by *morphogenesis*.

The MM process described above thus incorporates structure, agency, and culture, hence the acronym SAC.[71] Of course, to analyze

---

[67] Martin, "Personal Best."

[68] Roy Bhaskar (2009) *Scientific Realism and Human Emancipation* (New York: Routledge).

[69] Archer, "Morphogenesis versus Structuration"; Realist Social Theory. Again, there are CR dissenters from this view, notably Varela and Harré ("Conflicting Varieties of Realism") and Elder-Vass (*The Causal Power*).

[70] K. Marx (2000) "The Eighteenth Brumaire of Louis Bonaparte," in David McClellan, *Karl Marx: Selected writings* (New York: Oxford University Press).

[71] Margaret Archer (2013) "Social Morphogenesis and the Prospects of Morphogenetic Society," pp. 1–24 in Margaret Archer (ed.), *Social Morphogenesis* (Dordrecht: Springer).

the temporal interplay of elements belonging to these three categories, the categories themselves must remain analytically distinct. To conflate one with another is to lose the analytical ability to see how they interrelate. Such is the basis of Archer's principled opposition to conflation, which, as I say, has become canonical for CR. Seen thus, the acronym SAC stands not just for structure, action, and culture, but also for CR's affirmation of their distinctness as separate ontological categories.

Giddens too spoke of structure as both context and outcome of action. Is that not the same as the MM approach? Not quite. In the first place, as Archer notes, we can speak of an interplay of structure and agency only if the two are not collapsed into the same thing as Giddens proposes. Second, we must ever recall that Giddens fundamentally redefined structure so that it no longer is talking about the same thing as CR. Yes, provided they are not conflated, there is, as Archer maintains, also an MM cycle that obtains between rules or schemas on the one hand and action on the other. But then we are speaking of what CR would call culture, not structure.

Because Giddens renders social relations epiphenomenal, he does not apply the MM cycle to them. CR does. That is the difference. The difference is reclaiming what structure originally meant, deconflating, re-empowering relations. Thus, when Giddens speaks of structure as constraining and enabling, he does not mean the same thing as CR.

CR is happy to concede that culture too – whether in the form of rules or schemas – is constraining and enabling. Distinctly, however, there is another thing CR adds. The social structural relations that bind us are not just enabling and constraining, but motivating as well.[72] With the post-Wittgensteinian approach of the fourth conception of structure, running from Giddens through Swidler, motivation largely disappears, surfacing, Giddens tells us, only in those isolated moments when our routines break down. As observed, the conflationism of the fourth position dissolves not just structure understood as social relations but human personhood as well. That dissolution is the topic of the next chapter.[73]

---

[72] Archer, *Realist Social Theory*. Porpora, "Four Concepts of Social Structure," "Cultural Rules and Material Relations."

[73] Giddens, *The Constitution of Society*, p. 6. For counter-arguments see Archer, *Being Human*; Douglas V. Porpora (1983) "On the Post-Wittgensteinian

Let us return to motivation, which takes us back to Martin's discussion of fields and games. There, Martin uncommonly and refreshingly references *constitutive rules*. He notes that the constitutive rules of a game frequently establish unequal outcomes that represent various degrees of winning and losing.[74]

So far so good, but there Martin stops. He refrains from the further observation that such a schedule of contingencies already constitutes, relative to the game, an objective, relational, opportunity structure that the involved actors can ignore only at their own cost. Players have in a word, a word Martin does not mention in this context, an *interest*, a *material interest*, in those outcomes. And with such material interest, motivation for behavior.[75]

Moreover, since the actors (i.e., players) generally outnumber the most preferred outcomes, especially if there is only a single winner, the preferred outcomes constitute, relative to the players, a limited good that cannot be shared. The effect is to generate among the players the relational condition of mutual threat I spoke of earlier: The attainment of a preferred outcome by each player is threatened by its attainment by others. That threat generates for each position or player a further material interest in its counter. That ultimate goal in turn generates further material interests in whatever instrumental or strategic goals might serve it. If the game is chess, then, as noted, there becomes for each player an early material interest in controlling the board's center. If the game is Parker Brothers *Monopoly*, then those occupying the position of player each have a material interest in securing all the cards of a single color and erecting hotels as soon as possible.[76]

In short, the concept-dependent emergently objective relations generated by constitutive rules in turn generate equally objective, *positional interests* – interests that independent of subjective preferences are built into the social positions – that so motivate behavior that we

Critique of the Concept of Action in Sociology," *Journal for the Theory of Social Behaviour* 13 (2): 129–146; Smith, *What Is a Person?*; and Smith *To Flourish or Destruct*.

[74] John Levi Martin (2003) "What is Field Theory?," *American Journal of Sociology* 109 (1): 1–49; and also Martin, *The Explanation of Social Action*, pp. 268–320.

[75] Interests do make a pivotal appearance when Martin turns his attention to political parties, pp. 304ff., for example. It is unclear, however, how Martin understands that term.

[76] Toward that end, the railroads are fun but just a distraction.

typically are quite able to explain and even to predict it. As philosopher Daniel Dennett famously observed, even if you are playing chess against a computer, you would do well to play as if against an intentional agent best pursuing its interests.[77] To do so, you need to anticipate its interests, which include countering your own.

To be sure, no deterministic causal laws are operative. People can fail to perceive their interests or ignore them. Still, if the stakes are high (imagine a *Monopoly* game with real money) and the options constrained as in a game, most people will behave in a fairly predictable manner – not because they are following regulative rules but because they are strategically, rationally pursuing their material interests. Those neglecting their interests will soon enough disappear from the game, requiring of us no further notice.

There is nothing particularly mysterious or obscure in this picture connecting rules, relations, interests, and motivated behavior. Yet it is a picture rational choice theorists seem completely to miss. As we saw, for example, according to Peter Hedström, mechanisms always refer to actors and their actions.[78] Hedström thus overlooks how, even prior to action, the games of game theory, so integral to rational choice theory, are already mechanisms of related contingencies generating the interests motivating the rational behavior that rational choice theory expects. Likewise, as we saw, speaking for the pragmatists, Neil Gross tells us that mechanisms are "chains or aggregations of actors confronting problem situations."[79] But actors apart, what are problem situations? Might they not stem from relational conditions such as conflicts of interest? And as such would they not be ontologically objective, motivating mechanisms in themselves? Gross does not say, but to admit as much would move us outside the confines of his brand of pragmatism.

There seems, as I have suggested, a concerted will in American sociology to disregard ontologically objective relational conditions and with them the analytically pivotal concept of material interests.[80]

[77] Daniel Dennett (1989) *The Intentional Stance* (Cambridge, MA: Bradford Books).
[78] Peter Hedström (2005) *Dissecting the Social: On the Principles of Analytical Sociology* (New York: Cambridge University Press), pp. 24–26.
[79] Neil Gross (2009) "A Pragmatist Theory of Social Mechanisms," *American Sociological Review* 74: 358–379, p. 368.
[80] But for a strong, recent defense of the concept (by a non-American) see Jack Barbalet (2012) "Self-Interest and the Theory of Action," *The British Journal of*

That disregard – or outright refusal – is shared by Martin. His own pragmatist subjectivism likewise precludes admission of the ontologically objective. Hence, although he talks of fields as positioned actors oriented to each other, in contrast with Bourdieu, the orientation for Martin is always an interactionist one.

Put otherwise, for Martin, the field forces operating are always subjective – always feelings of "what should be done" – as if what were most important in a game were senses of normative obligation rather than strategic advantage.[81] Using the example of chess himself, Martin says that "to explain social action is akin to explaining why a grand master allowed a knight to exchange for a pawn."[82] I completely agree. That move, however, is not explained by any sense of normative obligation but rather in terms of positional advantage. That explanation requires reference to the objective relations and interests the constitutive rules generate and which have developed further in the course of play.[83] Without such, how does Martin actually explain

---

Sociology 63 (3): 412–429. Emirbayer and Johnson, "Bourdieu and Organizational Analysis," likewise speak of interests.

[81] Martin, "What is Field Theory?," p. 57.   [82] Ibid., p. 59.

[83] Again, Emirbayer and Johnson, "Bourdieu and Organizational Analysis," seem to write in the same spirit. To put the point in a way that addresses the concerns of Isaac Reed, it is the *import* of the move that cannot be unpacked without reference to the objective relations and interests that are generated by the constitutive rules of the game and game play itself. See Isaac Reed (2008) "Maximal Interpretation in Clifford Geertz and the Strong Program in Cultural Sociology: Toward a New Epistemology," *Cultural Sociology* 2: 187–200. My account here does not actually counter the cultural priority of the so-called Strong Program in Cultural Theory propounded by Jeffrey Alexander and Philip Smith. On the contrary, I freely admit that the mind-independent, ontologically objective relations at issue emerge from the culturally constructed, constitutive rules of chess. See Jeffrey Alexander and Philip Smith (2002) "The Strong Program in Cultural Theory: Elements of a Structural Hermeneutics," pp. 135–149 in Jonathan Turner (ed.), *Handbook of Sociological Theory* (New York: Plenum).

Coming himself from a Strong Program perspective with its emphasis on actors' own interpretations, Reed seems to me to misunderstand CR's concern with ontology. See Isaac Reed (2008) "Justifying Sociological Knowledge: From Realism to Interpretation," *Sociological Theory* 26 (2): 101–129. If we critical realists seem to harp on ontology, it is because the Interpretivists would rather absorb absolutely everything under the category of epistemology. Thus, Reed (p. 121) asserts that "no matter how objective – in the sense of external, unchangeable, and coercive – a set of social structures appear to the actors immersed in them, from a strictly epistemological perspective they are artifices of human creation." I actually might agree with this statement, but insofar as Reed

the move? As Wittgenstein observes, "what we cannot speak about we must pass over in silence."[84] It is silence Martin keeps.

Do we need material relations?

I have shown, I think, that the conceptions of social structure rival to CR's are both conflationist and actualist, leaving any kind of objective social relations out of account. But that showing counts as critique only if analytically we do in fact need ontologically objective social relations. Throughout this chapter – as just above, I have serially indicated in passing that we do need them. In this final section, I want to devote myself more concertedly to that point.

Let us begin simply. Is American sociology prepared to say that inequality is of no consequence? That *inequality* itself, as Collins might have it, is only an abstraction with no concrete causal effects of its own? If not, then what is inequality? Is it a behavior? An enactment? A cultural schema? Clearly, inequality – at least primordially – is neither a behavior nor a schema. Primordially, it is a relation: a certain distribution of something and as such objective or material. If, then, inequality is itself consequential, then what is consequential is a

---

is making a claim not about knowledge but rather about the nature of social structures in reality, his claim is not epistemological but, like CR's, ontological.

 I say that I might agree with Reed's statement above but not with his implied opposition between the objective and the socially created as if only what occurs naturally can be ontologically objective or consequential. Thus, what he says just prior gives me more pause. He says that from his interpretivist perspective, "constraining, external structures are considered as *objectivized* structures, which thus have their own historical trajectory and must be interpreted as presupposing their own meaningful logic (p. 121; italics in original)." I do not understand what Reed might mean as applied to our current context: My opponent has just exchanged his knight for a pawn, and as a result, my king is now threatened with mate in two moves. That threat is a relational property, an institutional fact that, given the game-assigned meanings, is ontologically objective. Its existence does not require any further objectification from my opponent or me; it is there even if neither of us notices it. Its existence may be discovered only decades later. If by having its own historical trajectory, Reed means the threat was created at one point in time and then altered by other actions, I am fine with that. It sounds like morphogenetic cycles. I am likewise happy to concede that talk of kings and threats has meaning only relative to the culturally constituted game. If Reed is pushing for something more, I do not know what it is. Nor do I know what objectification might mean here.

[84] Wittgenstein, *Tractatus Logico-Philosophicus*, p. 74.

material relation. With that concession, the match has just been won, but let us move on.

Forget Marx. I also mentioned Adam Smith. What did Smith mean by the market's invisible hand? Can it really be explained without reference to interests and to the relation of mutual threat that conditions them? Smith himself did not think so.

It is not from the benevolence of the butcher, the brewer or the baker, that we expect our dinner, but from their regard to their own interest. We address ourselves, not to their humanity but to their self-love, and never talk to them of our own necessities but of their advantages.[85]

As Smith uses them above, interest and advantage are not subjective qualities. Smith considers them objective properties to which we can appeal even if they have previously gone unnoticed by the actors to whom they apply. As I said above, the invisible hand refers to more than just some capitalist habitus. It refers to the prior force of mutual threat that makes a free market free. That relation is the basis of market efficiency. Without that relation or the interests it generates, we lose completely the entire market mechanism. Then we are in worse shape even than the economists.[86]

Let us now move back to where I began with the culture of poverty theory. Helpfully, the cultural sociologists tell us now that the poor are not motivated by pathological values – or at least not by values different from those of American society at large. That finding ought to drive a nail into the culture of poverty theory, except the nail immediately dissolves. The cultural sociologists tell us not to think of culture at all in terms of values. Instead we are to understand culture as repertoires and narratives and frames and other schema.[87]

Okay, but can we still not ask how much the problem of poverty is due to the cultural schemas that are being passed down as opposed to the number and types of jobs on offer to the poor, that is, to what used

[85] Adam Smith (1937) *An Inquiry into the Nature and Causes of the Wealth of Nations* (New York: Modern Library), p. 14.
[86] Yes, certainly, as Reed, "Justifying Sociological Knowledge," observes, in concrete reality, actually existing markets may all differ. It is unclear, however, whether, according to Reed, that precludes Weberian ideal types and, indeed, all abstraction. As a fellow holder of an undergraduate degree in mathematics, I ask him whether, although all real triangles actually differ, we cannot still speak abstractly of them under that one category.
[87] Swidler, "Culture in Action."

to be called the opportunity structure? The question does not go away.[88] What goes away only is our discipline's interest in answering it.

Let us move from the national to international level of analysis. What are we to make of the third and fourth conceptions of structure in relation to world systems or dependency theory? A nation's position in an international division of labor seems to involve something other than just behaviors or cultural schemas. A division of labor itself is a relational concept, as is dependency. At neither the level of individuals nor at the level of nations is dependency primordially an enactment; again, on the contrary, any behavior considered to enact dependency is already a response to dependency as a prior condition or relation. That simple logic is lost along with any ability even to conceptualize core and periphery when we construe structure as behavior or cultural schemas. Not even resources help here as many poor, peripheral countries are resource rich. To analyze such cases, there is no escaping relations.

I said earlier that, conceptually, relations creep back into the very accounts of those who would dismiss them. Let us now see how. Begin with Collins's *Violence: A Micro-Sociological Theory*.[89] It is a wonderful book, a fascinating book. But it also vitiates completely Collins's larger claim about social structure.

The entire thrust of the book is that human beings are so intimidated by violence that they will initiate it only when the odds of survival are highly in their favor as when supported against targets by overwhelming force. It is an important insight, but wait. What is meant by overwhelming force or the odds of survival? Both expressions are comparative and hence relational in nature. They refer to objective, relational features of the social situation.[90] True, the objective relational features gain purchase only if they are subjectively perceived by the actors, but if there were no fairly close correlation between perception and reality, not only would there be little point ever in speaking of

---

[88] See, for example, Orlando Patterson (2006) "A Poverty of the Mind," *New York Times*. www.nytimes.com/2006/03/26/opinion/26patterson.html? pagewanted=all&_r=0.

[89] Randall Collins (2009) *Violence: A Micro-Sociological Theory* (Princeton, NJ: Princeton University Press).

[90] Ibid., p. 19; Collins actually acknowledges that point in one passing sentence.

perception but Collins would have no theory. However surrepiti-
tiously, material relations occupy a pivotal role in Collins's account.

We find the same with Martin when, for example, he comes to
explain dominance. The third and fourth conceptions of structure
would reduce the dominance of, say, A over B to behavior patterns:
A behaves dominatingly and B dominatedly. But why does the behavior pattern run that way rather than the other way around? Why is it
not A who behaves dominatedly and B who behaves dominatingly?
Martin explains:

> Dominance orders can arise in different ways. In one, a preexisting difference
> in some attribute or attributes leads to an inequality (i.e., A is "greater" than
> B in some respect); relations of inequality are then the scaffolding for
> interaction. So if all animals have some individual characteristic ζ, animals
> i and j can compare themselves on degrees of ζ, with animal i submitting if
> $\zeta_i < \zeta_j$ and animal j submitting if $\zeta_j < \zeta_i$. For example, little animals may get
> out of the way when big animals approach.[91]

Say what? In an admittedly enthymematic way we will accordingly
need to unpack further, it sounds as if Martin has just introduced a
material relation that accomplishes the feat we earlier saw him describe
as fantastic: It explains the behavior pattern we call dominance. Certainly, again, there is a subjective component here: For the dominance
pattern to arise, the animals do need to compare themselves. But the
passage itself seems explicitly to acknowledge that the animals are
comparing themselves on an inequality that is objective – in this case,
their size differences.

The objective or material relation is analytically pivotal, although
the objective, unequal distribution of ζ is not enough. As I said, the
passage is enthymematic. Left unsaid is that ζ must somehow be
causally consequential. It must, as Martin would say, matter and
matter in a certain way.[92] Specifically, ζ must be a source of power, a
capacity that yields the relation of *power over*. That relation of power
in turn generates a material interest for the subordinate party not to
displease the superordinate. The superordinate conversely has an

---

[91] Martin, *Social Structures*, p. 106. Later (pp. 238ff.) Martin speaks of hierarchies
having various causal effects, but there the causal operator could still be
construed as a particular pattern of behavior. That construal is less possible here
in relation to inequality.

[92] Martin, "Personal Best," p. 9.

interest in exploiting whatever advantages derive from the power differential. It is such interests and not regulative rules that explain the behavior pattern. And the interests originate in the material relation. Martin describes the inequality relation as "scaffolding," but scaffolding is a causative word, indicating that the inequality – the relation – has causal consequences.

The aversion to material relations is endemic to much of the pragmatist tradition. We see it as well in Alex Dennis and Peter Martin's defense of Symbolic Interactionism's treatment of power.[93] First they cite Howard Becker's atypical reference to power as a material relation with causal effect attached to a social position:

Differences in the ability to make rules and apply them to other people are essentially power differentials (either legal or extralegal). Those groups whose social position gives them weapons and power are best able to enforce their rules.[94]

What Becker articulates above is straightforward CR ontology. So Dennis and Martin must immediately proceed to efface it. "Power," they say, "is not some kind of entity whose essence can be revealed or abstracted from its situations of use, let alone abstractly defined or measured."[95] Do they mean that Becker cannot do what he just did – i.e., speak of power in the abstract? Dennis and Martin elaborate.

Such [power] differentials, however, must be understood as the outcomes, over time, of social processes – often quite prosaic – which ultimately produce patterns of decisive advantages and disadvantages, often involving the accumulation (or loss) of significant resources – money, land, military might, prestige, and so on. To understand how these patterns come about, how they are perpetuated and challenged and so on, is for us an important opportunity in the exercise of the "sociological imagination."[96]

If we read this elaboration closely, we discover why, for all Dennis and Martin's effort, materialists remain frustrated with Symbolic Interactionism and its pragmatist roots. What Dennis and Martin are saying is

---

[93] Alex Dennis and Peter J. Martin (2005) "Symbolic Interactionism and the Concept of Power," *British Journal of Sociology* 56 (2): 191–213. http://onlinelibrary.wiley.com.ezproxy2.library.drexel.edu/doi/10.1111/j.1468-4446.2005.00055.x/full

[94] Ibid., pp. 199–200. Howard Becker (1963) *Outsiders: Studies in the Sociology of Deviance* (New York: Free Press), pp. 17–18.

[95] Dennis and Martin, "Symbolic Interactionism," p. 200.   [96] Ibid., p. 208.

that power is a pattern that is an outcome of social processes and that Symbolic Interactionists devote themselves to understanding how that pattern is produced, maintained, and challenged.

Describing a power differential as a pattern already moves in the direction of actualist behaviorism that depletes the differential of any explanatory power. A power differential is not a pattern; it is a relational condition that itself causally explains certain patterns. Thus, while it is all to the good that Dennis and Martin want Symbolic Interactionists to pursue the causes of this relational outcome, as Becker observed and I just suggested, outcomes too have outcomes. Yet missing from Dennis and Martin's proposed research agenda is any mention of the effects of power, i.e., of the causal powers of power as a material relation. Perhaps Dennis and Martin mean to include it under their second "and so on," but I doubt it. To talk of power that way, Dennis and Martin suggest, would be to reify it.[97] Which means what? To consider power something real, something objective? Yes, that is precisely what is needed and precisely what contemporary Symbolic Interactionism retreats from.

Younger scholars ask why we need CR and what difference it makes. CR's SAC affirms a three-legged analytical stool: material relations (structure); culture; and purposively motivated human agency. Mainstream American sociology would prefer to limp along on only two legs or, even worse, hop on one. Actually, as the practice turn tends also to de-agentify agency, what might have been a stool floats in the air. If, as I say, the discipline has lost interest in asking the questions to which material relations are the answer, then, indeed, in this regard, CR offers no benefits. Lenin referred to what results as "subjective sociology." He might just as well have labeled it bourgeois.

---

[97] Ibid., pp. 197–198.

5 | *Are we not men – or, rather, persons?*

For those too young to remember, the title of this chapter is an homage to the punk band, *Devo*, whose name signified its charge that, at least in America, humans were no longer evolving; instead we were devolving or going backward.[1] From what were we devolving? If we exchange the sexist designation *men*, we arrive at *persons* and at *personhood* as an ontological category.

Whether American society is devolving is a theoretical question that needs to be answered empirically. Whether American sociology is devolving is a question that is metatheoretical in nature. Within socio-logical theory, if the category of person is not quite devolving, it is at least under sustained attack from multiple directions.

What is a person? The question is the title of a CR book by Christian Smith.[2] He needs to ask because in sociology, we rarely speak of persons or of personhood. We speak rather of the self, as do the Symbolic Interactionists or as in poststructuralist circles of the subject or Cartesian subject. Person, though, is the technical term used in philosophy and law and is the term critical realists tend to favor.

Although person more or less coincides with what we in sociology call the self, it bears different connotations. Whereas the self conveys an image of something floating inside us, some mysterious I and me that we need to locate, person is not something we have but something we are. Put in sociological terms, persons do not have selves; they are selves. The full meaning of that declaration is something in this chapter we will explore further.

In Chapter 4 I spoke in passing of zombies. As I write, zombies are hot; in film and on television, they have replaced vampires as the

---

[1] The title question is also a famous line from H. G. Wells's (2013) *The Island of Doctor Moreau* (Los Angeles, CA: Hungry Girl Books).

[2] Christian Smith (2011) *What Is a Person? Rethinking Humanity, Social Life, and the Moral Good from the Person Up* (Chicago, IL: University of Chicago Press).

favored denizen of the supernatural.[3] *Wikipedia* provides a very apt definition of zombie: "a hypnotized person bereft of consciousness and self-awareness, yet ambulant and able to respond to surrounding stimuli."

Re-read *Wikipedia's* definition of zombie and behold: It also describes *in nuce* what has become of persons in much contemporary sociological theory. Contemporary sociological theory is uncomfortable with persons, selves, or Cartesian subjects. Contemporary sociological theory does not want consciousness or at least centered, reflective, self-aware consciousness. It expressly does not want intentionality. In their place, contemporary sociological theory wants – at most – the unconscious, hypnotized responsiveness to surrounding stimuli of Bourdieu's habitus.[4] I say at most. In such perspectives as relational sociology and poststructuralism, agency is often completely pried apart from actual agents to float away on its own, giving us, for example, discursive resistance somehow without the blood and guts of actual resisters.

And what of the human agents themselves? In much contemporary theory, human agency becomes *de-agentified*. In much contemporary sociological theory, what used to be human agents now shamble along, unmotivated, hypnotized by habit. Early on, Anthony Giddens warned us against the derogation of the lay actor. Yet his own effacement of human purposiveness ultimately contributed to a new form of that effect.

---

[3] Actually, they are hot too in philosophy of mind, especially in connection with philosophical functionalism. Don't get me started on that.

[4] We critical realists are actually split on Bourdieu, reflecting, I think, an ambiguity in Bourdieu's work. Philip Gorski, George Steinmetz, and Frédéric Vandenberghe, all very influenced by Bourdieu, believe he should be claimed as a critical realist, and Bourdieu's account of field certainly fits. See Philip Gorski (ed.) *Bourdieu and Historical Analysis* (Durham, NC: Duke University Press); and Frédéric Vandenberghe (1999) "The Real is Relational: An Epistemological Analysis of Pierre Bourdieu's Generative Structualism," *Sociological Theory* 17 (1): 33–67. Margaret Archer, on the other hand, who studied under Bourdieu, is very put off by Bourdieu's concept of habitus, which I am critiquing here. See, among other places, Margaret Archer (2012) *The Reflexive Imperative in Late Modernity* (Cambridge: Cambridge University Press). I share Archer's criticism but would also say that while the concept of habitus has been overblown by Bourdieu and certainly his followers, there is a more modest account of it I might accept, relating less to unconscious motivations than to styles of action and bases of judgment.

As usual, the French were there first. Thus, already in 1962, the French poststructural Marxist, Louis Althusser, famously pronounced Marxism an anti-humanism.[5] The place of thinking, feeling, reflecting humans in Althusser's theory was occupied by zombies, operating at best like Margaret Archer's "fractured reflexives," capable, that is, of response to their name but otherwise following along the iron tracks of social structure.[6] Large-scale social change, Althusser held, was never effected by human purposiveness but only by larger, tectonic forces beyond it.

Here is the curious thing. Marxism we are said to have passed because it was reductionist. But Althusser's zombies continue on undead. They continue on because they resonate with various currents of contemporary sociological theory, from poststructuralism to standard American practice theory, all of which have come to valorize "the body." And with zombies, sociological theory gets exactly that: Without anything going on inside, zombies are just moving bodies, perfect for an actualist behaviorism. Ultimately, zombies resonate particularly with a cultural trajectory that begins with Nietzsche pronouncing the death of God and ends with Foucault saying Kaddish for humanity.[7]

Against this backdrop, I say unabashedly, as Jean Paul Sartre said of existentialism, CR is a humanism.[8] It stands against the reduction of people to zombies. As is evident in Christian Smith's *What Is a Person?*, in Margaret Archer's *Being Human*, and throughout my own work, CR defends the special value and inviolable dignity of the human person. We need a fuller explication of that status, but the place to start is agency.

What is agency? Emirbayer and Mische vs. Bruno Latour

What is agency? This question too forms a title, the title of a very widely cited article in the *American Journal of Sociology* by Mustafa

[5] Louis Althusser (2006) *For Marx* (New York: Verso).
[6] Margaret Archer (2007) *Making Our Way through the World* (Cambridge: Cambridge University Press).
[7] See Michel Foucault (1994) *The Order of Things: An Archaeology of the Human Sciences* (New York: Vintage), p. 309. Those who know us will certainly regard it no coincidence that Margaret Archer puts the point in almost exactly the same way. See Margaret Archer (2001) *Being Human: The Problem of Agency* (Cambridge: Cambridge University Press), p. 1.
[8] Jean Paul Sartre (1975) "Existentialism is a Humanism," pp. 345–368 in Walter Kaufmann (ed.), *Existentialism from Dostoevsky to Sartre* (New York: Meridian).

Emirbayer and Ann Mische.[9] Of course, what Emirbayer and Mische
define and focus on is distinctly human agency. We know, however,
that according to Bruno Latour's ANT, agency is not limited to human
beings. Material things too have agency. Inanimate objects have
agency.[10]

What is the connection between human and non-human agency?
Emirbayer and Mische speak of human agency in terms of three
principal dimensions: a habitual element (what Emirbayer and Mische
speak of as iteration); a projective element (a future-orientation); and a
practical element (evaluation). Do the non-human components of
ANT's actor-networks manifest their agency in these forms as well?
Do hammers and particle colliders have what sociologists mean by
habits? Do they orient toward the future and, accordingly, evaluate
matters toward that end?

If human and non-human agency are different, then, again, what is
the connection between them? Why are both covered by the same
word? The trouble is that by zooming in from the start on distinctly
human agency, Emirbayer and Mische do not at all address the question. That omission is not in itself very serious since, as we will see, the
question is easily enough answered. The problem is that in omitting
address to the question, Emirbayer and Mische end up missing as well
the entire crux of human agency.

That assertion sounds incredible. Am I really suggesting that in an
immense and dense 61-page article with nearly endless references,
Emirbayer and Mische actually fail to put their finger on the signal
characteristic that makes human agency human agency? Yes, however
startling, such is my claim. I will now endeavor to substantiate it.

Let me start by saying that if agency involves doing, then the problem with Emirbayer and Mische's treatise is that there is no doing; they
never get to it. They cover endlessly how people work themselves up
to some doing – how they schematize and problematize, characterize
and deliberate, but all of these purely cognitive activities might just as
well be undertaken by someone in the passenger seat of a car; it is only
the driver who actually acts on the external world, and at that step, the
step of actual acting, Emirbayer and Mische desert us.

[9] Mustafa *Emirbayer* and Ann Mische (1998) "What is Agency?," *American
Journal of Sociology* 103 (4): 962–1023.

[10] Bruno Latour (2005) *Reassembling the Social: An Introduction to Actor–
Network Theory* (New York: Oxford).

This omission by Emirbayer and Mische long puzzled me. I now consider it no accident. To provide what is needed, Emirbayer and Mische would have to re-ensoul the zombies, but Emirbayer and Mische do not believe in souls – or in the centered consciousness that makes persons persons:

> We conceptualize the self not as a metaphysical substance or entity, such as the "soul" or "will" ... but rather as a dialogical structure, itself thoroughly relational. Our perspective, in other words, is relational all the way down.[11]

The problem we will see is precisely with the core commitment of relational sociology, its sweeping denial of the entire ontological category of particulars, its position that relations are everything, the only form of being there is. As is evident by now, we critical realists too are big on relations, but the ontological reduction of Emirbayer's "Manifesto for a Relational Sociology" is madness.[12] Of course, for many, particularly the young, madness has appeal.

Let us try, however, to be serious. To do so, we need to begin at the other end of the issue, that is, with Latour. What does Latour mean by his extension of agency beyond the human realm, which is the exclusive focus of Emirbayer and Mische? Latour explains:

> At first, bringing objects back into the normal course of action should appear innocuous enough. After all, there is hardly any doubt that kettles 'boil' water, knifes 'cut' meat, baskets 'hold' provisions, hammers 'hit' nails on the head, rails 'keep' kids from falling, locks 'close' rooms against uninvited visitors, soap 'takes' the dirt away ... and so on. Are those verbs not designating actions? How could the introduction of those humble, mundane, and ubiquitous activities bring news to any social scientist?[13]

It is, as Latour says, no news to any social scientist that the inanimate objects Latour mentions do in fact all of the things he specifies. All of the verbs he employs are, as he suggests, causative. Clearly, we are speaking here of agency in the broad context of causal power, of a capacity to make something happen. As we noted earlier, it is the context in which we might ask of an analgesic tablet, what is the active ingredient, what in the tablet is the causal agent that makes the pain go away?

---

[11] Emirbayer and Mische, "What is Agency?," p. 974.
[12] Mustafa Emirbayer (1992) "Manifesto for a Relational Sociology," *American Journal of Sociology* 103 (2): 281–317.
[13] Latour, *Reassembling the Social*, pp. 70–71.

In the most abstract sense then, agency centrally involves consequential doing. It does so at the human level too. What conscious and non-conscious agency share is the causal power to do something, to make something happen.

As I commented way back in Chapter 2, if by agency ANT means the manifestation of causal power, then from a CR perspective, what ANT asserts is perfectly reasonable and salutary. But of course, what is reasonable and salutary is not provocative or fun. What is provocative and fun is the heroic image of ANT stealing, like Prometheus, the fire of agency from the human gods and sharing it with heretofore inanimate objects.

Except that such heroics represent just a trick of the tongue, resting on ambiguity in the meaning of the word agency. Yes, in a broad sense, agency refers to causal power. The significant question, however, is whether in a more narrow sense, causal power *simpliciter* is all we mean by human agency and social action. And of course the answer is definitely not. Thus, what is news and, indeed, startling is Latour's bold pitch to equate human action with causal power *simpliciter*.

Going back to Weber, what we social scientists have traditionally meant by action is meaningful action. And insofar as Weber specifically distinguished meaningful action from mere reactive behavior, it is clear that for Weber and, indeed, following Weber for most social scientists, not even all human manifestations of causal power count as action.

If not even all human manifestations of causal power count as what sociologists have meant by action, why suddenly elevate the causal manifestations of inanimate objects to that status? With that question we approach the boundary between agency in the broad sense and agency in the specific, narrow sense we sociologists employ when speaking of human beings.

It is, again, a dividing line about which Emirbayer and Mische say little. They do define human agency as involving engagement, but what counts as engagement?[14] It is not just thinking and feeling about the world in all the ways Emirbayer and Mische catalogue but also eventually doing something in the world. If engagement involves doing something, what is the distinctive character of that doing?

---

[14] Emirbayer and Mische, "What is Agency?," p. 970.

What counts as engagement is just another way of asking what agentic action means, and the remarkable thing is that Emirbayer and Mische never directly answer that question. They simply note in passing that, "Agency, for Parsons, was captured in the notion of effort." Perhaps effort is what Emirbayer and Mische also mean by engagement for, again in passing, they say "we claim that even habitual action is agentic, since it involves attention and effort."[15] The implication here is that attention and effort form the sine qua non of human agency, but while *attention* receives more attention from Emirbayer and Mische, *effort* does not.

The inattention is strategic. Most dictionaries define effort as *an attempt*, which would exclude such reactive behaviors as knee-jerks and sneezes. On the contrary, *attempt* suggests goal-directed intervention in the world. If so, then, simply put, human agency involves purposiveness, that is, consciously attentive, goal-directed behavior. Yet, although Emirbayer and Mische speak a lot about projects and projection, because they never quite make it to action, they never endorse any explicit statement that human agency centrally means attentive, goal-directed behavior.[16] On the contrary, it seems a pronouncement they would rather avoid.

It is Latour, rather, who, in offering the specious reason he would obliterate the line between the broad and narrow conceptions of agency, at least utters the one word that marks the division:

If action is limited a priori to what "intentional," "meaningful" humans do, it is hard to see how a hammer, a basket, a door closer, a cat, a rug, a mug, a list, or a tag could act. They might exist in the domain of "material" "causal" relations but not in the "reflexive" "symbolic" domain of social relations. By contrast, if we stick to our decision to start from the controversies about actors and agencies, then *any thing* that does modify a state of affairs by making a difference is an actor – or if it has no figuration yet, an actant.[17]

To take Latour's reasoning first, we can of course make words mean anything we want them to mean. The question here is why sow

---

[15] Ibid., pp. 965, 973.

[16] Admittedly, purposive behavior may entail all the various cognitive activities Emirbayer and Mische detail but only insofar as they serve purposive activity. Moreover, to the extent that some of those activities themselves count as mental acts, they, too, are done with purpose.

[17] Latour, *Reassembling the Social*, p. 71.

needless confusion unless it is simply for the fun of introducing yet another form of madness. It is simply a non-sequitur to insist that we cannot combine lists, rugs, and people all in the same analysis – in the same actor-network, if you will – unless we pretend that all these things act in the selfsame way and impose that pretense by referring to them all indiscriminately as actors. The way rugs act is different from the way people do, and for that matter cats as well. The distinctive causal agency of beings with higher consciousness – like cats and people – is purposive.

In contrast with Emirbayer and Mische, however, Latour at least does get to actual doing; accordingly, he names the marker that distinguishes conscious from non-conscious doing.[18] That marker is intentionality. We encounter conscious agency in the world when we are confronted with intentional, purposive, goal-directed behavior.

Intentionality brings us to the most notable name missing from Emirbayer and Mische's extensive reference list: philosopher Donald Davidson. The omission is significant because as one of the towering philosophical figures of the late twentieth century, Davidson, in a seminal article titled "Agency," a quarter-century earlier already answered the title question of Emirbayer and Mische's article. Davidson's must just be an answer that Emirbayer and Mische – and sociology generally – wish not to entertain.[19]

Davidson quite definitively identifies intentionality or purposiveness as that which distinguishes conscious agency, what we in sociology have traditionally called action. In a famous passage, Davidson observed that while to count as action not all casual consequences of one's behavior need be intentional, there must be at least one description according to which the behavior that produced those consequences was intentional.

A man moves his finger, let us say intentionally, thus flicking the switch, causing a light to come on, the room to be illuminated, and a prowler to be alerted. This statement has the following entailments: the man flicked the switch, turned on the light, illuminated the room, and alerted the prowler. Some of these things he did intentionally, some not; beyond the finger

---

[18] Actually, ANT is too much about doings, tending in its own way toward actualism.

[19] Originally published in 1971, reprinted in Donald Davidson (2001) "Agency," pp. 43–62 in Donald Davidson, *Essays on Actions and Events* (Toronto and New York: Clarendon). www.uruguaypiensa.org.uy/imgnoticias/961.pdf.

movement, intention is irrelevant to the inferences, and even there it is required only in the sense that the movement must be intentional under some description. In brief, once he has done one thing (move a finger), each consequence presents us with a deed; an agent causes what his actions cause.[20]

"An agent," Davidson concludes above, "causes what his actions cause." We must read this assertion closely. What makes an agent a conscious agent, i.e., an agent in the narrow sense pertinent to sociology, is that he or she has caused something intentionally and thereby performed one or more actions. Some of those actions may not be intentional, but in the narrow sense pertinent to sociology, all that we call action originates in some intentional action, i.e., a behavior that under some description we can say the agent purposively performed.[21] Intentional action is behavior teleologically directed toward some purpose.

Just as intentional action is purposive action, purposive action in turn is motivated action. Purposive action is action motivated by reasons. Thus, as Elizabeth Anscombe (another famous name missing from Emirbayer and Mische's reference list) alternatively put it, intentional action is action performed for reasons. In which case, we could also say that reasoned behavior is what distinguishes the action of conscious creatures from the behavior of rugs and particle colliders and even from such reactive behaviors of our own as knee jerks and sneezes, which are not cognitively informed.[22]

The reasons that make for purposive action can be formulated in terms of wants and beliefs. In such terms, intentional action, then, is

[20] Ibid., p. 53.

[21] I speak of intentionality in the narrow sense (usually designated with a small i) as deliberateness or purposiveness in contrast with Intentionality (note capital I), in the broader sense of *aboutness* coined by Franz Brentano and still today often distinguished in philosophy. We will not even get into intensionality (yes, with an s).

[22] Reasoned action, it unfortunately needs to be said, includes more than just the utilitarian calculus of rational choice theory. Rejecting rational choice theory's crude account is thus no reason to reject the idea of reasoned action wholesale. To do so is to concede rational choice theory's account of rational choice. Together with emotions and other mental states, wants, and beliefs rather belong to the account of cognitively informed behavior professional philosophers call folk psychology. See Ian Ravenscroft (2010) "Folk Psychology as a Theory" *Stanford Encyclopedia of Philosophy Online*. http://plato. stanford.edu/entries/folkpsych-theory/.

behavior chosen by an agent because that agent believes the behavior will achieve a desired result or goal or purpose.[23] Such wants and beliefs are the reasons for the action.

With this understanding of agency, we are dealing not only with all the various preparatory forms of sense-making that Emirbayer and Mische catalogue, but also, more centrally, with the specific character of any ensuing doing or action that comes of it. We are ultimately dealing, that is, with the purposiveness we call intentionality.

Behind intentional action, moreover, there always lies a centered, concrete agent, one with wants and beliefs, capable of formulating and acting on intentions. There stands in other words, what the early Judith Butler sought to dispel: "A doer behind the deed," the dreaded "Cartesian cogito" that so much social theory wants to kill off.[24] If Emirbayer and Mische seem reluctant to equate agency with purposive behavior, it is perhaps in part because they too are party to the would-be assassination:

While what we have been calling 'agentic orientations' vary in their concrete manifestations, agency itself remains a dimension that is present in (but conceptually distinct from) all empirical instances of human action; hence, there are no concrete agents, but only actors who engage agentically with their structuring environments.[25]

Other than telling us that there are no agents but only *agentic orientations*, this comment is very obscure. Emirbayer, however, evidently likes it. He repeats it in multiple venues.[26] It never gets any clearer, but each time Emirbayer accompanies it with what he seems to regard as an authoritative remark by Jeffrey Alexander that to equate actors and agency is to commit the *fallacy of misplaced concreteness*.

---

[23] Such purposes can be either normative or instrumental. Both are equally intentional.

[24] See Judith Butler (2006) *Gender Trouble: Feminism and the Subversion of Identity* (New York: Routledge), p. 34.

[25] Emirbayer and Mische, "What is Agency?," p. 1004.

[26] Mustafa Emirbayer and John Goodwin (1994) "Network Analysis, Culture and Agency," *American Journal of Sociology* 99 (6): 1411–1454, 1443; Mustafa Emirbayer and John Goodwin (1996) "Symbols, Positions, Objects: Toward a New Theory of Revolutions and Collective Action," *History and Theory* 35 (3): 358–374, 370; Mustafa Emirbayer (1996) "Useful Durkheim," *Sociological Theory* 14 (2): 109–130, p. 11. In this last piece, intentionality makes a sudden and brief appearance without any real engagement by Emirbayer. So it is unclear how it fits in with relational sociology.

That fallacy sounds dire, but how exactly does it apply here? Alexander explains:

My objection to this identification of actor and agency is that it is guilty of misplaced concreteness. Rather than replacing or reinterpreting the familiar dichotomy between actors and structures, the identification of actor and agency actually reproduces it in another form. Rather than forming a hierarchy, actors and structures are placed horizontally – side by side but not interpenetrating and creating new forms. What results is a mixture rather than a solution, a compromise rather than a reformulation. The incantation "that structure controls actors who simultaneously reconstitute structure in turn" is simply that – an incantation. Because actor and structure are conceived to be concrete, or empirically distinct, the dichotomization is described in a way that no amount of juggling – keeping both balls in the air at the same time – can create a fundamentally different conception of the macro–micro link.[27]

Alexander's complaint here is against the analytic dualism upheld by Margaret Archer and CR. Instead of structure and agency being analytically distinct, Alexander wants them, as he says, somehow to interpenetrate.

It still remains unclear how the charge of misplaced concreteness applies – or at least how it applies more to analytic dualism than to the view Alexander favors. Essentially, in the extract above, via disparaging descriptors ("misplaced concreteness," "compromise," "mixture," "incantation"), Alexander just dismisses analytic dualism without argument. In particular, Alexander never actually identifies the putative difficulty in "juggling" structure and agency conceived as analytically separate. The feat seems easy enough: Merely observe the distinction Marx draws between the history people make and the circumstances in which they make it. What's the problem? On the contrary, to abstract agency from concrete agents and then to reify it Hegelian-style as something other seems the real commission of misplaced concreteness.

Worse, the whole maneuver is incoherent. In the first place, for two things – i.e. structure and agency – to interpenetrate, they must in some sense be distinct. Second, we must ask what it is that is agentic about Emirbayer and Mische's *agentic orientations* or what Alexander terms

---

[27] See Jeffrey Alexander (1992) "Recent Sociological Theory Between Agency and Social Structure," *Schweizerische Zeitschrift für Soziologie* 18 (1): 7–11, p. 8.

agentic processes.[28] All we have in Emirbayer and Mische are *attention* and *effort*, which, as we saw, cannot be unpacked without reference to conscious agents and their intentions.

Likewise, when we turn to Alexander, he tells us that "agency is the moment of freedom, or effort, which occurs within three structured environments, and ... two of these – culture and personality – exist ontologically only within the actor."[29] As with Emirbayer and Mische, this formulation reads as if Alexander is trying to de-agentify human agents, making actors seem to be just passive places where agency "occurs" rather than a quality of the holistic activity of the actors themselves.[30] Perhaps, however, the problem is just obscurity. Alexander himself goes on to acknowledge that "action is the exercise of agency by persons."[31] Let us not be misled by the passive voice: If persons exercise agency, then they must be its exercisers, and since exercisers of agency is all anyone means by agents, there must be agents after all. Whither the charge of misplaced concreteness?

Ultimately, the problem is that, like Emirbayer and Mische, who clearly follow him, Alexander stays inside actors' heads: "I will conceive of action as moving along two basic dimensions: interpretation and strategization."[32] Fine. To act, actors must interpret and strategize, but what is it about the doing that eventually comes of that internal activity that makes action action? Although, like Emirbayer and Mische, Alexander declines to say, the answer is intentionality.

There really is no escape from intentionality. Intentionality is not only important, it is fundamental to consciousness. As John Searle showed us, intentionality lies behind whatever words we speak, for

---

[28] Ibid., p. 9. He says, "There remains a dimension of agency which I have conceived as articulated through the processes of invention, typification, and strategization. By calling these agentic processes, I mean they embody, in the sense of giving shape to the exercise of free will." Again, the who or what that does the exercising can only be agents.

[29] Ibid., p. 8.

[30] There is an actualist tinge to such reading: Agentic processes or orientations are events; agents themselves are not.

[31] Alexander, "Recent Sociological Theory," p. 9.

[32] See Jeffrey Alexander (1987) "Action and Its Environments," pp. 289–318 in Jeffrey Alexander, Richard Giesen, Richard Münch, and Neil J. Smelser (eds.), *The Micro–Macro Link* (Berkeley, CA: University of California), p. 300.

although some people appear to talk without purpose, in fact, meaning is tied to what we intend to convey.[33]

Even more fundamentally, as Stuart Hampshire observed, as long as we are awake and conscious, even if we are "just chilling," we are always doing something intentionally.[34] Consciousness and intentionality are that intimately connected. Not just for humans but for cats too. For all creatures of higher mental functioning.

This consideration runs counter to the various forms of practice theory that, extolling habit, would limit intentionality and motivation to unusual circumstances as if intentionality were switched on and off as we move about. The mistake is to confuse purposiveness with attentiveness. But there is much we do with little attention that nevertheless remains purposive. The fact is that intentionality is so endemic to consciousness that it is more or less linguistically built into how we identify whatever it is we do. Look at any historical narrative and the causative verbs employed – exiling, contesting, charging, feasting, whatever – they virtually all implicitly connote intentionality and cannot be understood without it. And, again, behind every intention, there lies an intender, a center of consciousness, an agent. Without agents translating the various agentic orientations of relational sociology into intentional action, all those various agentic orientations are without any historical effect.

We have come a long way to arrive at the CR position on conscious agency, which gets actors out of their heads and into the world. In contrast with neo-functionalist obscurity and de-agentification, the CR position is sleek. For CR, conscious agency is just intentional (i.e., purposive) behavior. And behind intentional behavior there always lies a doer, a center of consciousness that is the intending agent.

This CR position again just recovers common sense. It is consistent, for example, with what we would find in the practice of law. Sociological departures from it produce only the obfuscation through which sociologists manufacture for themselves "make work."

The CR position is important not just for explanatory purposes. It has a moral dimension as well. Already, even below the level of humans, conscious agents confront us as thou's, centers of experience

---

[33] John Searle (1970) *Speech Acts: An Essay in the Philosophy of Language* (New York: Cambridge University Press).

[34] Stuart Hampshire (1981) *Thought and Action.* (Notre *Dame*, IN: University of Notre Dame).

that feel as well as think and with whom to varying degrees we can meaningfully communicate. As centers of experience that feel as well as think, what we do to them registers. At the higher levels at least, that means that, morally, we cannot respond to such agents as if they were just things, instrumentalities to be treated simply as means to our ends. Morally, even below the level of humans, we already encounter self-hood, conscious agents that already demand their treatment to some extent as ends in themselves.[35]

It is only in the context of what Martin Buber called the "I–Thou" relation that we respond to the moral call of the other.[36] The objects of our concern are not enactments, subject positions, or orientations. To none of those do we ontologically ascribe feelings or rights. Only a coherent thou can address us with moral claims, and in response to that address, we are called to be thou's ourselves, to respond as an I, agent to agent, self to self.

Of course, all that is especially true when the agents we confront are humans. Humans are not just conscious agents but conscious agents of special kinds. We humans are also persons. It is to personhood we now turn.

Personhood

The three CR sociologists who have most addressed the concept of personhood are Margaret Archer, Christian Smith, and me. Of the three, Archer leans most closely, like the practice theorists, on Merleau-Ponty and bodily practice whereas I, like the discourse theorists, lean most closely on language, indeed, approaching what Archer disparages as a conception of personhood as "society's gift." Smith would demur from my own Durkheimian understanding of person-hood as a socially emergent property and argue on the contrary, as would, I believe, realist philosopher Hugh Lacey, that we are persons even before language acquisition.

Although I will give some account of the differences among us, they represent more of an in-family squabble, for vis-à-vis sociology as a whole, our position is unified. As much as Archer speaks of practice,

---

[35] Ted Benton (1993) *Natural Relations? Ecology, Animal Rights, and Social Justice* (New York: Verso).
[36] Martin Buber (1971) *I and Thou* (New York: Touchstone).

she is not a practice theorist because she does not detach agency from centered self-consciousness. On the contrary, she points to our enduring selfhood even apart from language as it shows up in practice. Similarly, for all my claim that language makes us into a higher kind of being, unlike the poststructuralists, I do not dissolve selfhood into discourse and nor do I think like Rom Harré that selfhood is just a manner of speaking or, like Judith Butler, that our selfhood disappears between conversational encounters. I, too, like Archer and Smith and unlike Emirbayer and Mische, consider a self an ontological particular with, as Archer would put it, its own irreducible causal powers. Along with Smith, I am happy to call myself a *Personalist*.

Archer in particular has convinced me that human selfhood precedes language and that, indeed, even self-consciousness precedes language. Non-human animals, even without language, pass the so-called mirror test, and humans too pass it before acquiring language. There is, however, I think the three of us would all agree, something different and higher about human selfhood. We mark that higher difference with the category of personhood. Persons are enhanced kinds of selves. Although humans are not in principle the only beings to which the category of personhood might apply, we are the only species so far to which we would apply it. Vulcans, too, should we meet them, would be persons as also, in my opinion, might have been Alex, the grey parrot who was taught quite a bit of language by psychologist Irene Pepperberg.[37]

What is a person? While I am inclined just to say briefly that persons are moral agents, I would also enthusiastically accept Smith's more expansive definition:

By *person* I mean a conscious, reflexive, embodied, self-transcending center of subjective experience, durable identity, moral commitment, and social communication who – as the efficient cause of his or her own responsible action and interactions – exercises complex capacities for agency and intersubjectivity in order to develop and sustain his or her own incommunicable self in loving relationships with other personal selves and with the impersonal world.[38]

---

[37] See *Wikipedia* entry for *Alex (Parrot)*. http://en.wikipedia.org/wiki/Alex_ (parrot).
[38] Smith, *What is a Person?*, p. 61.

Smith's definition requires unpacking. Although I am not given to puns, the semantic center of Smith's definition is his use of the word center. In the definition above, Smith calls persons centers of conscious experience. In *To Flourish or Destruct*, he refers to persons as centers of purpose. Archer and I would join Smith in accepting either and both. The central point is that, to begin with, persons are selves and as such, contrary to Emirbayer and Mische, ontological entities, consciously experiencing, feeling, intending particulars.

Selves, Smith's definition goes on to stipulate, represent durable identities. To be clear, this assertion is not phenomenological but ontological. Let me explain. Part of postmodernism's assault on essentialism was to fracture unity wherever it was previously thought to exist. One such place was the Cartesian cogito. In place of a centered subject, postmodernism left us rather with disparate subject positions we discursively adopt. (Actually, though, without a subject, who or what is doing the adopting always remained unclear.)

The appeal of the postmodernist (now poststructuralist) view is largely phenomenological. Many of us may experience ourselves as, we might say, different persons in different circumstances. We might think of Erving Goffman's impression management. On one read of Goffman, there is nothing central to us beyond our different presentations of self to different audiences, no central manager managing impressions, no self that is really, authentically us.[39]

Postmodernism's fractured view of identity likewise speaks to the resistance many feel to the normative identity markers by which they find themselves socially classified. Thus, from that perspective, to challenge the Cartesian notion of stable identity is to strike against the oppression Foucault calls *governmentality*.[40]

Yet as satisfying as it may be to "stick it to the man" in whatever form "the man" takes (think also of Jacques Lacan's "name of the father"), we must think analytically about what we are saying. There is a difference between who we are phenomenologically and what we are ontologically. Phenomenologically, many today may not find themselves with what they consider coherent identities, and perhaps

---

[39] See Archer (2001) *Being Human: The Problem of Agency* (Cambridge: Cambridge University Press), p. 78.

[40] See Graham Burchell, Colin Gordon, and Peter Miller (eds.) (1991) *The Foucault Effect: Studies in Governmentality* (Chicago, IL: University of Chicago Press).

all of us to some extent exhibit a degree of incoherence. We may similarly be dissatisfied with how we find ourselves in between social classifications.

But what is it to which the adjectives incoherent and dissatisfied are attributed? Ontologically, that something is our enduring self, a particular, experiencing subject. In Meadian terms, it is the I reflecting on the me – or multiple mes that finds itself incoherent or dissatisfied or oppressed. Switching frames to Buber, if there were not an enduring thou there to so experience such things, there would be nothing to be the object of our care. Regardless of how we find ourselves phenomenologically, ontologically we are a thou, a who, a self.

Analytically as well, we cannot do without a doer behind the deed. Contrary to the postmodernist read of Goffman, something must be managing the self-presentations to various audiences, choosing to segregate them as need may be, and that something is the consistent I behind the presentations, a self that cannot simply disavow past transgressions as the responsibility of some other, different self-presentation.

Without singular, enduring selves, nor can there be any consistent narrative. Of course, postmodernism opposed consistent narrative too, historical or otherwise. Thus, to the extent that we embrace narrativity, we are already beyond the un-self selves of postmodernism. We are back to something very much like the Cartesian cogito. We are back to enduring selves.

But enduring selfhood is only the rock bottom nature of personhood. From there, Smith goes on to speak of persons as centered selves that are distinctly self-transcending, capable of responsible moral commitment and social communication.

Granting to Archer (against my own original position) that selfhood, even a degree of self-conscious selfhood, precedes language, I nevertheless maintain that the various distinct capacities that Smith associates with personhood are all to a great degree language-dependent. If, as Archer says and I would agree, language is an emergent phenomenon, I would further argue that as such, language exerts downward causality transforming us linguistic users into something new.

In fact, language, to me, is the most glaring example we have of emergence, an example of emergence that, moreover, is distinctly non-compositional. Language is a social product but not one that is built up of smaller components. It emerges as a cultural, social whole.

To the extent that it acts down on us, turning us into something new, it is an equally clear example of efficacious downward causation.[41]

In the first place, language vastly expands the richness of our lives, the range of things we can do. That is because language is not just a means of communicating thoughts we could have independent of language – although to be sure there are many such – but the means of formulating many important thoughts and cultural constructs we could not have without it.[42] Insofar as rules, including moral rules, need to be articulated, we accordingly need language for that purpose. That includes as well all the new cultural constructs we create via constitutive rules: games, institutions, and such. Likewise, the many speech acts we associate with Searle, of which Archer also speaks – commanding, promising, questioning, asserting, denying, and so forth – are all possible only once we have language through which to perform them. They are built on language.

Language is also central to our distinct capacities for self-transcendence and moral agency. Indeed, in the autobiographical words of Helen Keller, we can see both what comes before and after language.

Before my teacher came to me, I did not know that I am. I lived in a world that was a no-world. I cannot hope to describe adequately that unconscious, yet conscious time of nothingness. I did not know that I knew aught, or that I lived or acted or desired. I had neither will nor intellect. I was carried along to objects and acts by a certain blind natural impetus. I had a mind which caused me to feel anger, satisfaction, desire. These two facts led those about me to suppose that I willed and thought. I can remember all this, not because I knew that it was so, but because I have tactual memory. It enables me to remember that I never contracted my forehead in the act of thinking. I never viewed anything beforehand or chose it. I also recall tactually the fact that never in a start of the body or a heart-beat did I feel that I loved or cared for anything. My inner life, then, was a blank without past, present, or future, without hope or anticipation, without wonder or joy or faith.[43]

---

[41] Here, I am quite with Durkheim of *Suicide* (p. 213): "If, in other words, as has often been said, man is double, that is because social man superimposes himself upon physical man. Social man necessarily presupposes a society which he expresses and serves."

[42] Paul Gee says the same. In fact, his (2010) *Introduction to Discourse Analysis: Theory and Method* (New York: Routledge), shows remarkable affinities with critical realism.

[43] Helen Keller (1938) *The World I Live In* (New York: The Century Company), p. 113.

Keller describes her world before language as a time that was "uncon-scious, yet conscious." But what she means by unconscious is not literally unconscious. Hence, her gloss: an unconscious consciousness. Even before language, Keller describes herself as having fears, satisfac-tions, and desires. Such mental states are the attributes only of a being we would identify as conscious. Keller goes on to describe a kind of tactile consciousness that, even apart from anything social, is, as Archer maintains, necessary for us to move about the world so as not to bump into chairs or remain in the rain. As Keller goes on beyond the above extract, it is clear that even before language, she was still a self. There was a thou there to whom her family related as such and to whom Anne Sullivan could finally communicate, even across the divide of blindness and deafness.

So why then does Keller describe her former state as an unconscious consciousness? Because without language, Keller lacked the symbolic consciousness that affords not just a means of expressing thoughts already there but also a whole new world of thoughts not previously possible, thoughts that make for self-transcendence and moral agency. Keller describes this situation herself. Without language, she could not stand back and make an object of herself, could not engage in what Archer calls the internal conversation. In Meadian terms, there could be no I talking to a me.[44]

Although the evidence is that incipient morality may precede lan-guage, it also takes language to formulate moral codes and compelling moral ideals. It likely takes language to be morally inspired or morally called to action.

Although American sociologists may never have heard of it, it has been long now since philosopher Harry Frankfurt introduced the concept of *secondary preferences*. Secondary preferences are prefer-ences about our preferences. To illustrate, I may prefer to smoke – which after years of not smoking, I still do. But I have a secondary preference about that preference, a preference not to have that

---

[44] Margaret Archer, *Being Human*; also Archer (2003) *Structure, Agency and the Internal Conversation* (New York: Cambridge University Press). For an excellent treatment of the evolution of different forms of consciousness see Mark R. Leary and Nicole Buttermore (2003) "The Evolution of the Human Self: Tracing the Natural History of Self-Awareness," *Journal for the Theory of Social Behaviour* 33 (4): 365–404.

preference. And that secondary preference was key to the transcendence of my addiction.[45]

Without language, we cannot formulate secondary preferences and so cannot work on ourselves in this way. Without secondary preferences, we remain what Frankfurt calls *wantons*, rational choice beings who can only act on what we want or desire. Keller describes her pre-linguistic self just that way.

It takes language as well to identify not just secondary preferences but also phenomenally unifying ultimate concerns. Ultimate concerns are concerns to which we are devoted across contexts and that lend our lives and our life narrative a coherence and integrity.[46] Indeed, if many today experience themselves phenomenally incoherent, perhaps it is because they lack any ultimate concern that reaches high enough to gather their lives toward any overarching point. Instead, they remain attached to different, unintegrated, low-lying concerns that vary from situation to situation. If, phenomenologically, we are what we care about, what we love, then for many of us, what we ultimately care about – ourselves and our families – is not sufficiently encompassing to unify our lives.[47] This phenomenal condition, which theologian Paul Tillich describes as making ultimate that which is not truly ultimate, is a state of affairs that merits sociological exploration. It represents a condition that in Christian Smith's terms, represents a departure from human flourishing. Yet outside the circles of critical realism, this condition is not anything that sociology has explored in such terms.[48]

In *Being and Worth*, CR philosopher Andrew Collier follows a Spinozist line of reasoning to argue that we can speak of the relative worth of different sorts of beings in the world. On that analysis, given the range of their higher powers, particularly those that converge on the capacity for moral agency, there is an objective sense in which

[45] Harry Frankfurt (1975) "Free Agency," *Journal of Philosophy* 72 (8): 205–220.
[46] The term was coined by theologian Paul Tillich in (2009) *Dynamics of Faith* (New York: Harper Perennial).
[47] I make this argument in *Landscapes of the Soul: The Loss of Moral Meaning in American Life* (New York: Oxford University Press).
[48] It is the central issue I explore in *Landscapes*. Margaret Archer explores it in (2007) *Making Our Way Through the World: Reflexivity and Social Mobility* (New York: Cambridge University Press); and Smith in *What Is a Person?* and (2014) *To Flourish or Self-Destruct: A Personalist Theory of Human Goods, Motivations, Failure, and Evil* (Chicago, IL: Chicago University Press).

persons have much greater worth than, say, insects. In that assertion, the claim is staked that the dignity and sanctity we attach to humans are not just a form of speciesism, but judgments grounded in objective, ontological differences of real differential value. It is such judgments of objective worth that underlie the axiological direction of critical realism pursued by Bhaskar, Andrew Sayer, and Smith.[49]

Against the practice turn

In *To Flourish or Self-Destruct*, Christian Smith attacks what he, following Colin Campbell, calls *situationalism* in sociology.[50] Here, I will make a kindred attack on the so-called practice turn in sociology. Whereas CR upholds the ontological status of humans as persons, the so-called practice turn in sociology leaves us, as I have been saying, with zombies.

The practice turn now is quite a diffuse movement across multiple disciplines. It has left anthropology and sociology to find its way into education, organization studies, international relations, and management. Many uses of it are not objectionable. The strand of practice theory to which I object begins with Pierre Bourdieu and Anthony Giddens, who displace an emphasis on conscious, reflective, intentional action in favor of what they consider non-reflective, non-intentional routine or habitus.[51] In the United States, the most notable move in this direction was Ann Swidler's enormously influential "Culture in Action," which programmatically limits culture to what people do with it.[52] Along the way, human agency again becomes de-agentified, for the behavior that gets emphasized in this strain of the practice turn is routine or habit. Routine and habit can be construed in various

---

[49] In addition to Smith, *What is a Person?* ; *To Flourish or Self-Destruct*, see also Roy Bhaskar (2011) *Reflections on metaReality: Transcendence, Emancipation and Everyday Life* (New York: Routledge); and Andrew Sayer (2011) *Why Things Matter to People: Social Science, Values, and Ethical Life* (New York: Cambridge University Press).

[50] See Smith, *To Flourish or Self-Destruct*. Colin Campbell (1998) *The Myth of Social Action* (New York: Cambridge University Press).

[51] Again, it is helpful to keep in mind the distinction between intention and attention. You can have the former even without much of the latter.

[52] Ann Swidler (1986) "Culture in Action: Symbols and Strategies," *American Sociological Review* 51 (2): 273–286.

ways, but with routine and habit as construed in this strain of the practice turn, motivation and reflection disappear.[53]

Swidler's argument, recall, is behaviorist: Culture is to be understood not as "some abstract stuff in people's heads which might or might not cause their action," but as the way people make use of culture in practice.[54] Culture, for example, does not so much consist of shared values as shared repertoires or procedures or schemas that we can observe being deployed in practice. Thus, as Swidler goes on to say, "whether 'practices' refer to individual habits or organizational routines, a focus on practices shifts attention away from what may or may not go on in actors' consciousness – their ideas or value commitments – and toward the unconscious or automatic activities embedded in taken-for-granted routines."[55]

It is practice theory's depiction of human action as largely unconscious, automatic, and un-thought that constitutes its brand of de-agentification and that I mean to dispute here.[56] As I say, it is a

---

[53] In *To Flourish or Self-Destruct*, Christian Smith also allocates a great deal of agency to routine or habit, but he does not intend thereby the de-agentification of practice theory.

[54] Again, Stephen Vaisey has likewise already characterized Swidler in such terms. See Stephen Vaisey (2008) "Socrates, Skinner, and Aristotle: Three Ways of Thinking About Culture in Action," *Sociological Forum* 23 (3): 603–622. For her part, Swidler disputes the "situational determinism" attributed to her but still wants to avoid going inside people's heads. See Ann Swidler (2008) "A Comment on Stephen Vaisey's 'Socrates, Skinner, and Aristotle: Three Ways of Thinking About Culture in Action'," *Sociological Forum* 23 (3): 614–618.

[55] Ann Swidler (2001) "What Anchors Cultural Practices," pp. 74–92 in Karin Knorr Cetina, Theodore R. Schatzki and Elke von Savigny, *The Practice Turn in Contemporary Theory* (New York: Routledge), p. 75.

[56] Actually, Vaisey, "Socrates, Skinner, and Aristotle," too, drawing on psychologist Jonathan Haidt's dual process model, likewise appeals to the unconscious. See also Stephen Vaisey (2009) "Motivation and Justification: A Dual-Process Model of Culture in Action," *American Journal of Sociology* 114: 1675–1715. For a sociological critique of Haidt and his "New Intuitionism" in psychology, see Douglas Porpora, Alexander Nikolaev, Julia Hagemann, and Alexander Jenkins (2013) *Post-Ethical Society: The Iraq War, Abu Ghraib, and the Moral Failure of the Secular* (Chicago, IL: University of Chicago Press). A fuller critique, however, is still needed. Alternately, Omar Lizardo and Michael Strand try to ground practice theory in computational psychology. See Omar Lizardo and Michael Strand (2010) "Skills, Toolkits, Contexts, and Institutions: Clarifying the Relationship Between Different Approaches to Cognition in Cultural Sociology," *Poetics* 38 (2): 205–228. Fortunately, strong critiques of the computer model in psychology already exist. See Steven Horst (1996) *Symbols, Computation, and Intentionality: A Critique*

depiction that goes back to Giddens and to at least one strain of thought in Bourdieu. According to Giddens, "motives tend to have a direct purchase on action only in unusual circumstances, situations which in some way break with routines. ... Much of our day to day conduct is not directly motivated." Thus, as is said by Ira Cohen, one of Giddens's sympathetic commentators, "according to Giddens, it is often the case that large areas of social life are not directly motivated. ... In routine situations ... agents may maintain nothing more than generalized motivation to the integration of their conventional practices during the course of their day-to-day routines."[57] Cohen still speaks of agents here, but we are no longer dealing with conscious beings but rather with semi-conscious zombies.

Although Bourdieu is more sophisticated, at least one strand of his thought takes him to the same place. According to Loïc Wacquant, Bourdieu's philosophy "seeks to capture the intentionality without intention, the knowledge without cognitive intent, the pre-reflective, infra-conscious mastery that agents acquire of their social world by way of durable immersion within it ... and which defines properly human social practice." Wacquant goes on to say that for Bourdieu, "the relation between social agent and the world is not that between subject (or consciousness) and object, but a relation of 'ontological complicity' or mutual 'possession.'"[58]

In part, what Wacquant may be speaking of here is some kind of body knowledge or muscle memory. In part, the effort is to deny the image, often associated with rational choice theory, of all action as involving an extended, discursive calculation of means to ends. Against such an image, emphasized instead is habit or habitus, understood as behavior that is not just unreflective but also unmotivated or without conscious intention.

---

of the Computational Theory of Mind (Berkeley, CA: University of California Press). More recently see John Searle (2014) "What Your Computer Can't Know," *New York Review of Books*, October 9: 52–55.

[57] Anthony Giddens (1984) *The Constitution of Society* (Berkeley, CA: University of California), p. 6; and Ira Cohen (1989) *Structuration Theory: Anthony Giddens and the Constitution of Social Life* (New York: St. Martin's Press), pp. 51–52, 226.

[58] Loïc J. D. Wacquant (1992) "Toward a Social Praxiology: The Structure and Logic of Bourdieu's Sociology," pp. 1–60 in Pierre Bourdieu and Loïc Wacquant, *Invitation to a Reflexive Sociology* (Chicago, IL: University of Chicago Press), pp. 19–20.

It is, however, utterly untenable if not outright incoherent to split actions into a reflective, conscious, motivated category and an entirely unreflective, unmotivated, unconscious category. Of course, we do not reflect equally on all of our behavior. I have reflected a good deal on what I am writing now. Should you question me about it in person, what will come out of my mouth will likely represent less reflection. But it will still be motivated, conscious, and intentional. In fact, even unconscious responses – and these, certainly, need not be denied entirely – are motivated.

There is something conceptually wrong with the distinction practice theory is making. And what is wrong returns us to intentionality. Let us start with the idea of body knowledge or muscle memory. There are two questions to ask: Is the exercise of muscle memory conscious, reflective, and intentional and how much of our activity in the world can be so described? If we think of a boxer dodging a punch or of ourselves typing the letters that will form the words on a page, certainly there is something more automatic than reflective about these behaviors. To perform these behaviors successfully, there is no time for the reflection we would afford to philosophical quandaries. In fact, the more automatic the reaction, the better.

But even here, would we say the behaviors are unconscious and unintentional? Was the boxer's dodge not intentional? Was he (or she) not conscious of the incoming punch? Certainly, we are not talking here of declarative or discursive consciousness, but precisely as Archer points out in *Being Human*, we remain conscious in ways that are other than linguistic.

When I typed the letter c that ended the word linguistic above, I was certainly relying on the body knowledge I acquired through repetition in a high-school typing class. But did I not still also type that c intentionally?

Part of the problem stems from a mistakenly narrow view of intentionality as what would characterize long moments of strategizing behind a chess board. The phenomenological tradition – and notably Alfred Schutz – helped give rise to that misunderstanding.[59] But most instances of intentionality are not at all of that nature. I don't know about you, but whenever I speak, I intend virtually all I say and mean

---

[59] See Alfred Schutz (1967) *The Phenomenology of the Social World* (Chicago, IL: Northwestern University).

most of it. Yet, somehow, marvelously, I perform all this intentional action instantaneously. Insofar as speech is a paradigm case of intentional action, intentional action need hardly entail long reflection. A first point, then, is that reflection and intentionality are distinct.

As we saw earlier, in the narrow sense, what intentionality means is that what we did was cognitively informed, meaning that we did it for a reason, that in other words we were motivated to do what we did by that reason. And by that criterion, even when we are speaking of body knowledge, we are speaking of intentional behavior. The boxer dodging a punch or my typing the c were behaviors performed for reasons.[60] They were motivated and intentional.

Few, moreover, would argue that mere body knowledge and muscle memory account for much that social scientists seek to study. The more usual claim of practice theory is that it is habit or routine that accounts for most of what we do. These too are claimed to be mechanical behaviors, done without reflection, consciousness, or intentional motivation. It is only in unusual circumstances, we hear the practice theorists say, when we confront problems in our routines that we engage in conscious, motivated action.

Again, there is something profoundly wrong here. If, per Stuart Hampshire, whenever we are conscious there is always something we are doing intentionally, then our motivated intentionality does not switch on and off as we move from routine to non-routine situations. It is always on.

Are there differences in our levels of attention to what we may be doing? Absolutely. But to the extent that we are engaged in action rather than in what Weber called reactive behavior like sneezes or knee-jerks, in no case can what we are dong involve the suspension of intentional reflexivity and the mechanical movement of zombies.[61]

Consider some habits. I don't know whether it is a blessing or a curse, but now, as I have gotten older, my body wakes me up without an alarm at 4:30 in the morning – often, strangely, on the dot. That certainly is not something I intend. However, it is my habit after that to get up, shave, shower, and brush my teeth. I then lumber downstairs, make coffee and feed our now three cats. To make the coffee, I have to

---

[60] In the terms of Schutz, ibid., they are explained by an in-order- to motive.

[61] Although they do so in terms of attention and effort, Emirbayer and Mische, "What is Agency?," make this point as well.

boil water, transfer the coffee from bags into the jars where my wife seems to want it, then from the jars into coffee filters, having first poured milk into my cup.

We can describe this entire sequence as my habit, my routine. I do it all without much reflection. Normally, as I do it, I am thinking of something else, like why I have to attend some damn – not the word I actually use – meeting later that morning.

For all these reasons, we could describe my routine as mechanical. But do we really want to say the activity I just described is mechanical in a philosophically technical sense? That all the discrete actions I described are unconscious or motivated only by a general need for ontological security?[62]

To describe it as such, as the practice theorists do, makes it seem as if we operate in two very discrete, very different modes. There is the reflective consciousness we snap into on those rare occasions when we encounter problems and otherwise, when we are acting according to routine or habit, we operate along the lines of stimulus–response (S–R) behaviorism.

The problem with that view is the problem with S–R behaviorism, which did not work even for rats. The basic problem, as Charles Taylor amply demonstrated long ago, is that even within the S–R literature itself, the behavioral responses were identified functionally rather than structurally.[63] What that means is that responses did not represent so-called "colorless movements" but rather functions or goals accomplished. Think of it in reference to what I described as my habitual morning behavior. Whether it is shaving or getting the milk to pour into my cup, I haven't described any movements. You do not know whether I am using shaving cream or soap or an electric razor. Similarly, at a micro-level of analysis, there are all kind of different movements that might be required, beginning with where I initially am, for me to get to the refrigerator, open it up, grasp the milk, and pour it into my coffee.

---

[62] I am actually a rather spiritual person who derives his ontological security from sources I think of as more significant than my morning habits. Admittedly, though, my wife would say I am also like a rat – or *The Big Bang Theory's* Sheldon, who gets out of sorts if his routine is in any way disrupted.

[63] Charles Taylor (1964) *The Explanation of Behavior* (New York: Prometheus).

So what? So what that all the behaviors we just named in my morning routine are identified not structurally but functionally in terms of goals? What is the bearing of that distinction?

The bearing actually is critical. We have broken down my morning routine not into discrete movements but into discrete goals accomplished. We thus have not escaped teleological language. But careful here. It is not just a matter of our language. If in the case of each discrete action, we are talking about a goal accomplished, then we are also talking about a mechanism at work that is teleological or purposive rather than mechanistic – purposive, that is, rather than anything S–R.

Purposiveness, in turn, as we saw, can only be cashed out in terms of conscious, intending agents – motivated agents. Each discrete goal identified in other words (as opposed to colorless movements) is the motive of the action that accomplishes it, goals we are implicitly referencing in our very identification of the acts.

What I am saying is that it is a complete fiction to represent what we call habit as something mechanical in a technical, philosophical sense, that is, as something non-conscious and non-motivated.

What I am saying is that there is less purchase than the practice theorists suppose in differentiating between habit and more reflective behavior. There is less purchase because insofar as the two categories represent actions rather than reactive behaviors, they are alike in basic form and process, being conscious, cognitively informed, and performed for reasons.

Nor, really, can what the practice theorists refer to as our routines or habits be described as devoid even of reflection. Again, the practice theorists make out as if we are dealing with two entirely separate categories of phenomena: the category of standard conditions that call for automatic, standard movements; and the category of problematic situation where we need to sit and calculate. But as Archer argues in *The Reflexive Imperative*, action does not divide in such way. Instead, problematic situations are endemic to our daily routines.[64]

Go back again to my morning habits. I do not know about you, but things rarely run smoothly for me. I may be out of shaving cream or left with a dull razor. Where did "she," i.e., my wife, hide the milk? We

---

[64] Margaret Archer (2012) *The Reflexive Imperative in Late Modernity* (New York: Cambridge University Press).

don't have enough coffee. The cats are fighting, and I need to break them up. And from the moment I arise until I put the food down in front of them, one or another of them is under my feet or between my legs, requiring each day a novel acrobatic navigation. Viewed finely, ethnographically, my morning routine is complex, as, I am sure, is yours. My reflection is constantly being demanded.

Viewed from a more consequential, macro-perspective, we see the same thing. And that actually is the larger point of Archer's *The Reflexive Imperative*. If ever there was a period when human beings could function continuously and completely on what we might call habit, we are no longer in it. We seem to be in a period of extremely rapid morphogenesis, where things change over night. People my age can remember when cutting and pasting revisions was something we did literally with scissors and glue. Then came computers, and the Internet. We now routinely use smartphones more powerful than the devices used to send astronauts to the moon. And of course we have international capitalism heating in ways that have and will likely continue to cause worldwide disturbances. Mechanical action is less possible now than it ever was. Of course, my contention is that mechanical action never truly was possible anyway.

But what about the unconscious?

Let me say a last word about the unconscious and psychoanalysis as it seems of great appeal to many. Critical realists span the spectrum on the unconscious and psychoanalysis. Margaret Archer is perhaps staunchest among us in dismissing much appeal to either. Conversely, George Steinmetz has recently argued that Bourdieu would be improved by a dose of Lacanian psychoanalysis and faults Bourdieu for his dismissal of Jacques Lacan.[65]

My own position is in between but closer to Archer. I have hung out enough with and been impressed by psychoanalysts of the object relations variety to credit their insights. And I can see in my own life that I am not immune to unconscious motivation when my emotions get attached to the wrong object. Nothing I have said in this chapter

---

[65] George Steinmetz (2013) "Toward Socioanalysis: The 'Traumatic Kernel' of Psychoanalysis and Neo-Bourdieusian Theory," pp. 108–130 in Philip Gorski (ed.), *Bourdieu and Historical Analysis* (Durham, NC: Duke University Press).

excludes that possibility. Notice, however, that in speaking of motivation and emotions, we are still speaking in teleological categories that suggest some level of consciousness as opposed to a non-conscious process.

Even so, I agree with Archer that there is too much rush in social science to the unconscious and likewise caution that unconscious motivation will always apply more to isolated cases rather than to our behavior as a whole. Why do I say so? It is a point that again goes back to Donald Davidson, who expressed it more philosophically.[66] I will put the point in more Marxian terms. We are social animals who have always survived by way of collective action. Whether that collective action involves bringing down a mastodon or shooting rockets at the moon, it requires extensive and reliable coordination. Reliable coordination in turn requires that we each are sufficiently aware of and in control of how we behave as to guarantee and actually deliver on performance in the roles we are assigned to play. We could not do so if each of us were so beset by vast and imponderable motivations as to leave us without any idea of what we will do next, let alone next week or next month.

If you think about it, our very ability to give reliable accounts of our own behavior is avouched by our reliable ability to predict our behavior even months ahead of when we will act. The very degree that we take this ability for granted is indicative of how reliable and indispensible it actually is. For that reason as well, as Anscombe pointed out, we acknowledge a kind of first-person privilege, meaning that, if not always at least generally, each of us rather than any observer is in the best position to say what our motives for action are or were.[67]

What I have outlined above is a kind of CR transcendental argument: What is necessary for coordinated action to be possible? We can run through yet another version of transcendental argument. As John Searle has pointed out, "if I am trying to tell someone something, then (assuming certain conditions are satisfied) as soon as he recognizes that I am trying to tell him something and what it is I am trying to tell him, I have succeeded in telling it to him."[68] Why is that? Because, Searle goes on, there is a connection between linguistic meaning and

---

[66] Donald Davidson (1973) "Radical Interpretation," *Dialectica* 27: 314–328.

[67] G. E. M. Anscombe (1957) *Intention* (Oxford: Basil Blackwell).

[68] John Searle (1969) *Speech Acts: An Essay in the Philosophy of Language* (New York: Cambridge University Press), p. 43.

intentionality. "In speaking I attempt to communicate certain things to my hearer by getting him to recognize my intention to communicate just those things."[69] What is necessary for this linguistic mechanism to work? That even if not always, normally, what it seems to be a person's intention to communicate actually is what the person is intending to communicate. Again, language would be impossible if what motivates what comes out of our mouths were normally other than the motivations they appear to be.

So, are we susceptible to unconscious motives? Yes, but in the flux of our activities of daily living, unconscious – as opposed to tacit – motivation is relatively isolated, and the burden is always on the observer-analyst to demonstrate that some subject or another is in fact not consciously but unconsciously motivated. It is a burden those rushing to unconscious motivations often decline to bear.[70]

---

[69] Ibid. p. 43.

[70] Again, in psychology, Jonathan Haidt and the so-called "New Intuitionists" have newly made much of unconscious motivation. See particularly Haidt (2013) *The Righteous Mind: Why Good People Are Divided by Politics and Religion* (New York: Vintage). In our discipline, Haidt's work has strongly influenced Stephen Vaisey, "Motivation and Justification," and Steven Hitlin (2008) *Moral Selves; Evil Selves: The Social Psychology of Conscience* (New York: Palgrave). Although I am not going to devote space to it here, see Porpora *et al.*, *Post-Ethical Society*, for a critique of Haidt.

6 | *What and where is culture?*

Having gone through structure and agency, now, with culture, we come to the C portion of Margaret Archer's SAC. It is Archer's own *Culture and Agency: The Place of Culture in Social Theory* that represents the major CR statement on this topic, and for Archer, culture needs to be treated in parallel with structure.[1] That parallel means in the first instance to treat culture as something analytically distinct from agency. The two obviously interrelate causally, just as structure and agency interrelate causally. But, again, for two things to interrelate causally, they must be ontologically distinct. It is that ontological distinctness of culture and agency that first marks Archer's CR view.

Of course, for Archer and CR, structure and culture also are distinct. Neither reduces to the other. Whereas structure, as I have said, refers to social organizational relations, for Archer culture refers to *intelligibilia*.[2]

What does Archer mean by intelligibilia? Intelligibilia are anything with meaningful content produced by social intentionality. That formulation itself requires unpacking. As I made clear in the previous chapter, intentionality and reasoned motivation lie somewhere behind all human action. Action in turn can be social in two respects. It can be motivated or informed by social phenomena – such as rules, myths or ideologies. It can also be socially oriented as is anything designed to communicate to or to otherwise influence others. And, of course, what is social can be both informed by and oriented to what is social.

Because intelligibilia express intentionality, intelligibilia require hermeneutical interpretation to understand or explain. Why do I invoke this clumsy-sounding locution, *hermeneutical interpretation*? Ironically, for the sake of clarity. In one sense, to understand anything

---

[1] Margaret Archer (1996) *Culture and Agency: The Place of Culture in Social Theory* (Cambridge: Cambridge University Press).
[2] Ibid., p. xviii.

requires interpretation. It requires a kind of interpretation, for example, to discern whether or not in the cosmic background radiation, there is evidence that our universe once inflated astronomically. That kind of interpretation, however, is not the kind we mean when we speak of specifically hermeneutical interpretation.

What is distinctive of the kind of interpretation we mean when we speak of hermeneutical interpretation? The simplest answer is it refers to the distinction the interpretivists or Verstehen sociologists invoke to mark the difference between the natural and the human. Whereas natural phenomena, they say, need to be explained causally, human phenomena need to be understood hermeneutically. Whereas the former involves laws, the latter involves reasons.

As we now know, CR denies that even the natural realm is governed by laws – or at least by Humean laws specifying invariant regularities. Does it follow then that for CR the distinction between the natural and the human breaks down? Well, it breaks down more for CR than for the interpretivists. CR recaptures an overall unity of science that is lost by interpretivism. As we saw in Chapter 2, in rejecting the covering law model of causality, CR is able to recapture the sense in which reasons too may be causes – however nondeterministically they function. Thus, for CR, the human realm too requires explanation and not just understanding – or, alternately, part of what we are doing by understanding in the human realm is simultaneously causally explaining.

Nevertheless, CR recognizes a difference between the kinds of causal processes that operate across the natural and human planes. Although for CR, reasons, too, may be causes, not all causes are reasons. In addition to discursive causal mechanisms, there are also mechanisms that are extra-discursive. What proximally caused any cosmic inflation, for example, were not reasons, that is, the product of purposive consciousness.[3] In contrast, intentional action and its results are a product of consciousness, and therein lies the difference. That difference is why we must exercise Verstehen with regard to reasoned behavior and not in the case of non-reasoned phenomena like cosmic inflation or, in the human realm, non-discursive relations like inequality.

---

[3] More distally, given the many so-called *anthropic coincidences* of cosmology, it remains an open question whether there ultimately is some teleology behind the universe. See, for example, Paul Davies (2007) *The Cosmic Jackpot: Why Our Universe is Just Right for Life* (New York: Houghton-Mifflin).

If, in technical terms, we designate only what results from intentional action as meaningful – that is, as something that meant something to some agent, then we may say that hermeneutic interpretation is the distinct kind of interpretation we use to decipher the meaningful content of anything that results from intentional behavior. Through hermeneutics, we decipher what a product meant to whoever produced it. That meaningful content is what is referred to by intelligibilia.

There is another way to understand intelligibilia and, hence, culture. The designation, Archer says, "is roughly co-terminous with what Popper called Third World Knowledge."[4] Archer tells me that the Marxists in British CR never forgave her for drawing on Karl Popper, whose *The Open Society and Its Enemies*, was a broad critique of totalitarian thought, which for Popper included historical materialism.[5]

When it comes, however, to Popper's seldom-cited Tanner lecture, *Three Worlds*, delivered at the University of Michigan, I am all with Archer and happy to let bygones be bygones. With Archer, I consider *Three Worlds* a gem of a piece, anticipating the CR perspective in a number of important respects. Popper expressly identifies himself, for example, as a realist and expressly invokes what CR would later call the causal criterion of existence.

According to Popper, all reality is comprised of three separate domains or worlds. The first world is the realm of purely physical things without any sentience. World two refers to psychological reality, to the ideas, thoughts, motives and so forth that make up purely mental functioning. Embracing emergence himself, Popper, like CR, denies that the mental can be reduced to the physical, that world two can be reduced to world one. But besides worlds one and two, Popper also affirmed a third.

By world 3 I mean the world of the products of the human mind, such as languages; tales and stories and religious myths; scientific conjectures or theories, and mathematical constructions; songs and symphonies; paintings and sculptures. But also aeroplanes and airports and other feats of engineering.[6]

---

[4] Ibid., p. 104; see also p. xvii.
[5] Karl Popper (2013) *The Open Society and Its Enemies* (Princeton, NJ: Princeton University Press).
[6] Karl Popper (1978) "Three Worlds," the Tanner Lecture on Human Values. Delivered at University of Michigan, p. 144. www.thee-online.com/Documents/Popper-3Worlds.pdf.

Although in the above extract Popper describes world three as the products of the human mind, that designation would not sharply distinguish world three from world two. But if we consider Popper's examples of world three denizens, we see he means what I have been calling specifically social products – products informed by or oriented to (or both) the social – products like language and myths and works of art. And later, returning us back to Archer, Popper also says very expressly that what he means by world three coincides very closely to what anthropologists mean by culture.[7] It coincides closely as well with Orlando Patterson's understanding.[8] Finally, something we will examine more presently, Popper makes a number of important arguments to the effect that world three cannot be reduced to world two. Thus, coincident with what Archer calls intelligibilia, world three is eminently social.

It is likewise significant that Popper uses the term "product" to distinguish what resides in world three. Clearly, to the extent that all of our actions are products of our minds, those of our actions that are distinctly social all reside in world three. Thus, just as is held by practice theory, we definitely do have culture in action. Rituals come immediately to mind.

The question is whether all that is in culture can be equated with action, and here the answer is no. While actions, and specifically social actions, are products of our minds, our actions also have products, which insofar as they derive from actions, which derive from our minds, can likewise be designated products of our minds.

The products of our actions, however, are frequently not themselves actions. In the extract above, Popper adduces quite a few examples: stories, myths, works of art, airplanes and airports. Each of these things is produced by actions. Books do indeed get written, but the book you hold in your hand is not itself an action. Yet it is cultural. So the cultural is not reducible to action.

Of course, the practice theorists do not say that culture is entirely reducible to actions. They say culture consists of action and discourse. And a book, although physical, at least contains or conveys discourse. But are all intelligibilia that are not actions discourse instead? No.

---

[7] Ibid., p. 166.
[8] See Orlando Patterson (2014) "Making Sense of Culture," *Annual Review of Sociology* 40: 1–30.

To begin with, although it may have its discursive aspects, an airplane is not discourse. Nor really is language, which is rather a requisite for discourse.

What about values, stereotypes, morals, and taken-for granted beliefs? Do these represent discourse? Well, what is discourse? Here, we must be careful. By definition, talk is discursive. So whenever we talk about anything, we are discoursing. But we can discourse about planes and airports without planes and airports being themselves discourse. We must distinguish our talk from the objects our talk is about. Accordingly, we must distinguish values and stereotypes from our talk about them. Certainly, we can only express our values or articulate stereotypes linguistically, but then to express or articulate anything – like what a plane is or an airport – requires language.

If discourse is equated with anything linguistic, it becomes a fairly vacuous term. But even then, it is unclear that values and stereotypes are linguistic. Is justice – not our talk of it but the value itself – discourse? Is it even linguistic? Justice is a social relation or way of behaving. To describe it requires language, but its instances do not. An individual or a society can each be described as just or acting justly even if they lack any such concept.

One may be able to act justly without ever having heard of that concept, but without the concept can one value it? For the sake of argument, let us assume not. Let us assume that to value justice, one must at some point, using language, articulate that value to oneself and commit oneself to it. What is being valued, however, is still not a linguistic expression. It is not as if in valuing justice, what I value are particular words. What I value is a quality, the way of being, that the words express.

Similarly, if I hold a stereotype of certain people, it is an image or an association I hold and that I apply to those people indiscriminately as if it reflected something essential about them. We can only discuss this stereotype via language, but the image itself need not be at all linguistic.

Thus, however much we may communicate about them, if even to ourselves, values and stereotypes are not in themselves communications. Properly, then, they are not themselves discourse.

Although values are thus distinct from and irreducible to discourse and action, perhaps values are not really an important element of culture. Throughout this book, we have already encountered a number of places where Ann Swidler says as much.[9] In her *Talk of Love: How Culture Matters*, Swidler expands on this claim.

We often think of ourselves as goal-directed actors and, especially in America, we are likely to give an account of why we act the way we do by speaking of our "values." But as sociological explanation, such a view is theoretically implausible and empirically inadequate. ... First, the assumption that culture shapes people by shaping their values is not supported by the evidence. If deep, enduring values were dominant factors in individual behavior, we should expect people in changed circumstances to continue to pursue traditional values, perhaps using new methods to achieve their goals. In fact, we observe precisely the opposite.[10]

Can it really be that people are not motivated in important ways by values? Existentially, do we not choose who we are by what we love, what we stand for, for what we are willing to sacrifice, even die? Is Swidler telling us that she herself is not motivated by values or just that such is the case only for those she studies? We again see exemplified Christian Smith's observation of how ready sociologists are to accept visions of themselves the falsity of which should be obvious from their own lives.[11]

At long last, there is now some push back against Swidler's dismissal of values, but, given its continued hold, there remains need for more extended argument.[12] Let us begin with Josephus, the ancient Jewish historian who reports an incident involving the Pharisees early in Pontius Pilot's governance over Palestine. When he arrived, Pilot placed Roman banners bearing Caesar's image near the Jewish Temple. To the Jews, that image, especially so placed, was sacrilege.

---

[9] Ann Swidler (2001) *Talk of Love: How Culture Matters* (Chicago, IL: University of Chicago Press).

[10] Swidler, *Talk of Love*.

[11] Christian Smith (2011) *What Is a Person? Rethinking Humanity, Social Life, and the Moral Good from the Person Up* (Chicago, IL: University of Chicago Press).

[12] Stephen Vaisey initated the push back, but it is now endorsed as well by Orlando Patterson. See Stephen Vaisey (2009) "Motivation and Justification: A Dual-Process Model of Culture in Action," *American Journal of Sociology* 114: 1675–1715; and Orlando Patterson (2014) "Making Sense of Culture," *Annual Review of Sociology* 40: 1–30. For more on behalf of values, see Hans Joas's (2000) *The Genesis of Values* (Chicago, IL: University of Chicago Press); and also Steven Hitlin and Jane Alyn Piliavin (2003) "Values: Reviving a Dormant Concept," *Annual Review of Sociology* 30: 359–393.

When a crowd of Pharisees demonstrated in protest, Pilot had his soldiers surround them. In response, the Pharisees reportedly fell on the ground, exposing their necks to the soldiers' swords. Taken aback and mystified, Pilot acted pragmatically. He removed the banners.

Were values really not in play here in the Pharisaic behavior? Were values really absent as well from the Underground Railroad or from the bravery of the so-called righteous gentiles who saved Jews during the Holocaust? Is it really, as Swidler suggests, a false image of ourselves to imagine ourselves acting in accord with values?

Swidler's dismissal of values prompts us to ask what values are. "'Values,'" Swidler tells us in *Talking of Love*, again placing the word within quotation marks lest we mistake it for something real, "are usually seen as the ranking of options on a hierarchy of preferences."[13]

To say the least, Swidler's definition of values is exceedingly thin and emotionally barren, as if lifted from the pages of a treatise on rational choice theory. Not what one would expect from a doyenne of cultural sociology. Admittedly, we hold some values more strongly than others, which is why we have a rich vocabulary for labeling them: commitments, concerns, passions, ideals, interests, and so on. Preferences also is a word we use to label our values, but it is one of the weakest. I more than just prefer that justice be done, that my wife thrive, or that the earth abide.

Presumably as well, the Pharisees more than just preferred that Pilot remove Caesar's image. Workers on the Underground Railroad presumably more than just preferred that African slaves find freedom; those who risked their lives to save Jews during the Holocaust presumably were acting on more than just a preference that Jews live. In all cases, what seems at work are values as powerful emotional draws, callings – i.e., causes that motivate behavior in profound ways.[14]

Swidler suggests we dismiss all this apparent profundity as illusion. What prompts this suggestion? Let us start with the putative evidence. Like Swidler's definition, it is very thin. In *Talk of Love* she cites one example: "immigrants seeking wealth and prestige in market societies, while they may have sought family prestige and family honor in their homelands."[15] In her prior, seminal article, "Culture in Action," she

---

[13] Swidler, *Talk of Love*, p. 36.
[14] Perhaps the cultural sociologists need to catch up with the sociology of emotions. See Jack Barbalet (ed.) (2002) *Emotions and Sociology* (New York: Wiley Blackwell).
[15] Swidler, *Talk of Love*, p. 80.

cites two more examples. Against the culture of poverty theory, she says, values do not explain why some people are poor and others not; the poor seem to hold the same values as everyone else. Her second example is Max Weber's thesis concerning the Protestant Ethic. The behavioral orientation toward work remains, Swidler says, although the ends sought change over time. What culture does, Swidler concludes, is not so much provide values as what she calls "strategies of action" that organize our behavior in ways that could be applied to alternate goals.[16]

To this putative empirical evidence against values, Swidler adds two conceptual arguments. The first, from pragmatism, is that human beings typically do not act from a priori goals; instead, goals develop and change in encounter with the means available. The second conceptual argument is that a purposive means–ends account of action focuses us misleadingly on individual acts, which cannot be extracted from a broader, ongoing life strategy, or what we saw Swidler call an action strategy.

What are we to say about Swidler's argument? The first thing to say is that as in the case of others we have examined, we must detach the admittedly valuable sociological work Swidler does from what she says or thinks she is doing. As we have already seen in relation to others, Swidler's programmatic pronouncements often contradict her own project and analyses. To take a simple example, in her programmatic pronouncements, Swidler tells us that culture is not in our heads. Nevertheless, from the very opening pages of *Talk of Love*, her subjects' heads are just where she takes us.

I wanted to understand not only *what* my interviewees thought about love, but *how* they thought. I was interested in the varying views often held by the same people and in the circumstances under which one understanding would give way to another. ... I was interested not just in the conclusions people drew but in the ways they brought together cultural images, feelings, experiences, and ideas to think about a problem.[17]

What Swidler describes here is a very commendable sociological project, and, correspondingly, her whole book is of great sociological merit. But the project and analysis described departs radically from

---

[16] Ibid., p. 82; and Swidler (1986) "Culture in Action: Symbols and Strategies," *American Sociological Review* 51 (2): 273–286, pp.273, 275.

[17] Swidler, *Talk of Love*, p. 4.

what we saw the practice turn purportedly to be about. In the first place, where are Swidler's interviewees thinking these thoughts she wants to understand? Where are the varying views the interviewees entertain? Not in their practice but where practice theory tells us not to look: Inside their heads.

Further, the specific cultural elements that interest Swidler – images, feelings, experiences, and ideas – are neither practices nor discourse. From her opening pages, Swidler leaves the practice turn behind – or, perhaps, understood more charitably, reinterprets practices and repertoires to include what occupies people's heads, in which case we are returned to what culture meant prior to the practice turn.

Finally, despite Swidler's programmatic dismissal of values, people's holding and deploying alternate values is specifically much of what Swidler explores in *Talk of Love*. Consider what she says about an engineer she interviewed.

In the midst of this well-worked out picture of how two people should manage a relationship, Donald Nelson said something surprising. Asked what he would do if his wife should become ill and require constant care, he abandoned the language of autonomy and mutual respect in favor of an image of absolute commitment, sacrifice, and selfless love: "If you love [someone] . . . it is just something you do for them. It's something you want to do." Even if it means giving up hobbies, interests, freedom? "Yeah."[18]

Swidler wants to make the point that people shift frames and discourses depending on the scenarios with which they are presented. That may be, but it is hard to deny that what Swidler also uncovers in engineer Donald Nelson are strongly held, if conflicting value commitments, commitments to autonomy and respect on the one hand and to selfless love on the other.

So Swidler's own empirical data belie her dismissal of values. What are we to make of her general arguments for that dismissal? It is that they can be quickly dismissed. In the first place, empirically, Swidler's case rests on only three anecdotes, which I have countered with three of my own, but even the anecdotes Swidler advances hardly prove her point. It is not clear, that is to say, that the immigrants Swidler cites have abandoned their former values, and by Swidler's own admission, the poor actually do hold values. The fact that those values are not

[18] Ibid., p. 32.

what explains poverty is beside the point; and, in fact, as we saw in Chapter 4, without a non-cultural conception of structure, Swidler herself is left still with a version of culture of poverty theory.

Admittedly, as Swidler observes, in Weber's account of the Protestant Ethic, an action strategy survives with a transposed end. But it hardly follows from that case that values seldom figure in our lives. In fact, as we observed in Chapter 5 about effort, strategy is also a teleological term, implying, however tacitly pursued, some ultimate goal that is accordingly valued.

Conceptually, Swidler also is undoubtedly correct that our individual acts are frequently part of larger life-narratives that to be fully grasped must be examined in broad canvas. And she is also correct with pragmatism and against, for example, rational choice theory, that our goals frequently alter as we pursue what we originally had in mind.

Conceptually, however, neither point counts against a means–ends understanding of either individual acts or the larger action strategies Swidler endorses. As we saw in Chapter 5, all actions are subject to what philosophers call an "accordion effect," being describable in terms of purposes of lesser or greater scope – e.g., turning on a light, thereby alerting a prowler, and so on.[19] But purposes are involved at each level. Similarly, there may often be a temporal dialectic between objectives and possibilities, the former conforming to the latter, but, even then, purposiveness again reappears in each moment of that interplay.

With what would Swidler replace the purposive account? S–R behaviorism? We have already discussed in Chapter 5 the failure of that route. In the end, we cannot do without purposes or values, and not even Swidler herself does without them. Values remain an important element of culture.

Culture as world three

Archer would agree with Swidler that culture is not just in our heads – although, unlike Swidler, Archer would not deny that culture is there too. Thus, in contrast with Swidler, Archer does deny that culture resides just in our embodied actions. In addition to both our heads

---

[19] Joel Feinberg (1970) "Action and Responsibility," pp. 119–151 in Joel Feinberg (ed.), *Doing and Deserving* (Princeton, NJ: Princeton University Press).

and our actions, Archer says that culture is also in libraries and elsewhere, wherever there are intelligiblia to be interpreted. Culture, Archer would say, existed, for example, in the *Rosetta Stone*, even before anyone could decipher it. In such a case, culture can live on beyond even the life of the people who produced it.

The where of culture is ontologically peculiar, which makes us query also its whatness. That query in turn brings us back to Popper's world three. As noted, for Popper, world three consists of products of the human mind. One example Popper cites is Michelangelo's sculpture, *The Dying Slave*, which, he says, belongs simultaneously to world one and to world three. As an object of world one, i.e., as a block of marble, *The Dying Slave* has specific gravity. As an object of world three it has style and meaning. Popper goes on to cite other examples: Shakespeare's *Hamlet* or Beethoven's *Fifth Symphony*. He says that these are abstract objects, which are embodied in concrete objects. In his initial comments on embodiment, he sounds a bit like Giddens:

Hamlet is embodied in all those physical volumes that contain an edition of Hamlet; and in a different way, it is also embodied or physically realized in each performance by a theatrical company. Similarly, a symphony may be embodied or physically realized in many different ways. There is the composer's manuscript; there are the printed scores; there are the actual performances; and there are the recordings of these performances, in the physical shape of discs, or of tapes. But there are also the memory engrams in the brains of some musicians: these too are embodiments, and they are particularly important.[20]

When I say that Popper sounds like Giddens, I refer to Popper's talk of forms of embodiment – from practices to what Giddens will later call memory traces. But like Archer after him, Popper also says that world three objects may also be embodied in libraries.

Distinctly, however, Popper goes on to say something else. He says that the denizens of world three are abstract objects. Employing what in philosophy is called a type-token distinction, Popper does not equate the object type with its embodied tokens. He asserts a difference. It is the type that is the abstract object.

When I opened this chapter, I observed that Archer speaks of how the issues relating to culture parallel the issues relating to structure. We

[20] Popper, "Three Worlds," p. 145.

have already covered one such parallel: issues involving the relation of culture and agency mirror those relating to structure and agency. With Popper's invocation of abstract objects, we arrive at a second parallel, for, as in the case of structure, reference to abstract objects re-raises, now in the domain of culture, the matter of nominalism.

Nominalists deny the reality of abstract objects. So in the type-token terms I have introduced, nominalists deny that types exist apart from their token instances. For nominalists, reality consists only of concrete tokens-of-types and not also of types alone.

As abstract objects, types do not exist in space or time. If we ask, for example, where Beethoven's Fifth Symphony or the theory of evolution exist, the nominalist answer would be only in their concrete token instances – e.g., in the score for or in performances of the symphony and – for the theory – in texts and minds storing it. To attribute any further reality to the content of the symphony or of the theory is, according to the nominalists, a reification. As Popper puts it, "They say that in speaking of world 3 objects, I am guilty of hypostatization; which means, in English, that I make substances or things out of non-existing ghosts, or out of fictions."[21]

In "Three Worlds," Popper spends some time arguing against the nominalist view. He begins by invoking the causal criterion of existence: "I am trying to show that the objects of world 3 may be in a very clear sense not fictitious but quite real; they may be real in that they may have a causal effect upon us, upon our world 2 experiences, and further upon our world 1 brains, and thus upon material bodies."[22]

Popper's argument here is that we may, for example, be emotionally moved by a great symphony – say Beethoven's Fifth – and that this emotional reaction in world two is caused in large part by the artwork's objective aesthetic content. If that content does in fact have a causal effect, then that content is something real. As that content, however, is distinct from both our psychological dynamics or any particular performance, it does not reside in world two. It is rather a denizen of the cultural realm Popper calls world three.

Popper goes on to ask similarly whether theories, like Newton's and Einstein's of gravitation are something real. Is their content, that is, something real apart from their embodiment in our brains or manuscripts? Again, Popper invokes the causal criterion of existence, saying

[21] Popper, "Three Worlds," p. 146.   [22] Ibid., p. 150.

that these theories have proven effective in ANT-like causal networks that have profoundly changed the world.

Clearly, the theories have been causally effectual. Einstein's theory of special relativity was, after all, instrumental in the creation of the atomic bomb. So by the causal criterion, there's no doubt that the theories are real in some sense.

The question is whether the content of the theories is real apart from its embodiments in our minds, papers, or wherever. Popper cites a number of considerations that suggest an affirmative answer. First, he makes a distinction similar to the one we made earlier between values and our discourse about values. Just as those two are categorically distinct, so distinct, Popper suggests – and Archer after him, are the content of theories and anyone's thoughts about that content. Our thoughts about the content may take the form of brain processes, but those brain processes are not the content of the theory. It is the content, Popper says, and not any individual's thoughts about it that is supposed to remain invariant across translations. At least content is what a good translator attempts to keep invariant.[23]

Popper further points out that the different semantic elements comprising meaningful content can also "stand in logical relationships to each other," relations like "equivalence, deducibility, and compatibility."[24] Content like Einstein's theory of relativity could have gaps, inconsistencies, presuppositions and implications that no one has ever thought about, that instead remain to be discovered. If no one has thought about those gaps, inconsistencies, and implications, if they remain to be discovered, then clearly they have an objective existence independent of our thoughts and anything we have written down. Where is that existence? It must reside in the theoretical content itself. That content then must itself have an objective existence independent of our minds or indeed anything written down.

That implication begins to sound spooky. The gaps and presuppositions and so on are in the content. Fine. But if the content has an objective existence independent of our minds or anything written, where does that content reside?

---

[23] See Archer, *Culture and Agency*. The difference relates to the distinction Archer makes between cultural system and socio-cultural system.
[24] Ibid., p. 158. Again, Archer follows up closely on this point.

Hold onto that question a minute. I want first to address a different issue. We have arrived at yet another parallel between culture and structure. Recall that when we were talking of structure back in Chapter 4, I said that certain social relations could exist and exist consequentially even without anyone's notice. Inequality, for example, can exist with profound consequences even if no one in a society recognizes the inequality. As Archer observes, we see now that the same applies to culture.

As an emergent entity, the Cultural System has an objective existence and autonomous relations amongst its components (theories, beliefs, values, arguments, or more strictly the propositional formulations of them) in the sense that these are independent of anyone's claim to know, to believe, to assert, or to assent to them. ... Consequently contradictions exist independently of people noticing them or caring about them.[25]

There are, as Archer says, kinds of relations among elements of meaning that are ontologically objective. That is, they exist whether or not they are observed. Theoretical inconsistencies do not come into existence only the moment they are noticed. They were there before, awaiting notice. Where they exist, theoretical inconsistencies exist objectively.

We see the same in many other aspects of meaningful content. We say that the grading of essays is subjective, but what we really mean is that there are no formal measures of essay goodness. Still, an essay possesses very objective relational properties we can assess: Does the argument hang together? Does it contradict itself? Does the essay relate to the question it is supposed to address? Does it devote too much space to matters that are less important at the expense of matters that are more crucial? These are all relational considerations concerning content as a thing in itself apart from the mental activity that produced it or the particular media in which the content is embodied. And if something has ontologically objective properties, then it too must have an ontologically objective existence. Content, then, must be ontologically objective.

The same holds for mathematical relations. In one sense, mathematical constructs are cultural creations, ideas abstracted from reality or from abstractions from reality. The work of mathematics is to uncover

---

[25] Ibid., p. 107.

and demonstrate the structural relations among these constructs not previously known. To the extent again that those relations are there waiting to be discovered, they again must already exist objectively, independent of human knowledge. Of course, mathematical nominalists would deny that mathematical relations exist prior to their discovery, but nominalist approaches, like *fictionalism* or *formalism*, depart widely from the common sense view most sociologists would accept, namely that numbers are real and that mathematics is referential.

It is not only single works like poems, arguments, or symphonies that are structured. Archer's larger point is that cultural content as a whole is structured too. To put it otherwise, just as society is structured or organized as a whole, so is any society's culture. There is social structure and cultural structure. The two, however, should not be confused. Whereas social structure refers to relations connecting social positions or social positions and social objects, cultural structure refers to relations among ideas.

Swidler's notion of culture as a toolbox of ideas was in part a reaction to a view of culture as a homogeneous whole. To break with that view, however, we need not go the practice route of equating culture with actions. Indeed, Archer's *Culture and Agency* likewise broke with the homogeneity thesis without doing so. It is enough to treat the degree of cultural coherence as an empirical question. Some cultures may be more tightly integrated than others, as may be different parts of culture. Roman Catholicism, for example, may be a more integrated domain of ideas than Protestantism taken as a whole. Durkheim evidently thought so.

With its concept of hegemony, Marxian theory as well always recognized that culture does not consist of one, seamlessly integrated block of dogma. If culture as a toolbox simply means that what we call culture is an entire world of related and unrelated, consonant and sometimes incompatible ideas floating about a given society or part of society, then, yes, in one sense actors may treat culture as a toolbox.

But not completely. Indeed, the analytic limitations of the toolbox metaphor show up again in Swidler's own work, even in the example we earlier considered. A physical toolbox is a mere aggregation. Any individual tool can be used independent of any other. Ideas, however, are intrinsically relational and connected. We see such ideational relationality in Swidler's interview with engineer Donald Nelson. Recall Swidler's observation that Nelson suddenly shifts from the value of autonomy to the value of love and care. Nelson presumably shifts because love and care are deeper, more fundamental values than autonomy, and not just for Nelson himself. That difference in depth is already there in the cultural content through which Nelson is putatively rifling.

Thus, in contrast with a toolbox, culture is not just an aggregation of independent objects. The ideational objects of culture bear objective relations to each other about which we can argue and converse and which, like differences in depth, can exert causal influences on us.[26] All of that nature is missed by the toolbox metaphor and by what Archer calls the conflation of culture with action. It is, as in the case of structure, to an anti-conflationary position that Archer calls us. That call is decidedly against the contemporary American sociological current.

Let us return now to the question of location. I spoke above of culture floating around in a society. That vague formulation returns us to the question we postponed earlier: Where is culture or, alternately, where are the objects of culture or world three? It is precisely the difficulty of placing abstract objects in place and time that prompts nominalists to deny their reality.

To think through the issue more concretely, let us consider the game of chess. The game of chess clearly exists. We can pull out a set and readily play it. But where does chess exist? One nominalist answer would be that it exists wherever it is being played. There are two problems with that answer. The first problem is that with that answer, a single thing, chess, has, simultaneously, multiple locations. The second problem is that if at some moment in time no one in the world is playing chess, then it sounds like chess at that moment does not exist, in which case it seems to flicker in and out of reality.

The first problem may not be so bad. We have other such cases – properties, for example. Does redness exist? Of course, you say, but not so fast. The nominalist would say no. The nominalist would say that redness is a concept abstracted from reality that exists only in our minds. In reality, there are individual things or particulars that have the property of being red, but there is no redness as such, detached from particulars. The notion of redness itself is purely an abstract idea.

If, conversely, against the nominalist, you insist that redness too is an existent and not just individual red things, then it is an existent

---

[26] Ibid.

without definite location. The same would seem to be true for chess. Either it does not exist as such or it exists without definite location in space.

Or, for that matter, also without definite location in time. If redness as such exists, we cannot ask when. If it exists, redness appears to be eternal. Do we want to say the same of chess, that it and other cultural objects of world three are eternal? Well, certainly, we do not want to say they flicker in and out of existence, but they clearly are not eternal either. They at least have beginnings in time when they were created.

We could say that when chess is not being played, the concept exists in our minds and wherever else it is recorded in a form someone can decipher. But the concept of chess is not the same as chess itself, in the same way as a recipe for angel food cake is not the same as the cake itself. You may enjoy eating the one but not the other.

We know, as Popper and Archer observe, that worlds two and three must interact. We can play chess when two of us know how. That knowledge we each possess is subjective and hence within world two. But chess, the thing itself, exceeds our individual subjectivities. Somehow, via our individual subjectivities, world two can access world three, but the two worlds remain distinct.

I said at the beginning that cultural objects are ontologically peculiar. Their peculiarity regarding space and time has led Alexander Wendt in International Relations to explore the possibilities of understanding mind as a quantum phenomenon.[27] With quantum processes as well, space and time lose their definition.

Could mind be a mega-quantum phenomenon? Unfortunately, I do not have all the answers here. But in leaving the questions for philosophy alone, sociology cuts itself off from answers it should have; it thus leaves itself making pronouncements, like those of practice theory that fly in the face of our own lived experience.

Is culture everything?

Well, of course, my answer is no. I have just argued that structure and agency and even the subjective processes of world two are analytically separate from the meaningful products that comprise culture, which,

[27] Alexander Wendt (2015) *Quantum Mind and Social Science* (New York: Cambridge University Press).

I join Archer in suggesting, coincide with Popper's world three. Agency is not the same as culture because, among other things, the act of behaving purposively or intentionally is not the same as the meaningful content of the result. Similarly, although it may arise from culture, social structure is not the same as or reducible to culture because, among other things, meaning or hermeneutics is not the principal question to put to relations like power or inequality, which is to say that these relations have extra-discursive effects beyond their communicative content.

So culture is not everything. But the question can be put differently. Does culture ultimately trump everything? Or, to put the question still another way, in the human sphere, does interpretation take precedence over explanation? In his *Interpretation and Social Knowledge*, Isaac Reed answers that last question in the affirmative.[28] Against the realist account – and, along with John Levi Martin, Reed is one of the very few American sociologists to engage CR in any sophisticated way – Reed argues that "Explanation, as a goal for the study of human beings, can only function as a subcategory of the larger category of understanding."[29]

In Chapter 4 I expressed some disagreements with Reed, though not with his book. In fact, my previous references to his book have all been positive. Like others, I consider *Interpretation and Social Knowledge* a beautifully written book that challenges us in just the right directions. Because I consider it one of the most serious criticisms of CR, I want to engage it here.

As Reed's subtitle – *On the Use of Theory in the Social Sciences* – indicates, the book is about the role theory plays in sociology, particularly in realist and interpretive approaches. As mentioned in Chapter 2, Reed joins me in arguing that explanation involves theoretical re-description. Reed puts this quite beautifully.

It is the responsibility of the social researcher not only to report the facts, but to propose a deeper or broader comprehension of them. When investigators attempt to do this, we reach for our theories. We do this because we need some way of comprehending what is, to speak colloquially, "underneath" the facts. We want to know what generates them, what their consequences

---

[28] Isaac Reed (2011) *Interpretation and Social Knowledge: On the Use of Theory in the Social Sciences* (Chicago, IL: Chicago University Press).

[29] Ibid., p. 35.

are, how we should think about them politically, what their connection to the here and now is, and so on.[30]

Notice first that Reed believes in facts. He is already some kind of realist. Further, Reed says we explain the facts by re-describing them in terms of some theory, a process he calls *re-signification*. Re-signification, however, could be understood as interpretation or understanding. If so, all explanation would become interpretation, and Reed could rest his case.

To rest there, however, would be to overlook the distinction I made at the beginning of this chapter between interpretation per se and hermeneutic interpretation. Thus, resting there would end up proving too much – as then even natural science explanations of natural phenomena would become interpretations. True, but vacuous.

Thus, Reed does not rest his case there.[31] What Reed wants specifically to defend is the priority of cultural interpretation. Priority over what? Reed takes on board the CR position that reasons can be causes and that mechanisms need not be mechanistic in any positivist, determinist sense. There can be, Reed allows, purely cultural mechanisms at play.

If so, then cultural interpretations too are, as CR would have it, a form of explanation. In which case, we have the reverse situation: Reed's argument for the priority of interpretation (understanding) over explanation immediately fails. Which tells us that Reed must mean something different, that Reed, informed now by CR, is pushing beyond or deeper than the old distinction between explanation and interpretation. We must probe further.

Reed cogently argues that there are levels of motivation, that behind actors' proximal reasons for what they do, there are more diffuse cultural contexts, which he describes as landscapes. It is only within those contexts or landscapes, he says, that our proximate reasons and motivations find their sense. Thus, it is fine to say, for example, per Weber, that early Calvinists were motivated to accumulate wealth by a desire for eternal assurance and a belief that accumulated wealth would grant that assurance. Those motivating reasons for action, however, only make sense within a larger cultural landscape that include such diverse elements as God, heaven and the doctrine of

[30] Ibid., p. 17.   [31] Ibid. p. 124.

predestination. To understand any particular motivating mechanism, Reed wants to say, requires first an interpretation or understanding of the contextualizing culture that Reed calls the meaningful landscape.

To illustrate, Reed explores how interpretivists go about using theory to provide the deeper or broader comprehension of matters that comes from theory. One example he cites is Clifford Geertz's famous account of Balinese cockfights. Geertz shows us, he says, that what is important about that activity is not the simple gambling for money that seems to be going on at the surface, but a deeper, more subterranean conflict about status and masculinity in Balinese culture. Similarly, Reed cites Susan Bordo's account of how anorexia nervosa arises out of a confluence of deeper elements embedded in the content of Western culture, in particular three overlapping axes: mind–body; locus of control; and gender–power.

Reed's point is that to understand the actors' deeper motives and reasons, we need first to understand the conceptual landscape in which they are moving. That interpretive endeavor, he believes, falls outside the framework of CR:

> For these [interpretivist] theories are not, as we have seen in Geertz and Bordo, mobilized in a realist way. Rather, the theories merge with the meanings of the evidence so as to dig up "the double meaning" of the social actions under study – the hidden or tacit background within which actors act. Reconstructing the meanings of social life that are not consciously intended or obviously denoted by interviewees' statements or archival documents, but that underlie, form, and structure those very statements, is the primary intellectual goal of the interpretive epistemic mode. The meanings come in various layers, with various valences, and must be reconstructed using various theories. In doing this reconstruction, the investigator will move beyond her subjects' conscious understandings of what they are doing, and beyond her evidence, into the territory of maximal interpretation.[32]

Reed opens the above passage saying that the interpretive mode of inquiry does not proceed in a realist way. Why does he say so? Reed does speak a good deal in the passage of the unconscious about which some of us in CR – but by no means all – are cautious. But, then, as I said at the end of the previous chapter, CR does not rule out unconscious motivation.

[32] Ibid., pp. 104–105.

More to the point, it is not really unconscious motivation of which Reed is speaking. Even when actors are conscious of their motives, Reed seems to be saying, they remain less conscious of the embeddedness of those motives in the deeper cultural context, or at least actors do not necessarily call up that context in any explicitly discursive way when they act on the motives the contexts occasion.

Yet, however important the role of cultural background may be, that importance does not seem to rule out a CR take on matters. In CR terms, the cultural background itself can be conceived as a mechanism with causal effects. Reed has a more fundamental reason for thinking the interpretive mode of inquiry rules out CR.

As many historians and sociologists influenced by Geertz and Bordo (and Foucault) have realized, the commitment to the reality of social meaning that orients interpretive analysis implies that all other social ontologies must be historicized. The classic terms of debate in social theory – agency, structure, mechanism, solidarity, rationality, etc. – which are taken to be both general and referential, and thus to transcend historical particularity in their ontological status, now have to be analyzed relative to shared meanings, which are historically variable.[33]

What Reed is saying here is subtle. He is saying (1) the cultural background is crucial to any further understanding of actors' motives; (2) that the background varies historically; and (3) that the historical variability of that background precludes any more permanent ontology such as CR posits. Although Reed does not quite say so in the passage above, he is also contending (4) that insofar as the cultural background is a realm of meaning, it will always be meaning that takes precedence in the human realm over non-hermeneutic explanation.

I can easily stipulate to points (1) and (2). They are not at issue. Reed's point (3), however, rests, I think, on two misunderstandings of CR and on a conflation of theoretical and metatheoretical levels of analysis. Let us address these matters before moving on to point (4).

First the misunderstandings, which are related. The first misunderstanding is that Reed seems to think that ontological posits necessarily imply the permanence or trans-historical nature of what is posited. He says, for example, that "One presumes that gravity was the same for Henry II as it is for Barack Obama; the semiotic sources of legitimate

---

[33] Ibid., p. 105.

domination are not."[34] He goes on to ask, "Can we really go on to ascribe to the signifiers of social theory 'ontological status' if what we mean by this is the sort of permanence that, say, the natural kind 'gold' has?"[35]

The answer is that no such permanence is implied by ontological status. First of all, ontology is not the preserve of CR. The CR point, which I have been making throughout, is that all perspectives – and not just CR – from positivism to interpretivism bear ontological commitments. CR just asks that we come clean about them. Thus, what Reed calls "the semiotic sources of legitimate domination" must have some ontological status. The question is what that status is. And Reed's very comment implies that the status he himself accords those sources is objective reality. I say so because Reed implies that those sources have real causal powers, specifically the power to socially empower. Reed's suggestion is that there were objectively real semiotic sources that once socially empowered Henry II and different but just as objectively real semiotic sources that today socially empower Obama.

If so, then Reed's very comment undoes itself. Reed himself is implicitly making ontological posits without implying any trans-historical permanence. That certain semiotic sources of empowerment once prevailed as an objective reality does not mean that they must endure forever any more than the once objective existence of trilobites or Shakespeare necessarily implies that either is still with us. In short, ontological commitments cannot be avoided, and saying that something is or was ontologically real does not necessarily imply its permanence.

Given the obscurity of some CR texts, Reed can hardly be blamed, but he likewise misunderstands what we critical realists mean by *intransitivity*. Thus, he asks, "In what way is 'society' or 'social structure' intransitive?" "If, however, the social object is unstable or 'transitive' then it is also possible that cases could be incommensurable in the sense that they do not have, underneath them, different arrangements of the same basic social forces, or mechanisms, or relational entities."[36]

For CR, the distinction between the transitive and intransitive again does not have to do with the permanence of the object, or at least not in the sense that Reed speaks of it. The distinction has to do with the difference between an ontologically real object and our knowledge of

[34] Ibid., p. 61.   [35] Ibid., p. 62.   [36] Ibid., p. 62.

it. In one sense, there is something permanent about an ontologically real object even if the object is impermanent. If trilobites, for example, once existed, then what they actually were never changes. What trilobites actually were is in CR terms intransitive. Our knowledge of them, however, is, CR says, transitive, meaning that that knowledge could change over time. We might finally discover, for example, that William Shakespeare truly was Christopher Marlowe. If so, he always was. The intransitive past does not change with our transitive knowledge of it.

So the transitive–intransitive distinction refers to the difference between knowledge and object and not to the endurance of the object over time. So, contrary to what Reed suggests, CR has no problem countenancing different social structures or different semiotic systems at different times or different places. CR has no problems with historicism in that sense.

But Reed also seems to conflate theory and metatheory. In a number of the places I have quoted from his book, Reed suggests that the historicism of the cultural implies that we cannot speak in general about agency, structure, and rationality because agents, structures, and so on vary historically. But, as I say, that claim confounds the theoretical with the metatheoretical. Particular social structures may vary, but there will always be some structure. Cultures may differ in how they regard personhood or agency, but that does not mean that our best understanding of personhood or agency will not apply across the board. If, as I argued in the previous chapter, unconscious motivation cannot be our dominant mode of operation, that feature will not be different just because some culture or sub-culture – like American sociology – thinks otherwise. Reasons will vary historically with cultural backgrounds just as Reed maintains, but in all times and all places, people will be motivated by reasons. They will continue to be intentional actors, empowered variously by the semiotic sources Reed himself cites, however much those sources vary in content. Reed's historicism really does not effect the meta-level of general theory, which is what CR principally addresses.[37]

---

[37] François Dépelteau makes what I consider the same kind of mistake. Dépelteau complains that Archer continually trots out social structure in application to every social situation, as if Dépelteau thinks social structure even in the abstract – as opposed to any specific social structural configuration – is something that ought to come and go. See Dépelteau (2008) "Relational Thinking: A Critique of Co-deterministic Theories of Structure and Agency,"

We come, finally, to Reed's point (4). Does hermeneutic understanding take precedence over extra-discursive explanation? Yes, actually, in some broad sense it does. I have already conceded as much in Chapter 4. In human affairs, those things that are extra-discursive, like certain social structures or physical events like global warming, have their effects only through human agents and their actions. Thus, the effects of the extra-discursive on human actions will always need to be hermeneutically understood.

Even, moreover, where social structures are extra-discursive, such as, for example, class relations, I have already admitted that they frequently emerge from or arise out of prior constitutive rules, such as rules of property ownership. Ontologically, therefore, those rules come first.

Of course, historically, the rules may not come first. Instead, there is always, as Archer argues, a morphogenetic dialectic involving rules, agents, and structures. Within their structured positions arising from an initial set of rules, agents' struggles may change the rules and hence the structures and their future actions. Where we break into the circle is an analytical decision that reflects our pragmatic interest.

With my concession to the broad picture, there is, however, something misleading about the Geertz and Bordo examples to which Reed has directed us. In both of those cases, the mechanisms at issue – surface motivations and cultural background – are exclusively discursive in nature. Thus, those examples privilege what Reed calls the interpretive epistemic mode.

Other sorts of inquiries, however, will require much more that is extra-discursive. Consider, for example, the great financial crisis of 2008. *The Great Financial Crisis: Causes and Consequences* is actually the title of a terrific book by sociologist John Bellamy Foster and economist Fred Magdoff. A similar book, also excellent with similar diagnosis, is Lim Mah-Hui and Lim Chin's *Nowhere to Hide: The Great Financial Crisis and Challenges for Asia.*[38] A crisis itself is an extra-discursive event. While people may recognize themselves to be in

---

Sociological Theory 26 (1): 51–73; and (2013) Structure and Agency Again ... And Much More," *Contemporary Sociology* 42 (6): 815–817.

[38] John Bellamy Foster and Fred Magdoff (2009) *The Great Financial Crisis: Causes and Consequences* (New York: Monthly Review). Mah-Hui Lim and Chin Lim (2010) *Nowhere to Hide: The Great Financial Crisis and Challenges for Asia* (Singapore: Institute of Southeast Asian Studies).

crisis, the recognition follows rather than creates the crisis, which can obtain whether people recognize it or not. And it is not just the event itself that is extra-discursive but its primary causes as well. Consider the summary statement by Foster and Magdoff:

> Our argument in this book, derived from Magdoff and Sweezy in particular, is that a realistic assessment of recent economic history is best conducted within a framework that focuses on the interrelationship between the stagnation tendency of monopoly capital and the forces that to some extent counter it. The largest of the countervailing forces within the past three decades is financialization – so much so that we can speak today of "monopoly-finance capital." The expansion of debt and speculation that characterized the U.S. economy (and advanced capitalism as a whole) since the late 1960s represented the main means by which the system managed to avoid sinking into a deep slump, while not enabling it to overcome the underlying stagnation tendency. Hence, it is in this complex dynamic that the answers to the present economic predicament are to be found.[39]

The above narrative is complex, and highly wrought by re-signification in terms of theoretical language: monopoly capitalism, financialization, stagnation, and so on. Each such term references a causal mechanism or causal process that together constitutes a conjuncture. That conjuncture in turn constitutes a historical explanation, one that in exact form may well apply uniquely.

Our point, though, in looking at a narrative this time around is different. What we want to observe here is how this narrative differs from the explanations to which Reed drew our attention. In this one, cultural meaning figures less prominently. That is not to say that cultural meaning (for the actors) does not figure at all or perhaps even ultimately. Financial instruments and even capitalism rest on meanings and ultimately on constitutive rules.

But meaning (for the actors) is not what is doing the principal explaining in the passage. Certainly, there is a cultural background, or as Reed would put it a landscape in which the actors are moving. The cultural meanings and background, however, do not themselves explain the particular state of affairs, the crisis, under discussion. What chiefly does the explaining is an extra-discursive relational contradiction and a particular agential attempt to deal with it that results in yet another non-discursive, relational contradiction.

---

[39] Foster and Magdoff, *The Great Financial Crisis*, p. 19.

And, indeed, there is something else very important about the passage, something missing from Reed's own examples. The relevant landscape here is not entirely discursive. Fundamental to the explanation is the whole background signified by the phrase monopoly capitalism. What is so signified is not an element of meaning, of culture, but of non-discursive social structure. Monopoly capitalism is a stage of capitalism so dominated by oligopolies that price competition is no longer the prime mover among powerful individual firms and where, even more relevantly, avenues for new profitable investment have dried up. Certainly, that condition may mean something to the actors who find themselves in it, and certainly it means something to those who have so named it, but in its first instance, monopoly capitalism is not an element of culture, not an intelligible.

What does that mean to say that the designation monopoly capitalism is not an intelligible? Monopoly capitalism certainly sounds intelligible. Remember that we are using intelligibilia as a term of art for cultural content that needs to be understood by specifically hermeneutic interpretation because that content is intrinsically a communication.

Thus, remember that hermeneutic interpretation is distinct from interpretation per se. To understand anything requires interpretation of some sort. That we are in a period of global warming is an interpretation, but it is not a hermeneutic interpretation. Insofar as global warming is an unintended consequence of our collective actions, no one intended it. Thus, that we are in a period of global warming is not a hermeneutic interpretation of discursive reasons but a non-hermeneutic interpretation of causes that are not reasons.

Monopoly capitalism is, similarly, an extra-discursive, unintended consequence of human activity, specifically capitalist activity. As monopoly capitalism was nobody's intention, it has no intended meaning which we might fruitfully subject to hermeneutic interpretation.

The kind of interpretation to which we must subject monopoly capitalism is distinctly non-discursive. By non-discursive interpretation, I mean an examination of monopoly capitalism's non-discursive effects. Chief among them is stagnation. If at the stage of monopoly capitalism productive avenues of investment have dried up, capital will decline to invest, endangering the economic growth requisite for the health of a capitalist economy.

Like the monopoly capitalism that produces it, stagnation itself is extra-discursive, not something with an intended meaning. It is, rather, a structural effect of a structural condition. Because the stagnation confronts investors with a problem, it may eventually bring itself to their attention. With that step, we complete what Archer calls a morphogenetic cycle:

Capitalist competition $\rightarrow$ Monopoly capitalism $\rightarrow$ Stagnation
$\rightarrow$ Capitalist realization

The morphogenetic cycle begins with the structured agency we call capitalist competition – the activity of capitalists within a framework where one's loss is another's gain. That structured agency produces the structural reorganization we call monopoly capitalism, which produces the deleterious structural effect we term stagnation. If, as actually happened, the embedded -actors become aware of the deleterious effect, they may resolve to do something about it. They thus initialize a second morphogenetic cycle, the one to which Foster and Magdoff adduce to explain the crisis.

Financialization $\rightarrow$ Monopoly-finance capitalism
$\rightarrow$ Over-speculation $\rightarrow$ Crisis

By financialization, Foster and Magdoff mean capital's turn from investment in consumer products, the profitable opportunities for which have dried up, to investment in the new financial instruments with which we have all become familiar. And that tendency, which Foster and Magdoff's magazine, *Monthly Review*, closely tracked since the 1980s, has by now become so dominant as to have structurally transformed the system yet again, turning it into what Foster and Magdoff call monopoly-finance capitalism. With diminished opportunities for sound investment, the mode of monopoly-finance capitalism fosters less sound investment, even very unsound investment. In the end, the over-speculation produced the financial crisis.

Our interest here is not whether this explanation of the crisis is right or wrong, but the form it takes. Certainly, what we have here is nothing like a set of positivist equations. Event-regularities play no part. At most there are what might be called regular connections between structural mechanisms and structural forces such as obtains between monopoly capitalism and stagnation. These regularities in the domain of the real do not, however, yield necessarily any specific events because the structural forces can be counteracted, and indeed counteracted in utterly creative ways that exceed any causal closure. Financialization is in fact an eminent example of such agential creativity.[40]

So, clearly, we are far from positivism. But neither does the explanation conform to what Reed calls the interpretive mode of explanation. What is centrally going on in this explanation is not the kind of double-meaning that Reed says characterizes the interpretative mode. That is to say, the mechanisms in play here like stagnation and risk are not at deeper than surface levels of consciousness, but rather not conscious at all.

Admittedly, consciousness and agential interpretation do enter into the explanation. But in contrast with the interpretive mode, they do not govern the whole. Structure, agency, and culture are rather tightly interwoven into different moments of the different morphogenetic cycles. And the relevant background feature or landscape itself is as much structural as it is cultural.

I think in short that I have at least fought Reed to a draw, but a draw may be all I need. In the example I cite, non-discursive explanation is not, as Reed contends, a sub-category of hermeneutic understanding. If anything in my example, hermeneutic understanding is an ingredient of the overall explanation, which also invokes the interplay of extra-discursive mechanisms. In general, I would venture to say, whenever extra-discursive mechanisms play a role in human affairs, say, in the accounts of ANT, the overall form of explanation will not be understanding; understanding will be only an ingredient within.

Alongside such mixed cases, there will be cases like those Reed cites where interpretations of different depth are all that are at issue. In those cases, the overall form of explanation will be interpretive. So if I have made the case for another, non-hermeneutic form of explanation in sociology, I have not thereby ruled out the purely hermeneutic form of explanation that interests interpretivists. That is why I say the match perhaps has been a draw.

Why do I say a draw is all I need? Because in the larger sense of explanation, CR can encompass both sub-forms, the mixed form of explanation and the purely discursive one that Reed calls interpretive.

---

[40] Somehow, too, we are managing easily to juggle structure and agency, a possibility we saw Jeffrey Alexander dismiss. See Alexander (1992) "Recent Sociological Theory Between Agency and Social Structure," *Schweizerische Zeitschrift für Soziologie*, **18** (1): 7–11.

In some cases, the mechanisms at issue will be purely discursive and in some cases not. The explanation will take different forms depending on the case. CR has no problem with that outcome. Conversely, if it attempts to rule out the mixed form, interpretivism unduly deprives sociology of analytical tools otherwise at its disposal and becomes itself a form of idealist reductionism.

7 | *Do we need critical realism?*

Again, please forgive the predictability. I am hardly going to answer this chapter's title question negatively. Clearly, I would not have brought you this far to conclude that we do not need CR after all.

The point of this chapter is to bring everything together, to see how CR compares in terms of similarities and differences with various other theoretical and philosophical positions in sociology. My hope is that even if you are un-persuaded by what I have said so far about CR, the discussion here will at least help you better navigate through the thicket of philosophical commitments across sociological perspectives.

I speak of philosophical commitments, and hopefully by this time it is clear we cannot escape them. We have them and they influence us, whether we recognize them or not. Such being the case, as we sociologists counsel others, so should we think critically ourselves. We should make sure that the positions to which we are philosophically committed are the those that are most defensible.

Although much good social science can still come from faulty philosophical premises, it will not be the best social science it could be. With faulty philosophical premises, moreover, much that might be potentially good social science will not even be entertained. Under the long dominant positivism, for example, ethnography has been devalued and discouraged. Under CR, it is not. So there is a pragmatic payoff here. Like the pragmatists, we in CR – or at least I – do not believe in philosophizing without practical point. However long our sojourn in philosophy may last, our work there should all ultimately relate back to some practical problem of life. In this case, the practical problem is how we best go about doing social science – and how, even more pertinently – we avoid practicing a sham discipline, one that looks like science but is not.

I promised that in this chapter there would be a handy chart, and there it is as Table 7.1. It will facilitate our task of examining similarities and differences across theoretical positions. First, I need to explain a bit what you are seeing, and the first thing to say is that the chart is sort of a mixed bag as it includes both theoretical and metatheoretical positions. The top four positions are philosophical metatheories; the bottom nine are more standard theoretical perspectives in sociology.

Why the mixture? It is true that, in comparison with the metatheoretical positions, it may be less fair to expect the standard sociological perspectives to have explicit commitments on all philosophical concerns. Must standard network theory or Bourdieu, for example, have explicit positions on truth? As far as I know, they do not. At the same time, as they conduct their research and present their results, they must be operating with some idea of truth. Is that idea positivist, postmodern, or what? It is helpful to know which standard sociological perspectives are in need of explicit answers to which questions. For those questions for which the sociological perspectives do have explicit answers, it is also helpful to know where the various answers fall philosophically.

The chart is a mixed bag in two other regards. First, postmodernists would rightly accuse it of essentialism. In more modernist terms, the philosophical and theoretical positions listed ignore or collapse various internal differences within each. Who, for example, are the intepretivists? Here, I have collapsed Symbolic Interactionists, cultural sociologists, hermeneuticists, and others who subscribe to a Verstehen approach to sociology. Do they all agree on everything? Surely not.

Not even do we critical realists all agree on a number of the philosophical matters that run across the columns of the chart. Nor likewise is there complete agreement among the pragmatists or even among Symbolic Interactionists.

So are those X's and dashes not meaningless? No, the positions indicated are not meaningless, but neither should the chart be reified. Consider the chart rather a conversation piece, a place to begin reflection on the different positions represented. For the most part, the X's and dashes reflect what I fallibly consider the main line for each perspective. As we discuss the chart, I will try to reference alternate lines.

Speaking of the X's and dashes, they represent a second way in which the chart is a mixed bag. Both because of the plethora of internal divisions and because of nuanced responses to the listing of philosophical issues, it is not so easy to construct such a chart that has any practical use. To do so, I employed two devices. First, I constructed the

Table 7.1 *Theoretical perspectives by theoretical commitments*

	Agents Humanism (cogito)	Objective Human relations	Intensive methods	Extensive methods	Metatheory	Truth (non-relativist)	Value orientation
Positivism	–	–	–	X	–	X	–
Critical realism	X	X	X	X	X	X	X
Postmodernism/ poststructuralism/ Discourse theory*	–	–	X	–	–	–	X
Pragmatism	X	?	X	–	X	?	X
Interpretivism	X	–	X	–	–	–	?
Social constructionism	–	–	X	–	–	–	–
Analytical sociology	X	–	X	X	–	X	–
Relational sociology	–	X	X	–	–	–	–
Practice theory	–	–	X	–	–	–	–
ANT	X	X	X	–	–	–	–
Standard network theory	–	X	–	X	–	X	–
Marxism / Frankfurt School	X	X	X	?	?	X	X
Bourdieu	–	?	X	X	X	–	X

X Explicitly endorses the category.

– indicates either no explicit position or no support.

* Discourse theory different from discourse analysis.

? Clearly divergent lines within perspective.

headings of philosophical issues to represent explicit endorsements of a position. So, for example, the *Agents* column asks whether the perspectives represented down the rows explicitly endorse humanist accounts of consciously centered agents, what postmodernists disparage as the Cartesian cogito. Similarly, the *Truth* column does not ask whether the different philosophical perspectives have an explicit position on truth but whether they endorse a non-relativist conception of truth. The *Intensive methods* column asks whether intensive research methods are endorsed and the *Value orientation* column whether the perspective departs from value neutrality and the fact/value distinction. And so on.

Formulating the issues in this tendentious way permitted a second device that makes for a clearer chart. It permitted me to collapse lack of any explicit position with explicit opposition to the position represented by the column heading. Both are equally represented by the dashes, which is why I say they too represent a mixed bag.

Is that bag not untenably large? I appeal to the pragmatists among us. The chart is meant to be a tool, a helpful map. With too many symbols across the page, its utility is diminished. It gets harder to read and absorb. So I opted for simplicity and clarity at the expense of precision – which is always a matter of intents and purposes. And the chart is to be accompanied by this text. So we will make the distinction glossed by the dashes, and all will be well – or as John Levi Martin might say, well enough.

The X's too, finally, represent a mixture. Different perspectives may endorse the position of the column heading but in different ways. Such difference shows up most obviously in the commitment to a non-relativist truth shared by both positivism and CR. Positivism holds an epistemic and CR an alethic conception of truth, the two conceptions being quite different. Similarly, although positivism and CR both endorse extensive methods of research, those methods function very differently for the two. Rejecting the covering law model of causal explanation, CR never regards a regularity, however stable, as an explanation in itself. For CR, there is always a need for an explanatory mechanism, involving some kind of causal powers. There are other such differences masked by the common crosses that we also will need to distinguish in our discussion.

I used question marks to designate where perspectives have more than one strong line on the position but where at least one endorses and one opposes it.

Interpreting the chart

Now that the meaning of the chart should be clear, we can begin discussing it. Let us start with the chart's features that are most striking overall. The first striking feature is that only CR has X's entered across all categories. Was that pattern deliberately designed to make CR look uniquely good? Not consciously. Certainly, the chart is designed to highlight the similarities and differences between CR and the other perspectives. Whether that design also makes CR look uniquely good depends on whether it is in fact good to have an X in all columns. If so, then, however value-oriented the design, the design does in fact illuminate an objective difference that is also objectively good. Whether CR comes out looking uniquely good is for the reader to decide in the course of our discussion.

One implication of the X's for CR across all categories is that at some level, CR shares something with each of all the other perspectives. That quality means that CR at least has some potential for unifying sociological practice, although much depends on whether what CR shares with each perspective is in all cases worth sharing. Again, that remains for you to decide.

The second striking feature of the chart taken as a whole is that Marxism and the Frankfurt School seem very closely to coincide with CR. Like CR, they have no dashes but all X's or at least question marks under every category. This pattern is unsurprising. CR was born in a milieu of radical politics and many of its originators – although not all – saw it as the philosophy of science implicit in Marx's work. There are of course differences between standard Marxian approaches and the distinctive views of the Frankfurt School, but on the issues arrayed in the chart they mostly agree if not always in the same way.

A surprise to me personally when I created this chart is how closely Bourdieu aligns with CR. At first, I did not have Bourdieu listed, and he is the only individual there. At first, I had collapsed Bourdieu in with practice theory, and an argument can be made for doing so. Upon reflection, I considered Bourdieu important enough to break out separately and to consider him himself as opposed to the way Americans have appropriated him. So with regard to him, keep in mind that it is Bourdieu himself I will be considering and not Bourdieu's American followers who fall more under practice theory and are placed there.

Let us now look more closely at how the different perspectives approach the different issues listed across the top of the chart. We begin with agency.

Agents

The *Agents* column asks whether the perspectives listed down the rows endorse something like the Cartesian subject – that is, a substantial or ontologically particular center of conscious experience.[1] Certainly, I have argued that CR does endorse such a subject. In this respect, I referred to CR as a humanism.

Just as clearly, poststructuralism does not endorse anything like such a subject. The Cartesian cogito is in fact poststructuralism's coinage to dismiss essentialism in the domain of subjectivity. For the postmodernists and poststructuralists and for postmodernist/poststructuralist discourse theorists, there are no centered persons but only, as with Quine's gavagai, person slices or person phases, or, like the virtual particles of a physical vacuum, subject positions intermittently *interpolated* into fleeting existence by language.[2] Bourdieu as well, it seems to me, resists the Cartesian image, which is one of the features of Bourdieu's sociology I – and Archer – strongly oppose.

I put an X for humanism under Marxism, despite the fact that Louis Althusser's French structuralist version expressly considered Marxism an anti-humanism. Although some critical realists are attracted to Althusser, I consider his line rather a proto-postmodernist abomination.[3] It is unsurprising to me that most still living, former Althusserian Marxists left the Marxist fold completely to become full-fledged postmodernists, or poststructuralists as they now prefer to be called. In its main lines, Marxism is humanist not Lacanian. For its part, the

---

[1] Again without any necessary implication of Cartesian disembodiment, which is not endorsed by CR.

[2] The gavagai reference comes from Norman V. O. Quine (1964) *Word and Object* (Cambridge, MA: MIT Press).

[3] Andrew Collier was very sympathetic to Althusser although not, I think, to his anti-humanism. See Andrew Collier (1990) *Socialist Reasoning: An Inquiry in the Political Philosophy of Scientific Socialism* (New York: Routledge). George Steinmetz likewise seems attracted not only to Althusser but also to Lacan. See George Steinmetz (2013) "Toward Socioanalysis: The 'Traumatic Kernel' of Psychoanalysis and Neo-Bourdieusian Theory," pp. 108–130 in Philip Gorski (ed.), *Bourdieu and Historical Analysis* (Durham, NC: Duke University Press).

Frankfurt School likewise was and continues to be under Habermas humanist in orientation.

For their own different reasons, both relational sociology and standard network theory likewise deny centered agents. Both are relationally reductionist.[4] American relational sociology, we saw, opposes any substances. All substances – their word for ontological particulars – are to be dissolved into yet other relations. Somehow, there will be relations without relata. In place of agents, American relational sociology admits only "agentic orientations" which visit actors, who are ontologically distinct from these visitations.

Although network theory is not all alike, much of it suffers from what Christian Smith calls a "missing persons" problem.[5] According to Barry Wellman, one of the key founders of standard network theory, behavior in network theory "is interpreted in terms of structural constraints on activity, rather than in terms of inner forces within units (e.g., 'socialization into norms') that impel behavior in a voluntaristic, sometimes teleological push toward a desired goal."[6] Thus, in contrast with relational sociology, standard network theory does not so much deny the existence of inner forces like motives; instead, in Durkheimian fashion, standard network theory simply relegates agency entirely to psychology.

Network theory thus becomes a version of Structural Sociology, which imagines that structural explanations can subsist apart from human agency. To the extent that network theorists limit themselves to the constraints that various network arrangements pose to action, the enterprise may be successful. Without appeal to human agents and their motives, however, network theory can explain neither the reproduction nor the transformation of network relations.[7]

Practice theory, equally, as we have seen, would like to do without agents who have anything in their heads. Instead, practice theorists

---

[4] Again, I distinguish American relational sociology from Donati's Italian version, which does not share this quality. See Pierpaolo Donati (2012) *Relational Sociology: A New Paradigm for the Social Sciences* (New York: Routledge).

[5] See Christian Smith (2010) *What Is a Person? Rethinking Humanity, Social Life, and the Moral Good from the Person Up* (Chicago, IL: University of Chicago), pp. 220–276.

[6] Barry Wellman (1997) "Structural Analysis: From Method and Metaphor to Theory and Substance," pp. 19–61 in Barry Wellman and S. D. Berkowitz (eds.), *Social Structures: A Network Approach* (New York: Emerald), p. 20.

[7] Smith, *What is a Person?*.

think – or at least say they think – that structures and culture both can be found entirely embodied in material behavior. To the extent that it pursues this course, practice theory becomes a form of sociological behaviorism.

For its part, ANT does not deny intentional human agency with the implication behind it of centered agents. ANT simply thinks that too much ado is made of this distinction vis-à-vis non-human and even non-conscious agency that does not function in an intentional matter. Whether or not ANT's contention is fruitful or illuminating, as pragmatists would put it, is a separate question. Technically, however, ANT does not deny human agents.

Nor is human agency denied by analytical sociology. On the contrary, to the extent that it is built around rational choice theory, analytical sociology presupposes a very definite model of centered consciousness. Certainly, from the CR perspective, analytical sociology's conception of the human agent is crude and narrow, overly deterministic and overly infused with a logic of utility maximization that underplays the role of quantitatively incommensurable goods.[8] Still, whatever its weaknesses, it is a coherent, consciously centered human agent that analytical sociology endorses.

I did not put an X under agency for social constructionism only because I am unsure there is a main line with an explicit position on the matter. Certainly, in Peter Berger and Thomas Luckmann's classic statement of the position, conscious agents are strongly implied. Berger and Luckmann were, after all, coming from the phenomenological tradition of Husserl, for whom conscious agency was central.

On the other hand, social constructionism has moved far since Berger and Luckmann, often, to Berger's consternation, adopting a postmodern sensibility, so that human agency itself as in performative orientations is represented as mere appearance. In other applications, as in the social studies of science or knowledge (SSK), the whole issue of agency may be marginal. There is, however, no reason in principle for agency to be denied by social constructionism per se.

What about positivism? Strictly speaking, for high positivists like David Hume, there are no coherent selves, just bundles of traits or perceptions that co-occur in consciousness. A committed Humean like

---

[8] See Martha Nussbaum (1992) *Love's Knowledge: Essays on Philosophy and Literature* (New York: Oxford University Press).

Earl Babbie, who, we saw, at least once denied the existence of unobservables like love, would presumably for the same reason deny the
existence of selves. Sociology, however, has few such out-and-out
positivists but instead sociologists who only more or less conform to
positivist principles.

There is no reason in principle why positivistically oriented sociologists must deny the existence of a human self, but that self will not do
much. As ANT suggests, once there is adopted some version of the
positivist covering law model of causality, all causal power is leached
out from the things of the world and deposited instead in the putative
laws. Thus, even should positivists admit the existence of selves, at
most, positivist analyses will simply correlate what they consider
events – prevailing social conditions, mental states, and behaviors.
As again Christian Smith observes, positivist discourse "suggests that
variables, not persons, are the real social agents or actors. Persons, if
anything, are simply the background medium or vehicles through
which variables act or operate."[9]

We come to pragmatism and interpretivism. It seems clear that, like
CR, pragmatism is a humanism strongly committed to consciously
centered agents. In *Experience and Nature*, Dewey sets up experience
and experiencing consciousness as the foundation of philosophy.[10]
William James similarly focused on experience and consciousness.
CR and the pragmatists, then, are allies in this regard.

Allies, similarly, I would say in this regard, are the Symbolic
Interactionists. Yes, there is a tendency for Mead and others to represent consciousness more as a relation than a centered particular, which
Margaret Archer and Christian Smith both find disturbing.[11] I am
inclined to be more accepting. In the sociological lay of the land, it
seems to me that the Symbolic Interactionists clearly mean to affirm
consciously centered agency.

Clearly, as well, the variety of perspectives I am referencing under the
label of interpretivists – Weberians, hermeneuticists, phenomenologists,

---

[9] Smith, *What is a Person?*, p. 285.
[10] John Dewey (1929) *Experience and Nature* (London: George Allen & Unwin).
[11] See Margaret Archer (2001) *Being Human: The Problem of Agency*
(Cambridge: Cambridge University Press); and Christian Smith (2014) *To
Flourish or Destruct: A Personalist Theory of Human Goods, Motivations,
Failure, and Evil* (Chicago, IL: Chicago University Press).

and so forth – all equally endorse a notion of consciously centered agents. The matter is so clear in fact as to warrant no further comment.

Objective human relations

Clearly, as this book contains an entire chapter on the subject, CR certainly endorses objective relations among social positions – human relations like competition, dependency, power, inequality, and the like. Together, these are what CR thinks of as social structure. The same would be true for Marxian perspectives, including the Frankfurt School.

Positivist sociology also certainly endorses a conception of objective social structure, but in its conception, social structure does not consist so much of human relations that connect individuals to each other but rather relations among social facts. These may be causal relations, like the relation Durkheim posited between size and differentiation or more functional relations, but in any case, they generally obtain over the heads of individuals and thus are understood to operate independent of human agency.

Insofar as postmodernists, poststructuralists, and postmodernist or poststructuralist discourse theorists profess to disbelieve in anything ontologically objective, so do they disbelieve in objective social relations. For them, all social relations are discursive and therefore subjective. These approaches – the so-called new materialists aside – fully embracing what CR considers the epistemic fallacy, do not allow for anything extra-discursive.

Also ignoring the extra-discursive are interpretivism and standard social constructionism. Admittedly, from a CR perspective as well, social structural relations are human constructions. They derive from human behaviors and possibly from human constitutive rules. But, for CR, such social structures need not be directly created discursively to exist. Nor do their existence and consequence necessarily require anyone's recognition. In this sense, they are extra-discursive. To the extent that interpretivism and standard social constructionism do not recognize the extra-discursive, they also do not recognize extra-discursive human relations.

For differing reasons, neither analytical sociology nor practice theory acknowledges objective human relations; analytical sociology because it is committed to methodological individualism and practice theory because it is committed to a form of behaviorist reductionism that privileges only practice.

In contrast, relational sociology, standard network theory, and ANT all, like CR, believe in objective social relations. Those on which network theory focuses are a bit narrow – i.e., almost exclusively network ties or flows, but they are, nevertheless, ontologically objective.

I put a question mark under Bourdieu, because as I have remarked in a number of places in this book, I think there are two of him. The Bourdieu of fields believes in objective social relations, although they seem to be very limited – in contrast with Marx – to relations of power and status.[12] On the other hand, there is the more Heideggerian Bourdieu who opposes the subject–object distinction, precluding any notion of classically objective social structure. This would also be the Bourdieu who via an internalized – and hence ultimately subjective – habitus putatively overcomes the structure–agency dichotomy.

What about pragmatism? I put a question mark there too. The reason is that the pragmatists seem all over the map on this one, without what I can see as a main line. In Dimitri Shalin's view, pragmatism also challenges the subject–object dichotomy, which seems to preclude ontologically objective social relations.[13] Also coming from a pragmatist tradition, John Levi Martin tells me that he and his line of

---

[12] It has been my view for some time now that Bourdieu is American sociology's Marx substitute, safely diverting us from political economy to cultural areas of concern. When I look at the sharply upward trajectory of Bourdieu citations that Phil Gorski records, it seems to me likely to coincide with a sharp downturn in Marx citations. See Philip Gorski (2013) *Bourdieu and Historical Sociology* (Durham, NC: Duke University Press). Gorski himself suggests Marxian theory as a major rival to Bourdieu. To my mind, in this comparison, Gorski dismisses Marx too quickly as tied to working class dynamics. To me, rather, capitalist competition rather than power – although that too – is the real pivotal mechanism for Marx. There is in Bourdieu precious little about capitalist competition, which has, accordingly faded from the attention of American sociology. Economic sociology in particular seems to want little to do with it. See comments on this point by Richard Swedberg (2005) "Markets in Society," pp. 233–253 in Neil J. Smelser and Richard Swedberg (eds.), *The Handbook of Economic Sociology* (Princeton, NJ: Princeton University Press).

[13] Dimitri Shalin (1986) "Pragmatism and Social Interactionism," *American Sociological Review* 51 (1): 9–29; and (1991) "The Pragmatic Origins of Symbolic Interactionism and the Crisis of Classical Sociology Symbolic Interactionism," *Studies in Symbolic Interaction* 12: 223–251. For Shalin, relations reduce to social interactions.

it tends more toward nominalism. On the other hand, when I look at William James, I find the following:

The statement of fact is that the relations between things, conjunctive as well as disjunctive, are just as much matters of direct particular experience, neither more so nor less so, than the things themselves. . . . The great obstacle to radical empiricism in the contemporary mind is the rooted rationalist belief that experience as immediately given is all disjunction and no conjunction, and that to make one world out of this separateness, a higher unifying agency must be there.[14]

I don't know, but the above exposition hardly sounds to me like either nominalism or anything that departs from the subject–object distinction. Moreover, it appears a strong endorsement of ontologically objective relationality. Hence, my question mark for pragmatism under this category.

Intensive versus extensive methods

One of the strengths of CR, I have been arguing, is its explicit endorsement of both intensive and extensive methods of research. That strength, I went on to argue, gives it the potential to unify the discipline. With the exception of Bourdieu himself, who actually employed both kinds of methods, all other perspectives either explicitly endorse only one type of method but not the other or do not explicitly address the matter at all. Positivism, of course, endorses only extensive methods, while the standard anti-positivist traditions – interpretivism and postmodernism – favor only intensive methods. Standard network theory as a kind of positivist structural sociology also endorses mostly extensive methods. Although analytical sociology does not say anything explicit on the matter, it does seem at least compatible with either type of method. Social constructionism, ANT, and relational sociology seem to be more associated with intensive methods, although I can imagine at least ANT and relational sociology employing extensive methods as well. In the absence, however, of explicit statements addressing the matter, I entered dashes for them under this category.

What methods are sanctioned by pragmatism? To the extent that pragmatism is associated most with Symbolic Interactionism, we might

---

[14] William James (1909) *The Meaning of Truth: A Sequel to "Pragmatism"* (Prometheus Books). www.authorama.com/meaning-of-truth-1.html.

suppose it sanctions intensive methods. What about extensive methods? As I find no explicit statement within pragmatist writings that speak to that question, I entered a dash for it under extensive methods.

Marxian research has been more associated with intensive methods in general and history in particular, but there is no principled reason that analytical statistics also cannot be used to make Marxian points. The same holds for the Frankfurt School. Nevertheless, given their strong tendencies, I entered only a question mark for these perspectives under this category. Practitioners of these perspectives might thus benefit from a CR take on analytical statistics and its differences from the positivist account of those methods.

Metatheory

I have been calling metatheory the language of inter-paradigm dialogue. It is not so much a distinct language as a register, a theoretical posture that reflects conceptually on theory. It is the theory of theory and as such an analytical level removed from theory.

Put alternately, metatheory is inquiry into the philosophical grounding of our theories, an examination of their most basic philosophical assumptions. It is essentially philosophy of social science. As such, metatheory is anathema to empiricists. From its beginning, empiricist positivism privileged the empirical over the conceptual and accordingly rejected metaphysics as virtually meaningless assertions. Positivism in general therefore is hostile to metatheory.

As a discipline virtually born of positivism, the hostility to philosophy is deeply engrained in sociology. Along with psychology, philosophy is one of sociology's *others*. It is as it were one of the disciplines against which sociology distinguishes its own identity. To embrace metatheory then is to threaten disciplinary boundaries; it is almost disciplinary treason.

It is no wonder then that CR is the only perspective on the chart where I could confidently place an X. Certainly, as I just explained, positivism would not receive an X. It actually should receive an anti-X. Similarly, those perspectives that are positivist in nature – analytical sociology and standard network theory – likewise receive no X's.

By now, it may be less surprising than it might have seemed at first that the avowedly anti-positivist perspectives likewise receive no X's for metatheory. That is because perspectives like postmodernism are empiricist as well. Like positivism, postmodernism rejected metaphysics and embraced just the surface of things. Principled superficiality was, after all, one of the hallmarks of postmodernism.

Social constructionism likewise has its positivist roots. In the original statement of the position, Peter Berger and Thomas Luckmann tried to export philosophical matters – specifically whether there is a real reality – to philosophy, i.e., the discipline. The philosophical question of reality, they maintained, was not the business of sociology.[15] More recently, Harry Collins and Steven Yearley had maintained that the social construction of science should be considered more or less a positivist enterprise, immune to reflexive social constructionism trained on itself.[16] Although some social constructionists may embrace metatheory, my sense is that its appreciation is still largely missing from this tradition.

I again placed a question mark under metatheory for Marxism and the Frankfurt School. Both perspectives have strong philosophical commitments and both encourage philosophical inquiry. But these perspectives do not entirely coincide with the discipline of sociology, and, aside from their specifically CR adherents, it is not clear how many other sociologists within these folds actually do metatheoretical analysis. My sense is that in America it is not many.[17] Thus, while again there is no principled reason for Marxism or critical theory to exclude metatheory as a research agenda, I still would not describe their sociological versions as so far supportive of it. I did enter an X for Bourdieu under this category, largely because Wacquant and Bourdieu's invitation to a reflexive sociology at least sounds like a bid for philosophical self-examination.

Certainly, for many of the perspectives listed, the originating manifestos were actually metatheoretical documents. Herbert Blumer's early articulation of Symbolic Interactionism attacked positivist

---

[15] Peter Berger and Thomas Luckmann (1967) *The Social Construction of Reality* (New York: Anchor).

[16] Harry Collins and Steven Yearley (1992) "Epistemological Chicken," pp. 301–326 in Andrew Pickering (ed.), *Practice and Culture* (Chicago, IL: University of Chicago Press). Collins has now backed off some from this position. He at least himself reflects considerably on the philosophical implications of his approach.

[17] The work of Lauren Langman comes close. See, for example, Langman (2003) "Culture, Identity, and Hegemony: The Body in a Global Age," *Current Sociology* 51: 223–247.

sociology as "variable analysis." Mustafa Emirbayer's "Manifesto for a Relational Sociology" amounted in part to a philosophical critique of the metaphysics of substance. And in their originating statements, analytical sociology and standard network theory as well launched critiques of other perspectives.

For a perspective to receive an X for metatheory, however, it was not enough for the perspective to have been born of a metatheoretical statement. It must also encourage metatheoretical, inter-paradigm dialogue as part of its research agenda. None of the perspectives I just mentioned does so. The intention rather of the originating statements, once the new perspective was so articulated, was for followers simply to conduct a new form of normal science within the new perspective's new parameters. Once born, the inter-paradigm dialogue and the metatheory of the originating statement was supposed to end.

What makes CR different? Well, to be fair, in contrast with the sociological perspectives I have been talking about, CR is not a sociological theory but a philosophical perspective. Its function is not to promote any particular theoretical perspective but to specify what makes for productive scientific activity. From that perspective, it counsels confronting rather than ignoring important scientific differences where they exist. If that requires largely conceptual rather empirical analysis, then, from the CR perspective, so be it.

Pragmatism too seems to encourage metatheoretical argument across paradigms. Certainly John Levi Martin engages in it and seems to encourage it in others. Dimitri Shalin as well explicitly defends it. Asking whether metaphysical issues should be left to philosophers, Shalin cites Kuhn to the effect that all scientific theories contain metaphysical assumptions that need to be scrutinized as part of the scientific enterprise.[18] In that connection, Shalin cites as well mathematician and philosopher Alfred North Whitehead: "If science is not to generate into a medley of ad hoc hypotheses, it must become philosophical and must enter into a thorough criticism of its own foundations."[19] Of course, a medley of ad hoc hypotheses is how many would prefer sociology to be.

---

[18] Dimitri Shalin (1986) "Pragmatism and Social Interactionism," *American Sociological Review* 51 (1): 9–29.

[19] Cited by Shalin, ibid., p. 9.

Truth

Ah, truth. Truth has to do not just with truth but also with our access to objective reality, once again the extra-discursive. And once again it is no surprise to find no X's for postmodernism and its aligned perspectives or for social constructionism and interpretivism. In their main lines, these anti-positivist perspectives all tend toward relativism.[20]

Postmodernist approaches in fact tend to consider truth a device of power. Foucault said as much, drawing attention to regimes of truth.[21] Of course, as I have said all along, to be intelligible, that very claim can only be evaluated as either true or false. Even so, there is merit to examining what Foucault calls regimes of truth, but in doing so, analysts, to make whatever statements they make, still need to reserve their own take on the truth apart from whatever regimes they examine.

To challenge regimes of truth is to engage in ideology critique, something that was done by Marxists and critical theorists long before Foucault. It was not as if Foucault invented the enterprise. What was new –or at least new in the contemporary scene – with Foucault (or at least his epigoni) was the neo-Nietzschean assertion that power was all that truth was about. That claim, I have maintained, is just incoherent.

Some views listed on the chart like relational sociology, ANT, and practice theory, simply offer no explicit statement on truth. We might make inferences based on their positivist or anti-positivist leanings, but in these cases I did not consider the leanings strong enough to be sure. In the absence of anything firmer, I entered dashes. Conversely, I did consider standard network theory and analytical sociology positivist enough to align them with that philosophical perspective.

Positivism, like CR, definitely does believe in truth and in its main line tends to be realist about at least what can be observed. The main difference here is that positivism, supporting an epistemic account of truth, is foundationalist in its orientation, whereas CR, holding to an alethic account of truth, is explicitly fallibilist in orientation.

Marxian perspectives in general and the Frankfurt School in particular believe in truth and in a strong extra-discursive or materialist element. Certainly, the Marxian concepts of ideology and false

---

[20] We did see, however, that Herbert Blumer at least believed in truth and reality.
[21] Michel Foucault (1982) *The Archaeology of Knowledge* (New York: Vintage).

consciousness, implicitly shared by the Frankfurt School, make little sense without correlative concepts of truth and true interests. As I argued at the very beginning, moreover, what postmodernist critiques seemed to forget, if there is no truth, then moral critique completely loses its bite, becoming as a Foucauldian analysis would have it, just another, manipulative manifestation of power. Unless what is criticized is truly objectionable, there is no reason for anyone to heed the critique. There is no reason to pay any attention to an unpleasant, unflattering view that has no more validity than a self-congratulatory one.

Both in its early and later Habermasian phase, the Frankfurt School may have had its own distinct, Hegelian account of truth, but it shares with Marxian perspectives in general an underlying commitment to objective reality. It thus was not difficult to place an X in this box. Bourdieu may have a conception of truth that informs his sociology, but at the very least it is not clear. I therefore entered a dash here for him.

I again entered a question mark for pragmatism under truth. Once again that was because I detect three separate lines. One line again comes from Dimitri Shalin, who strongly disputes the subject–object distinction and therefore objective reality in the classical ontological sense. His view, following Mead, is that the world as we encounter it is always in part the creation of our interpretations of it, implying he says, "the possibility of multiple realities, or to use James's favorite expression, 'the pluralistic universe,' comprising many worlds, each one rational in its own way, each reflecting alternate lines of action, ends, and situations."[22] Such a world, Shalin goes on to say, "is not objective in the traditional sense – it has no being in itself; it is not a world of independent realities such as might be known by some ideal absolute subject."[23]

In *How to Make Our Ideas Clear*, on the other hand, as Shalin admits, Charles Sanders Peirce offered a more classically objective view of truth and reality, depending on triangulation in science to arrive at consensus:

This [scientific] activity of thought by which we are carried, not where we wish, but to a fore-ordained goal, is like the operation of destiny. No modification of the point of view taken, no selection of other facts for study, no natural bent of mind even, can enable a man to escape the predestinate

[22] Ibid., p. 11.   [23] Ibid., p. 13.

opinion. This great hope is embodied in the conception of truth and reality. The opinion which is *fated* to be ultimately agreed to by all who investigate, is what we mean by the truth, and the object represented in this opinion is the real. That is the way I would explain reality.[24]

In contrast with CR's alethic view of truth, Peirce's ideal consensus theory of truth is, like Habermas's ideal speech situation, epistemic. It is nevertheless realist. Interestingly, although Shalin observes that among the pragmatists William James had the most difficulty distancing himself from charges of subjectivism, James actually embraces explicitly, like CR, the correspondence theory of truth:

"Truth," I there say, is a property of certain of our ideas. It means their agreement, as falsity means their disagreement, with reality. Pragmatists and intellectualists both accept this definition as a matter of course.[25]

Like CR, James is explicitly saying that correspondence with reality is the meaning – not necessarily the criterion – of truth. From there, of course, James goes on to specify more pragmatic criteria of truth. He asks what is the "cash value" of truth in pragmatic terms. One answer he gives is not far from what a critical realist would say:

TRUE IDEAS ARE THOSE THAT WE CAN ASSIMILATE, VALIDATE, CORROBORATE, AND VERIFY. FALSE IDEAS ARE THOSE THAT WE CANNOT. That is the practical difference it makes to us to have true ideas; that therefore is the meaning of truth, for it is all that truth is known as. (Capitals in original)[26]

A critical realist would largely agree. In *Experience and Nature*, Dewey as well seems to want a distinction between subject and object, arguing that "we believe many things not because the things are so, but because we have become habituated through the weight of authority, by imitation, prestige, instruction, the unconscious effect of language, etc."[27] The distinction Dewey makes here between what is so and what we think is so is exactly the work done by our concepts of truth and reality. Suggested in fact is the correspondence theory, and Dewey goes on to identify mind-independent, objective reality in a manner CR likewise would affirm:

[24] Charles Sanders Peirce (1878) *Popular Science Monthly* 12 (January) 286–302. www.peirce.org/writings/p119.html.
[25] James, *The Meaning of Truth.*   [26] Ibid.
[27] Dewey, *Experience and Nature*, p. 14.

Even in such a brief statement as that just quoted, there is compelled recognition of an object of experience which is infinitely other and more than what is asserted to be alone experienced. There is the chair which is looked at; the chair displaying certain colors, the light in which they are displayed; the angle of vision implying reference to an organism that possesses an optical apparatus. Reference to these things is compulsory, because otherwise there would be no meaning assignable to the sense qualities which are, nevertheless, affirmed to be the sole data experienced.[28]

Again, no critical realist would disagree. Nor would any critical realist disagree with what Dewey goes on to assert: "the primacy and ultimacy of the material."[29]

If Peirce, James, and Dewey reflect a more realist, second stream of thought in pragmatism, John Levi Martin represents yet a third alternative. Martin reflects the tradition we more usually associate with pragmatism: That truth refers more to the productive results of practice; that in more mundane contexts, what we mean by true is what repays our practical efforts.

Critical realists would not dispute that what Martin mentions is an aspect of truth or, more properly, a consequence of truth. I say more properly because as realists, critical realists would ask of Martin why it is that some activities repay our efforts, our suggested answer being that the beliefs on which those activities rest are true – or at least true enough. "True enough" might well satisfy Martin.

Here and now, however, is not the place to haggle out all these differences. The point here was to explain the question mark under truth for pragmatism. I presume that objective has been accomplished.[30]

Value orientation

We come finally to value orientation, which we should be able to cover fairly quickly. Positivism of course, which strongly upholds the fact/value distinction, completely opposes any kind of value orientation in

---

[28] Ibid., pp. 17–18.   [29] Ibid., p. 18.

[30] I have neglected here the neopragmatism of Richard Rorty, of which CR – and Bhaskar in particular – is highly critical. The various positions it encompasses – the superfluity of truth, the denial of centered consciousness, our imprisonment in language, and so on – have been covered here as they relate to other perspectives. For a full critique of Rorty himself, see Roy Bhaskar(1989) *Reclaiming Reality* (New York: Verso).

research. Similarly, for that reason, equally opposed to value orientations would be all perspectives aligned with positivism. Here, I would include analytical sociology and standard network theory. Although not necessarily positivist, standard social constructionism as well. Peter Berger, for example, always tried to hew toward value-free sociology.[31] I would also place ANT in that category. At least I see no social cause that ANT particularly champions. I similarly see no encompassing cause – beyond the promulgation of an odd view of culture – that is endorsed by practice theory. Ditto for relational sociology. Individually, relational sociologists may have a value orientation, but as far as I can see, the perspective as a whole does not.

Just as clearly, both postmodernism and CR, being strongly antipositivist and strongly opposed to the fact/value distinction, just as strongly support value orientations in research. Postmodernism and its allied perspectives are closely associated with the value orientations represented by the politics of identity, most especially the LGBTQ movement. Similarly, CR is strongly supportive of value-oriented research, as is Marxism and the Frankfurt School. Pragmatism, too, as Shalin argues, was associated with progressive politics and therefore endorsed, if just as a matter of pragmatics, value orientations. I include Bourdieu here as well, as his own work was a challenge to institutionalized power in the cultural sphere.

It may seem surprising to see a question mark under value orientation for interpretivism, but remember this category is a bit of a mixed bag. It was that arch-interpretivist, Max Weber, who penned our most important statement of value neutrality in social research. Similarly, as Shalin argues, I think correctly, Symbolic Interactionism has not generally exhibited any strong value orientation. Why then the question mark? Because there is some evidence of value orientation in this tradition. I think especially of Howard Becker's *Outsiders* or, later, of Rick Fantasia's *Cultures of Solidarity*.[32] And as Shalin goes on to argue, there is no reason why Symbolic Interactionism ought not to be more value-oriented.[33]

---

[31] See, for example, Peter Berger (2011) *Adventures of an Accidental Sociologist: How to Explain the World Without Becoming a Bore* (New York: Prometheus).

[32] Rick Fantasia (2001) *Cultures of Solidarity* (Berkeley, CA: University of California Press). Howard Becker (1997) *Outsiders: Studies in the Sociology of Deviance* (New York: Free Press).

[33] Shalin, "Pragmatism and Social Interactionism."

But must I become a critical realist?

"Okay, fine," you say. "I agree with X's everywhere that CR has them. All across the board. But must I become a critical realist?" No, clearly, you need not. Of course, if you agree with all the X's where CR has them and, moreover, agree with the line CR takes where those X's are placed, then are you not already a critical realist?

"But I do not want to identify myself as such." Okay. Is that because you must be free of all labels? Would you at least label yourself a sociologist?

Perhaps it is just philosophical labels you eschew. That predilection is understandable. I have been saying all along that philosophy is one of sociology's others. So as a sociologist, it is quite understandable that you might resist identifying with any specific philosophy of science. You are being true to your kind.

Remember though that CR is not a sociological theory. No one is asking you to do what might be called CR research. What you are being asked to do is what Bourdieu asks you to do: Pay at least some attention to the philosophical grounding of your research, to what ontology you assume, what views of causality you hold, and so on. And to continually reflect on those matters in a manner that might be described as fallibilist or open to correction.

When you engage in such critical reflection, where do your answers locate you? Are you a positivist, a pragmatist, a poststructuralist, what? In the landscape I have elsewhere called *critical space*, the issue concerns self-positioning. Positioning ourself in a critical space of arguments and counterarguments and constantly requiring ourselves to defend or modify that position is what we sociologists mean by critical thinking. And to do that, it helps, however tentatively we may hold it, to articulate for ourselves what our current position actually is. Given the complexity of the issues, it is always legitimate to answer "none of the above" or "nowhere yet," but if we are committed to critical thinking, we do not forget the *yet* and keep trying to place ourselves somewhere.[34]

---

[34] That is, somewhere defensible.

8 | *So what do we do with it?*

First, let me answer a question not asked by the title: What do we not do with CR? I said it at the end of the last chapter, and Christian Smith says I always say it. I say it again here: CR is not a theory; therefore do not treat it as such. Strictly speaking, there is no CR explanation of anything. No more than there is a positivist or post-positivist account of this or that. What is the positivist theory of social stratification? There may be multiple theories of stratification all positivist in nature, but there is no particular theory that is singularly *the* positivist theory of stratification or of anything. The same goes for CR.

Like positivism, postmodernism, or pragmatism, CR is a metatheory rather than a theory. As such it parameterizes – from its criteria – what good theories are. Thus, it provides grounding for what it considers tenable research and challenge to research that departs from its premises. But that is all it does.

Is that enough? Enough to explain anything? No, but it is still something. Something needed and something important.

So how do we use CR? In the first place we use it for defense and for attack. We know that from the positivist point of view, which still reigns in sociology, that ethnography and historical narrative are suspect. Not so from the standpoint of CR. From the standpoint of CR, neither of these approaches is second best. Instead, from a CR perspective, even purely descriptive work is scientifically important. It is important to know what is out there, especially if attention has not previously been drawn to what is described and especially if, in the process, what is identified is described in theoretical language that highlights the significance of what is identified.

From a CR perspective as well, neither ethnography nor historical narrative need encompass only description. Insofar as CR separates causation from generality, ethnographic description of operative mechanisms can contribute to causal explanation even if what operates does so in only one place and time. Historical narrative, on the other

hand, is the only way to bring together the causal effects of conjunctures of mechanisms. As I said before, narrative, not a regression
equation, is the canonical form of a CR explanation as it is of any
scientific account of anything in the real world outside the laboratory.

Narrative is particularly apt, in fact, for showing the combined effect
of structure, culture, and agency. On the one hand, the effects of
structure and culture show up mainly in the thoughts and actions of
individuals. But because those socially structured thoughts and actions
remain creative, they do not necessarily follow regular patterns. Given
what is perhaps a unique conjuncture of structural and cultural mechanisms, the ensuing thought and behavior may well itself be unique.
Unlike a statistical correlation, narrative can trace how thought
and action, while remaining creative, were still nevertheless a (nondeterministically) caused cultural reaction to structural forces.[1] This
whole explanatory possibility is opened up by CR in a way that is just
precluded by positivism, or even postmodernism, which denies both
coherent agents and objective structures – not to mention coherent
narratives.[2] It is not, however, just defense or philosophical warrant
that is being served here – as important as that function is – but also a
greater understanding of all that intensive research approaches can
afford.

It is not only ethnography and narrative history that receive philosophical legitimacy from CR, but value-laden research as well. From
the positivist perspective, activist research is highly suspect. The positivist image of the proper scientific observer is one who is absolutely
neutral about whatever he or she is proposing to study. That stance
precludes study of a social movement in which one participates oneself.
Not so from a CR perspective. CR expressly challenges the equation of
objectivity with neutrality. From the CR perspective, it is not neutrality
that is to be demanded of competent scientific researchers, but intellectual honesty – the honesty to admit when their own expectations go
unmet, the honesty to admit when rivals have the better argument. Of
course, given the ever-present possibility of counterargument, it is not

---

[1] Again, I take this to be part of the point of Iddo Tavory and Stephen
Timmermans (2013) "A Pragmatist Approach to Causality in Ethnography,"
American Journal of Sociology 119 (3): 682–714.

[2] For a fuller account of narrative as the way to reconcile structure and agency, see
Douglas Porpora (1980) *The Concept of Social Structure* (Westport, CT:
Greenwood Press).

always easy to say when these moments have arrived, when, that is, the available defensive arguments lose their plausibility. That moment will be different for different researchers, but all must maintain an openness to its arrival.

Defense is not the only function served by CR. The various ontological commitments of CR also afford resources for attack. Sociologists often don't think in terms of attack and defense, but in part science is a contentious practice, a matter of conjectures and refutations. A conjecture or claim is put forward and stands only if it resists criticism – which is a form of attack.

From whence does criticism come? Sometimes it comes from our guts, which means one of two things. One thing our guts might reflect is our own lived experience. Our lived experience, like our passion, is a theoretical resource. It directs us to issues. Sociology often trains us out of it. As Christian Smith observes in *What is a Person?*, we have been trained to accept as sociological truths theories that run completely counter to the way we live our lives.[3]

In some important ways, our critical thinking is actually turned off by disciplinary conventions. Turn it back on! Like the child in the fable of *The Emperor's New Clothes*, start asking the embarrassing questions from your own lived experience that sociology prefers you not to ask. And don't just ask those questions: Turn them into research projects, projects that challenge disciplinary shibboleths.

It is not, however, always just our lived experience to which our guts direct us. Our guts may also signal our tacit reliance on one or another theoretical framework we have absorbed without ever having articulated it to ourselves. How much better, how much more deployable to articulate it?

As a formal metatheory or philosophy of science, CR articulates a range of ontological commitments that foster a corresponding range of theoretical questions to be lodged against any theory that is encountered. Does the theory – say a Bourdieusian account of academia – involve a defensible understanding of agency? Does it account for structure? How does it understand causality?

Similarly, can we effectively in Foucauldian fashion treat discourse as if it were not produced by actors motivated to produce it from

---

[3] Christian Smith (2010) *What is a Person? Rethinking Humanity, Social Life, and the Moral Good from the Person Up* (Chicago, IL: Chicago University Press).

specific structured sites? Can we, as per Branwyn Davies and Rom Harré's social positioning theory, talk of how actors position each other in conversation without similarly assuming that there are such things as actors who do such positioning work?[4] And can there be positions without relations? Or, per relational sociology, relations without relata?

These questions are not just ammunition for the delivery of inter-paradigmatic bombs. To the extent that science progresses through conjectures and refutations, it grows through scientific practitioners knowing with which questions to challenge each other and from there what further research might be fruitful. Thus do sites of attack turn into potential research projects, projects that lead somewhere theoretically interesting and not just to record another county heard from. CR in particular prompts questions that sociology – and especially American sociology – does not currently ask.

In the end, however, although CR is a valuable heuristic for asking important research questions, CR is not generally, in my opinion, the place to begin formulating a research study. Those looking for a place to begin should begin with whatever passionately engages them.

That advice is not necessarily easy to follow. Undergraduates often come to me asking my advice about graduate programs in sociology. "Well," I ask them, "What are you interested in?"

"Sociology," they tell me. Not a great answer. I have to do deep therapy with them to elicit something more helpful. Perhaps I can get them to say, "gender." They are interested in gender.

"Well, what about gender?" It is like pulling teeth. The promising researcher, however, eventually learns to pull these teeth himself or herself. The promising researcher learns to internalize a voice like mine. To internalize it and to answer it.

These questions are not particularly CR questions. As I said, I do not think CR is the place to start. I advise against asking oneself how to do a CR study of gender. That question is not what one should be asking.

What should beginning CR researchers be asking? Well, they should be asking first whether the literature on gender or whatever it is they are interested in has answered all the questions that are of interest. Have all questions been answered satisfactorily? Here, as I suggested

---

[4] Bronwyn Davies and Rom Harré (1990) "Positioning: The Discursive Production of Selves," *Journal for the Theory of Social Behaviour* 20 (1): 43–63.

above, CR can help as a heuristic. Do the answers to the questions employ defensible accounts of agency? Has social structure been adequately taken into account. Culture? What remains to be done?

Once prospective researchers determine what remains to be answered, they still are not necessarily ready to bring in CR in any formal way. The next step is to determine with what theoretical perspective they resonate. Is it Symbolic Interactionism? Marxism? Bourdieu or Foucault? Perhaps, then, prospective researchers should accept Bourdieu and Wacquant's invitation to a reflexive sociology so as to ask themselves whether their favored perspective gives us a full picture and whether it entails any philosophically untenable positions that at least need repair.

The repair may itself be the point of a research project aimed at bolstering a perspective to which one is overall attracted. I personally think, for example, that Davies and Harré's account of social positioning is a wonderful piece of work that provides almost an algorithm for future study. But I also think they are seriously wrong in what they say about structure and about agency. So someone attracted to this perspective might, following CR, do some empirical research from the social positioning perspective that brings to empirical light how important to that perspective is structure or agency or both. Attack, therefore, need not be deployed just to undermine but also to build up.

So a beginning question is whether theoretical repair is to be part of the work the prospective researchers plan to undertake or whether the prospective work will just entail a philosophical assumption different from that perspective's philosophical mainstream. That type of question, stemming from CR considerations, is the type of issue that prospective researchers should consider.

There is another category of question to which CR may prompt us. Our discipline goes through sensibility cycles. I came up in an era when many of the New Left entered the academy, a Left that was pretty much a political economic Left. A prominent research agenda then was directed at social change, political economy, corporate power, inequality, and war. The questions asked and perspectives addressed to them reflected those interests. In sociology, functionalism was abandoned in favor of a whole range of new perspectives better able to address social change and human action. Shortly thereafter, the political economic Left was eclipsed by a new cohort of graduate students reflecting a more cultural Left, reflecting social identity movements.

The dominant research agenda accordingly changed, and with that change there changed too the theoretical perspectives sociology came to emphasize. In America, the culture section mushroomed and the Marxist section withered.

Like lay people, even we sociologists tend to reify the present, to suppose in a Whiggish fashion that what prevails now is the culmination of best sense and not just a historically accidental sensibility. So one question that researchers might ask themselves is what questions the discipline is not or no longer even asking and whether they are important. Canvassing the various ontological categories represented by CR – agency, structure, truth, values, and so forth – may help to prompt such larger questioning of the discipline and the research direction one comes to pursue. It would be salutary for the discipline if more sociologists asked what important questions were going unanswered in the discipline, if more would traverse roads less followed.

As any dissertation chair will advise, whatever question one decides to pursue, it is necessary for the prospective researcher to narrow down the prospective topic of study, to formulate a project doable in the time to be allotted to it. Again, although the issue is not specific to CR, it may be that what one thinks one wants to study actually depends on prior findings that need to be studied first. Here, CR can help by orienting one toward interacting mechanisms and their conjuncture. It may even be a version of CR transcendental argument that prospective researchers need to entertain: What needs to be true for the phenomenon a researcher wants to study even to be a possibility? Does the researcher know that those prior possibilities obtain? If not, then maybe the existence of those prior conditions are actually what needs to be studied.

I stated the above issue in terms that are highly abstract. Can I supply a concrete example? Yes, sort of. At the risk of boring, I refer once again to my own work for *Post-Ethical Society*. I set out wanting to know what explains the privatization of morality, the retreat of moral reasoning from the public to the private domain. What causes that retreat? That question is a very good one if I do say so myself, but the prior question is whether there truly is such a privatization of morality. Certainly, if there is no such phenomenon, then nothing is going to explain it. So prior even to searching for the causes of the thing – in this case the privatization of morality, I needed to do something that had not originally occurred to me as a research project: Determine whether what I think I want to explain even obtains. As I mentioned in Chapter 2, following Isaac Reed, who follows Merton, often the first thing we need to do is "establish the phenomenon."[5] That prior task meant I actually needed to reformulate the research work I had to do.

It is such self-critical process that moves us back a step that is what I am talking about. What is required to do here is less empirical than careful conceptual analysis and a knowledge of what the literature on the topic so far has shown or failed to show.

Speaking of the literature on a topic, whether one plans statistical work or ethnography, one should enter research with two different conversations in one's head – and actually keep those conversations going throughout. One conversation is a dialogue between the theoretical literature and one's own theoretical expectations. How does what I intend to say add to what others have said? Whose positions am I supporting and whose am I challenging? The other conversation is between what one thinks one is going to say, come the time to report in, and what one actually finds, whether the findings come in the form of statistics, ethnographic field notes, or interviews.

Within this double dialectic, there is constant need for revision: "That is what I thought was happening, but now I find this. What is the relevance of this finding to the literature? What can I now say and is it still important?" This double conversation between self and data and self and literature needs to go on constantly. It is a version of grounded theory, although not the original, simplistic, positivist version that imagined we could go into research as blank states and just let the data affect us.

So this double dialectic of the research process is not specific to those who subscribe to a CR perspective. What CR can allow one, though, should time permit, is to think in terms of mixed methods. Because there are no canonical CR methods – at least from my perspective, one is free to entertain and utilize all methodologies.

Yet, although CR countenances analytical statistics, it must always be remembered that it does not do so in service to general laws. What that comment means is that for us, statistical equations never become the

[5] See Isaac Reed (2011) *Interpretation and Social Knowledge: On the Use of Theory in the Human Sciences* (Chicago, IL: University of Chicago), pp. 15–16.

explanation for what is happening but only evidence that one thing or another is happening with some frequency or perhaps that more of one thing is happening than another. Even when we insert an intervening variable into our regression equations, the new, more complex equation does not attain the status of an explanation. The intervening variable may signal the operation of a mechanism, but what that mechanism is and how it operates still need to be explained discursively.

The bottom line is to question the methodological type of research question we are asking, and this meta-question does take a CR form. In particular, is our research question a matter of how and why or is it more a matter of whether and where?

Again, the above formulation, meant to be pneumonic, is a bit too compact and abstract. Let me elaborate. If our question is a matter of how and why, then we are asking how or why it happens that something occurs. In that case, we are asking for the identification of a mechanism or a conjuncture of mechanisms. Our answer, then, if it is not to be just conjecture, which is sometimes appropriate, suggests research that is more intensive or qualitative in nature. We may want to show ethnographically, as in *Tally's Corner*, how a particular structure exerts its effects on behavior or, as in *Talking of Love*, how people draw on culture differently all to like effect. If conjunctures are at issue, then the research will likely take the form of narrative history.

As I have said, in my own research for *Post-Ethical Society*, my colleagues and I eventually realized we needed to show how in the secular press moral matters are consistently reframed as matters of strategy or prudence. That was a *how* question that accordingly called for a mechanism. The operative mechanism is textual reframing, not something that can be explicated via statistics. The how of textual reframing needs to be shown descriptively. It requires qualitative discourse analysis.

What did constitute a statistical question, because it was a matter of counts, was whether such textual reframing was general to secular American discourse. And when our question turned to whether such reframing occurred more in secular than in religious discourse, our question became an issue of where: Where (or in which discourse) did such framing appear with greater frequency and where (in which discourse) did it occur with less? Because that question was a matter of comparative counts, it too called for quantitative, statistical analysis.

The quantitative question is important too. Still, however, the statistical analysis did not explain why – why, as we found, secular publications are much less likely than religious publications to engage in moral reasoning. Our answer there we did leave as a conjecture, which means it is left for someone else potentially to research further.

The research questions with which the prospective researcher enters the field depend in part on the theoretical state of play in the literature on that topic. There seems only a very few sociologists concerned with macro-moral discourse, i.e., discourse about macro-moral matters like war, genocide, terrorism, and torture. Because there had been little written on this topic by anybody, when my colleagues and I began our research for *Post-Ethical Society*, we did not have much by way of expectation. A number of people, like Stephen Hart, Michèle Lamont, and Thomas Luckmann, had suggested that, like religion, morality might be privatized. That was about it.

As I said, with that state of play, it was premature to ask a causal question like "What is causing the privatization of morality?" We first had to confirm whether indeed morality is privatized. That task called not for causal analysis but description, appropriate description, and operationalization: What validly counts as the privatization of morality?

My point is that we enter the research process informed by the theoretical literature on the topic and with questions that result from the state of play in that literature. Actually, though, the state of play determines more than just the research questions we ask. From a CR perspective, it also determines to an extent what counts as good research.

Positivism sets up an ideal, decontextualized standard for all research. Being a foundational perspective, for positivism, if there is no certainty, there is no truth. Of course, no research study, particularly no non-experimental study in the social sciences, can hope to avoid all the threats to validity that we learn. So in reality, it is the rare social science study that comes close to the ideal, that establishes anything with certainty. I say rare, but I actually don't know of any.

The question is how far can your study depart from the ideal and still be good? Although positivism offers no answer to that question, in practice, the answer depends on two factors: (1) how hard-assed peer reviewers are likely to be; and (2) what passes for good research in that area, given the theoretical and scholarly state of play and the research difficulties involved in the topic's study.

On its own, the first criterion is clearly arbitrary. There is no empirical research study – not even one that is experimental in form – that can escape criticism. As the sociologists of science have shown us, even the best experimental findings are fodder for debate.[6] The second criterion – what passes for good research in an area – is a much fairer criterion. Suppose it is difficult for anyone to administer a truly randomized opinion poll somewhere on some topic. It may be, then, that all scholars who research that topic in that place rely on convenience samples. In such cases, it would seem inappropriate to reject for publication an individual paper on the grounds that it failed to employ random sampling.

Any deficiency applies instead to the sub-field as a whole rather than any individual paper. Of course, it may be quite appropriate to fault the entire sub-field on such grounds, particularly if better methods are possible. In the absence of better methods, the question is whether faulty data are better than no data.

Positivistically minded thinkers may say no, feeling that, unlike no data, faulty data can lead to faulty conclusions. But faulty conclusions can be corrected whereas silence cannot. Instead of being cowed by those who worry that our account harbors some unknown errors somewhere, we should ask in turn what error they think there is and invite them to do their own research to confirm it. The point is that truth does not spring full-blown from our methods like Athena from the head of Zeus. Truth is instead something toward which we often grope, and as such something we often obtain only through slow, individually erroneous steps.

In practice, sociologists are always working with faulty data. It would seem better to embrace a philosophy of science that actually admits or allows for that clear reality. CR does. CR epistemology, remember, is alethic. According to that perspective, the truth is what it is apart from our methods, although we only know what is true through our methods. Or, to be more precise, we have only our best chance of knowing what the truth is through our methods, because our knowledge of the truth is always fallible.

Thus, in science, CR does not expect the truth to emerge necessarily from a single study. It may take a range of different studies on an issue,

---

[6] Harry Collins is excellent on this point. See Collins (1992) *Changing Order: Replication and Induction in Scientific Practice* (Chicago, IL: University of Chicago Press).

all with different faults but all pointing the same way before we begin to get some confidence about what the truth might be. Such being the case, the CR advice to the individual researcher is to do the best one can methodologically, minimally as well as what passes for good research in that field of study, better if one can, perhaps correcting for methodological deficiencies in the literature even if it means incurring others, and not to sweat the remaining deficiencies over much. Of course, if one can employ a new method that comprehensively challenges all that came before, better still, but that prospect does not often present itself.

There is a final way to use CR that is truly distinctive and which brings us back to my opening remarks in this book. It is the most subversive way to use CR so far and not for the faint of heart. As I said at the very beginning of this book, sociology – American sociology particularly – socializes its new recruits into normal science, routine work within a paradigm.

There is absolutely nothing wrong with normal science. Science would not get done without it. The problem is when absolutely everyone is steered exclusively to normal science, when they are counseled against asking the big questions that cut across paradigms. It is especially a problem when, as in sociology, what we have is a plethora of paradigms of unclear compatibility. Can they all be completely right? Is there no way to work toward larger synthesis? Sociology has dubbed itself a multi-paradigm discipline, and we all nod our heads as if that christening completely legitimates the state of affairs.

By rights, however, our current multi-paradigm condition is a scandal. It suggests the discipline's inability to offer any comprehensive account that can cut across particular issues. It is not a state of affairs in which to take pride but one that betokens synthetic failure. In physics, the reconciliation of quantum mechanics and general relativity is a matter of keen concern. In sociology, the lack of reconciliation among our different paradigms leaves us indifferent. That lack of concern signals the reign of abject empiricism and a disciplinary inability to stomach long conceptual questions that cannot be answered with more data. Unfortunately, as the postmodernists in general and social constructionists in particular have amply demonstrated, data alone cannot adjudicate across paradigms.

What is needed to adjudicate across paradigms is not more data but deeper conceptual analysis. What is needed is a philosophical step back from each particular paradigm so as to examine their taken-for-granted assumptions. That is a metatheoretical task that often moves us outside of empirical sociology into metaphysics. The very word evokes horror in empiricists, which includes both positivists and post-modernists alike. Yet, as long as we decline to enter into metaphysical debate about fundamental ontology, the postmodernists are right that what we are left with is a relativist aporia.

Whereas empiricism in either its positivist or postmodern form discourages metaphysical inquiry, CR positively encourages it. It is CR therefore that distinctly promotes what is needed for inter-paradigm communication and for the great synthetic task left undone by a multi-paradigm discipline.

Yet, as the needed conceptual work does not conform to the positivist picture of science, our discipline actively discourages it. Were sociologists physicists, they would have complained about Schrödinger's cat and the Einstein–Rosen–Podolsky argument: "Away with all these silly thought experiments! Serve us more data." Then quantum mechanics would have been left in the same condition as sociology today. Fortunately, although real scientists think they are positivists, they actually do not act that way. Unfortunately, sociologists do. We need more intrepid souls. For them, CR is waiting.

Bibliography

Alexander, Jeffrey, "Action and Its Environments," pp. 289–318 in Jeffrey Alexander, Richard Giesen, Richard Münch, Neil J. Smelser (eds.), *The Micro–Macro Link*, Berkeley, CA: University of California, 1987.

"Recent Sociological Theory Between Agency and Social Structure" *Schweizerische Zeitschrift für Soziologie* 18 (1) (1992): 7–11. http://ccs.research.yale.edu/alexander/articles/1992/alexander_agcyrmk2.pdf.

Alexander, Jeffrey and Philip Smith, "The Strong Program in Cultural Theory: Elements of a Structural Hermeneutics," pp. 135–149 in Jonathan Turner (ed.), *Handbook of Sociological Theory*. New York: Plenum, 2002.

Alston, William, *A Realist Conception of Truth*. Ithaca, NY: Cornell University Press, 1997.

Althusser, Louis, *For Marx*. New York: Verso, 2006.

Anscombe, G. E. M., *Intention*. Oxford: Basil Blackwell, 1957.

Apel, Karl Otto, *The Response of Discourse Ethics to the Moral Challenge of the Human Situation as Such and Especially Today*. Belgium: Peeters, 2003.

Appiah, Kwame Anthony, *Experiments in Ethics*. Cambridge, MA: Harvard University Press, 2010.

Archer, Margaret, *Being Human: The Problem of Agency*. Cambridge: Cambridge University Press, 2001.

Culture and Agency: The Place of Culture in Social Theory. Cambridge: Cambridge University Press, 1988.

Making Our Way through the World. Cambridge: Cambridge University Press, 2007.

"Morphogenesis versus Structuration: On Combining Structure and Action," *British Journal of Sociology* 33 (4) (1982): 455–483.

Realist Social Theory: The Morphogenetic Approach. Cambridge: Cambridge University Press, 1995.

"Social Morphogenesis and the Prospects of Morphogenetic Society," pp. 1–24 in Margaret Archer (ed.), *Social Morphogenesis*. Dordrecht: Springer, 2013.

Structure, Agency and the Internal Conversation, New York: Cambridge University Press, 2003.

The Reflexive Imperative in Late Modernity, Cambridge: Cambridge University Press, 2012.

Babbie, Earl, *The Practice of Social Research*. Independence, KY: Wadsworth, 2011.

The Practice of Social Research. Belmont, CA: Wadsworth, 2013.

Barbalet, Jack (ed.), *Emotions and Sociology*. New York: Wiley Blackwell, 2002.

"Self-Interest and the Theory of Action," *The British Journal of Sociology* 63 (3) (2012): 412–429.

Barbour, Ian, *Issues in Science and Religion*. New York: HarperCollins, 1971.

Barrow, John D. and Frank J. Tipler, *The Anthropic Cosmological Principle*. New York: Oxford University Press, 1988.

Baudrillard, Jean, *Simulacra and Simulation*. Ann Arbor, MI: University of Michigan, 1981.

Baxter, Leslie A. and Earl Babbie, *The Practice of Social Research*. Independence, KY: Wadsworth, 2011.

Becker, Howard, *Outsiders: Studies in the Sociology of Deviance*, New York: Free Press, 1963.

Benton, Ted, *Natural Relations? Ecology, Animal Rights, and Social Justice*. New York: Verso, 1993.

Philosophy of Social Science: The Philosophical Foundations of Social Thought. New York: Palgrave Macmillan, 2010.

"Some Comments on Roy Bhaskar's *The Possibility of Naturalism*," *Radical Philosophy* 27 (1981): 13–21.

Berger, Peter, *Adventures of an Accidental Sociologist: How to Explain the World Without Becoming a Bore*. New York: Prometheus, 2011.

Berger, Peter and Thomas Luckmann, *The Social Construction of Reality*. New York: Anchor, 1967.

Bhaskar, Roy, *A Realist Theory of Science*. New York: Routledge, 2008.

"Contexts of Interdisciplinarity," pp. 1–25 in Roy Bhaskar, Cheryl Frank, Karl Georg Hayer, and Peter Naess, *Interdisciplinarity and Climate Change: Transforming Knowledge and Practice for Our Global Future*, New York: Routledge, 2010.

Dialectic: The Pulse of Freedom. New York: Routledge, 2008.

Plato, etc.: The Problems of Philosophy and Their Resolution. New York: Routledge, 2009.

Reclaiming Reality. New York: Verso, 1989.

Reflections on metaReality: Transcendence, Emancipation and Everyday Life, New York: Routledge, 2011.

Scientific Realism and Human Emancipation. New York: Routledge, 2009.

The Possibility of Naturalism: A Philosophical Critique of the Contemporary Human Sciences. New York: Routledge, 1998.

Blalock, Hubert, *Theory Construction from Verbal to Mathematical Formulations*. Upper Saddle River, NJ: Prentice-Hall, 1969.

Blau, Peter, *Inequality and Heterogeneity: A Primitive Theory of Social Structure*. New York: Free Press, 1977.

Bloor, David, *The Enigma of the Airofoil: Rival Theories of Aerodynamics: 1909–1930*. Chicago, IL: University of Chicago Press, 2011.

Blum, Alan and Peter McHugh, "The Social *Ascription* of Motives," *American Journal of Sociology* 36 (1971): 98–109.

Blumer, Herbert, "The Metholodological Position of Symbolic Interactionism," pp. 1–60 in Herbert Blumer (ed.), *Symbolic Interactionism: Perspective and Method*. Englewood Cliffs, NJ: Prentice Hall, 1969.

"Sociological *Analysis* and the Variable," *American Sociological Review* 21 (6) (1969): 683–690. *Reprinted* as pp. 127–139 in Herbert Blumer *Symbolic Interactionism: Perspective and Method*. Englewood Cliffs, NJ: Prentice Hall.

Bohman, James and William Rehg, "Jürgen Habermas," *The Stanford Encyclopedia of Philosophy* (Winter 2011), Edward N. Zalta (ed.), http://plato.stanford.edu/archives/win2011/entries/habermas/.

Bourdieu, Pierre, *The Field of Cultural Production*. New York: Columbia University Press, 1993.

The Rules of Art. Stanford, CA: Stanford University Press, 1996.

Bourdieu, Pierre and Loïc Wacquant, *An Invitation to a Reflexive Sociology*. Chicago, IL: University of Chicago Press, 1992.

"The Principles of Economic Anthropology," pp. 75–89 in Neil J. Smelser and Richard Swedberg (eds.), *The Handbook of Economic Sociology*. Princeton, NJ: Princeton University Press, 2005.

Bourget, David and David J. Chalmers, "What Do Philosophers Believe?" http://philpapers.org/archive/BOUWDP, 2013.

Brentano, Franz, *Psychology from an Empirical Standpoint*, transl. by A.C. Rancurello, D.B. Terrell, and L. McAlister. London: Routledge, 1973.

Brower, Jeffrey, "Medieval Theories of Relations," *Stanford Encyclopedia of Philosophy*. http://plato.stanford.edu/entries/relations-medieval, 2009/

Buber, Martin, *I and Thou*. New York: Touchstone, 1971.

Burchell, Graham, Colin Gordon, and Peter Miller (eds.), *The Foucault Effect: Studies in Governmentality*. Chicago, IL: University of Chicago Press, 1991.

Butler, Judith, *Gender Trouble: Feminism and the Subversion of Identity*. New York: Routledge, 2006.

Callinicos, Alex, "Anthony Giddens: A Contemporary Critique," *Theory and Society* 14 (1985): 133–166.

Campbell, Colin, *The Myth of Social Action*. New York: Cambridge University Press, 1998.

Cartwright, Nancy, *How the Laws of Physics Lie*. New York: Oxford University Press, 1983.

　The Dappled World: A Study of the Boundaries of Science. New York: Cambridge University Press, 1999.

Chalmers, Alan, *What is this Thing Called Science?* Indianapolis, IN: Hackett Publishing Company, 1999.

Chalmers, David, *The Conscious Mind*. New York: Oxford University Press, 1996.

Charmaz, Kathy, *Constructing Grounded Theory: A Practical Guide to Qualitative Analysis*. Thousand Oaks, CA: Sage, 2006.

Cohen, G. A., *Karl Marx's Theory of History*. Princeton, NJ: Princeton University. Press, 2000.

Cohen, Patricia, "'Culture of Poverty' Makes a Comeback," *New York Times* www.nytimes.com/2010/10/18/us/18poverty.html?pagewanted=1&_r=2&hp&, 2010.

Collier, Andrew, *Being and Worth*. New York: Routledge, 1999.

　In Defense of Objectivity. New York: Routledge, 2007.

Collins, Harry, "A Note on Kuhn," *Social Studies of Science* 42 (3) (2012): 420–423.

　Changing Order: Replication and Induction in Scientific Practice. Chicago, IL: University of Chicago Press, 1992.

　Gravity's Ghost and Big Dog: Scientific Discovery and Social Analysis in the Twenty-first Century. Chicago, IL: University of Chicago Press, 2011.

Collins, Harry, Robert Evans and Mike Gorman, "Trading Zones and Interactional Expertise," *Studies in History and Philosophy of Science Part A* 38 (4) (2007): 657–666.

Collins, Harry and Steven Yearley, "Epistemological Chicken," pp. 301–326 in Andrew Pickering (ed.), *Practice and Culture*. Chicago, IL: University of Chicago, 1992.

Collins, Randall, "On the Microfoundations of Macrosociology," *American Journal of Sociology* 86 (1981): 984–1014.

　Violence: A Micro-Sociological Theory. Princeton, NJ: Princeton University Press, 2009.

Coole, Diana and Samantha Frost (eds.), *New Materialisms: Ontology, Agency, and Politics*. Durham, NC: Duke University Press, 2010.

Coulter, Jeff, *Mind in Action*. Cambridge, MA: Polity Press, 1989.

Corbetta, Piergiorgio, *Social Research: Theory, Methods and Techniques*. Thousand Oaks, CA: Sage, 2003.

Danermark, Berth, Mats Ekstrom, Liselotte Jakobsen, and Jan ch. Karlsson, *Explaining Society: An Introduction to Critical Realism in the Social Sciences*. New York: Routledge, 2005.

Davidson, Donald, "Agency," pp. 43–62 in Donald Davidson, *Essays on Actions and Events*. New York: Clarendon, 2001.

"Radical Interpretation," *Dialectica* 27 (1973): 314–328.

Davies, Bronwyn and Rom Harré "Positioning: The Discursive Production of Selves," *Journal for the Theory of Social Behaviour* 20 (1) (1990): 43–63.

Davies, Paul, *The Cosmic Jackpot: Why Our Universe is Just Right for Life*. New York: Houghton-Mifflin, 2007.

Dennett, Daniel, *The Intentional Stance*. Cambridge, MA: Bradford Books, 1989.

Dennis, Alex and Peter J. Martin, "Symbolic Interactionism and the Concept of Power," *British Journal of Sociology* 56 (2),(2005): 191–213.

Dépelteau, François, "Relational Thinking: A Critique of Co-deterministic Theories of Structure and Agency," *Sociological Theory* 26 (1) (2008): 51–73.

"Structure and Agency Again... And Much More," *Contemporary Sociology* 42 (6) (2013): 815–817.

Derrida, Jacques, *Of Grammatology*. Baltimore, MD: Johns Hopkins University Press, 1997.

Dewey, John, *Experience and Nature*. London: George Allen & Unwin, 1929.

Diehl, David and Daniel McFarland "Toward a Historical Sociology of Historical Situations," *American Journal of Sociology*, 115 (6) (2010): 1713–1752.

Donati, Pierpaolo, *Relational Sociology: A New Paradigm for the Social Sciences*. New York: Routledge, 2012.

Duhem, Pierre, *The Aim and Structure of Physical Theory*. Princeton, NJ: Princeton University Press, 1991.

Durkheim, Emile, *Suicide*. New York: Free Press, 1951.

Elder-Vass, Dave, *The Causal Power of Social Structures: Emergence, Structure, and Agency*. Cambridge: Cambridge University Press, 2011.

Elster, Jon, *Alchemies of the Mind: Rationality and the Emotions*. New York: Cambridge University Press, 1999.

Emirbayer, Mustafa "Manifesto for a Relational Sociology," *American Journal of Sociology* 103 (2),(1997): 281–317.

"Useful Durkheim," *Sociological Theory* 14 (2),(1996): 109–130.

Emirbayer, Mustafa and John Goodwin "Network Analysis, Culture and Agency," *American Journal of Sociology* 99 (6),(1994): 1411–1454.

"Symbols, Positions, Objects: Toward a New Theory of Revolutions and Collective Action" *History and Theory* 35 (3),1996: 358–374.

Emirbayer, Mustafa and Victoria Johnson "Bourdieu and Organizational Analysis," *Theory and Society* 37 (2007): 1–44.

Emirbayer, Mustafa and Ann Mische "What is Agency," *American Journal of Sociology* 103 (4) (1998): 962–1023.

Ermakoff, Ivan, "Rational Choice May Take Over," pp. 89–107 in Phil Gorski (ed.) *Bourdieu and Historical Analysis*. Durham, NC: Duke University Press, 2013.

Evans-Pritchard, Edward E., *Witchcraft, Oracles, and Magic Among the Azande*. New York: Oxford University Press, 1976.

Fantasia, Rick, *Cultures of Solidarity*. Berkeley, CA: University of California Press, 2001.

Feinberg, J., "Action and Responsibility," pp. 119–151 in Joel Feinberg (ed.) *Doing and Deserving*. Princeton, NJ: Princeton University Press, 1970.

Feyerabend, Paul, *Against Method*. New York: Verso, 2010.

Fish, Stanley, "Truth But No Consequences: Why Philosophy Doesn't Matter," *Critical Inquiry* 3 (2003), http://brandon.multics.org/library/Stanley%20Fish/fish2003truth.html.

Foucault, Michel, *The Archaeology of Knowledge*. New York: Vintage, 1982.

   The Order of Things: An Archaeology of the Human Sciences. New York: Vintage, 1994.

Foster, John Bellamy and Fred Magdoff, *The Great Financial Crisis: Causes and Consequences*. New York: Monthly Review, 2009.

Frankfurt, Harry "Free Agency," *Journal of Philosophy* 72 (8) 1975: 205–220.

Galison, P., *Image & Logic: A Material Culture of Microphysics*. Chicago, IL: University of Chicago Press, 1997.

Gee, Paul, *Introduction to Discourse Analysis: Theory and Method*. New York: Routledge, 2010.

Geertz, Clifford, *The Interpretation of Cultures*. New York: Basic Books, 1977.

Gelman, Andrew "Causality and Statistical Learning," *American Journal of Sociology* 117 (3) (2011): 955–966.

Giddens, Anthony, *A Contemporary Critique of Historical Materialism*. Berkeley, CA: University of California Press, 1981.

   Central Problems in Social Theory. Berkeley, CA: University of California Press, 1979.

   The Constitution of Society. Berkeley, CA: University of California Press, 1984.

Glaser, Barney and Anselm Strauss, *The Discovery of Grounded Theory: Strategies for Qualitative Research*. Piscataway, NJ: Transaction, 1967.

Goffman, Alice, *On the Run: Fugitive Life in an American City*. Chicago, IL: University of Chicago Press, 2014.

Gorski, Philip (ed.), *Bourdieu and Historical Analysis*. Durham, NC: Duke University Press, 2013.

"Social 'Mechanisms' and Comparative Historical Sociology: A Critical Realist Proposal," pp. 147–196 in Peter Hedstrom and Born Wittrock (eds.), *Frontiers of Sociology*. Boston, MA: Brill, 2009.

"The Poverty of Deductivism: A Constructive Realist Model of Sociological Explanation," *Sociological Methodology* 34 (1) (2004): 1–33.

Gould, Stephen Jay, *Wonderful Life*. New York: Norton, 1989.

Gouldner, Alvin, "Anti-Minotaur: The Myth of a Value-Free Sociology," *Social Problems* 9 (2) (1961): 199–213.

Groff, Ruth, "The Truth of the Matter: Roy Bhaskar's Critical Realism and the Concept of Alethic Truth," *Philosophy of the Social Sciences* 30 (2000): 407–435.

Gross, Neil, "A Pragmatist Theory of Social Mechanisms," *American Sociological Review* 74 (2009): 358–379.

Guth, Alan, *The Inflationary Universe*. New York: Basic Books, 1998.

Habermas, Jürgen, *Between Facts and Norms*. Cambridge, MA: MIT Press, 1998.

Moral Consciousness and Communicative Action. Cambridge, MA: MIT Press, 2001.

Truth and Justification. Cambridge, MA: MIT Press, 2003.

Haidt, Jonathan, *The Righteous Mind: Why Good People Are Divided about Religion and Politics*. New York: Vintage, 2013.

Hampshire, Stuart, *Thought and Action*. Notre Dame, IN: University of Notre Dame, 1981.

Haraway, Donna J., *Simians, Cyborgs, and Women: The Reinvention of Nature*. New York: Routledge, 1991.

Harré, Rom and Edward Madden, *Causal Powers: Theory of Natural Necessity*. New York: Blackwell, 1975.

Hart, Stephen, *Cultural Dilemmas of Progressive Politics: Styles of Engagement among Grassroots Activists*. Chicago, IL: University of Chicago Press, 2001.

Hartwig, Mervyn, *Dictionary of Critical Realism*. New York: Routledge, 2007.

"Introduction," pp. ix–xxvi in Roy Bhaskar, *A Realist Theory of Science*. London: Verso, 2008.

Hedström, Peter, *Dissecting the Social: On the Principles of Analytical Sociology*. New York: Cambridge University Press, 2005.

Hesse, Mary, *Revolutions and Reconstructions in the Philosophy of Science*. Brighton: Harvester, 1980.

Hitlin, Steven, *Moral Selves; Evil Selves: The Social Psychology of Conscience*. New York: Palgrave, 2008.

Hitlin, Steven and Jane Alyn Piliavin, "Values: Reviving a Dormant Concept," *Annual Review of Sociology* 30(2003): 359–393.

Hollis, Martin and Steven Smith, *Explaining and Understanding International Relations*. New York: Oxford University Press, 1990.

Homans, George C., "What do we Mean by Social Structure?" pp. 53–65 in Peter Blau (ed.), *Approaches to the Study of Social Structure*. New York: The Free Press, 1975.

Horgan, John, *The End of Science: Facing the Limits of Knowledge in the Twilight of the Scientific Age*. New York: Broadway Books, 1997.

Horst, Steven, *Symbols, Computation, and Intentionality: A Critique of the Computational Theory of Mind*. Berkeley, CA: University of California Press, 1996.

James, William, *The Meaning of Truth: A Sequel to "Pragmatism"*. Prometheus Books, 1909. www.authorama.com/meaning-of-truth-1.html.

Jerolmack, Colin, *The Global Pigeon*. Chicago, IL: University of Chicago Press, 2013.

Joas, Hans, *The Genesis of Values*. Chicago, IL: University of Chicago Press, 2000.

Joseph, Jonathan and Colin Wight (eds.), *Scientific Realism and International Relations*. New York: Palgrave Macmillan, 2010.

The Social in the Global: Social Theory, Governmentality and Global Politics. Cambridge: Cambridge University Press, 2012.

Keller, Hellen, *The World I Live In*, New York: The Century Company, 1938.

Kim, Jaegwon, "Causation and Mental Causation," pp. 227–242 in Brian McLaughlin and Jonathan Cohen (eds.), *Contemporary Debates in the Philosophy of Mind*. New York: Basil Blackwell, 2007. http://colbud.hu/bloewer/Kim_Causation_and_Mental_Causation_-_Debates-1.pdf.

"Emergence: Core Ideas and Issues," *Synthese* 151 (2006): 547–559.

Kincaid, Harold, John Dupré, and Alison Wylie (eds.), *Value-Free Science? Ideals and Illusions*. New York: Oxford University Press, 2007.

Kuhn, Thomas, "Reflections on my Critics," pp. 123–175 in J. Conant and J. Haugeland (eds.), *The Road Since Structure*. Chicago, IL: University of Chicago Press, 2000.

The Structure of Scientific Revolutions. Chicago, IL: University of Chicago Press, 2012.

Lacey, Hugh, *Is Science Value-Free? Values and Scientific Understanding*. New York: Routledge, 1999.

Lakatos, Imre, "Falsification and the Methodology of Scientific Research Programmes," pp. 91–196 in Imre Lakatos and Alan Musgrave (eds.), *Criticism and the Growth of Knowledge.* New York: Cambridge University Press, 1970.

Lamont, Michèle, *Money, Morals and Manners: The Culture of the French and the American Upper Middle Class.* Chicago, IL: University of Chicago Press, 1992.

Langman, Lauren, "Culture, Identity, and Hegemony: The Body in a Global Age," *Current Sociology* 51 (2003): 223–247.

Latour, Bruno, *Reassembling the Social: An Introduction to Actor Network Theory.* New York: Oxford University Press, 2007.

Laudan, Larry, *Progress and Its Problems: Towards a Theory of Scientific Growth.* Berkeley, CA: University of California Press, 1978.

Law, John, "Actor Network Theory and Material Semiotics," pp. 141–158 in Bryan S. Turner (ed.), *The New Blackwell Companion to Social Theory.* New York: Wiley-Blackwell, 2009.

Law, John and John Urry, "Enacting the Social," *Economy and Society* 33 (3) (2005): 390–410.

Law, John and Marianne Lien, "Slippery: Field Notes on Empirical Ontology," www.sv.uio.no/sai/english/research/projects/newcomers/publica tions/working-papers-web/Slippery%20revised%2013%20WP%20ver sion.pdf, 2012.

Lawson, Tony, *Reorienting Economics.* New York: Routledge, 2003.

Economics and Reality, New York: Routledge, 1997.

Leary, Mark R. and Nicole Buttermore, "The Evolution of the Human Self: Tracing the Natural History of Self-Awareness," *Journal for the Theory of Social Behaviour* 33 (4) (2003): 365–404.

Lenin, V. I., *What the "Friends of the People Are" and How They Fight the Social Democrats.* Moscow: Progressive Publishers, 1970. www. marxists.org/archive/lenin/works/1894/friends/01.htm#v01zz99h-131-GUESS

Leslie, John, *Universes*, New York: Routledge, 1996.

Liebow, Eliot, *Tally's Corner: A Study of Negro Streetcorner Men.* New York: Rowman & Littlefield, 2003.

Lim, Mah-Hui and Chin Lim, *Nowhere to Hide: The Great Financial Crisis and Challenges for Asia.* Singapore: Institute of Southeast Asian Studies, 2010.

Little, Daniel, *New Contributions to the Philosophy of History.* New York: Springer, 2010.

Varieties of Social Explanation, Amazon Digital Services, 2012.

Lizardo, Omar, 2010 "Beyond the Antimonies of Structure: Levi-Strauss, Giddens, Bourdieu, and Sewell," *Theory and Society* 39: 651–688.

Lizardo, Omar and Michael Strand, "Skills, Toolkits Contexts, and Insti-
    tutions: Clarifying the Relationship Between Different Approaches to
    Cognition in Cultural Sociology," *Poetics* 38 (2) (2010): 205–228,

Lynd, Robert, *Knowledge for What? The Place of Social Science in American
    Culture*. Princeton, NJ: Princeton University Press, 1939.

Lyotard, Jean-François, *The Postmodern Condition: A Report on Know-
    ledge*. Minneapolis, MN: University of Minnesota Press, 1984.

Maccarini, Andrea, Emmanuele Morandi, and Riccardo Prandini (eds.),
    Sociological Realism, New York: Routledge, 2011.

Malazita, James, *Ontic Communities: Speculative Fiction, Ontology, and the
    Digital Design Community*. PhD dissertation, Drexel University, 2015.

Manicas, Peter, *A Realist Philosophy of Social Science: Explanation and
    Understanding*. Cambridge: Cambridge University Press, 2006.

Marcus, Eric, "Why There are No Token States," *Journal of Philosophical
    Research* 34 (2009): 215–241.

Margolis, Joseph, "Action and Causality," *Philosophical Forum* 11 (1979):
    47–64.

    Persons and Minds: The Prospects for a Non-reductive Materialism. New
        York: Springer, 1979.

    "The Ontological Peculiarity of Works of Art," pp. 253–260 in Joseph
        Margolis (ed.), *Philosophy Looks at the Arts*. Philadelphia, PA: Temple
        University Press, 1986.

Martin, John Levi, "Personal Best," *Contemporary Sociology* 42 (1) (2013):
    6–11.

    "John Levi Martin's Response to Christian Smith," *Contemporary Soci-
        ology*, 42 (1) (2013): 16–18.

    Social Structures. Princeton, NJ: Princeton University Press, 2009.

    The Explanation of Social Action. New York: Oxford University Press,
        2011.

    Thinking Through Theory. New York: Norton, 2014.

Marx, Karl, "The Eighteenth Brumaire of Louis Bonaparte," pp. 300–325 in
    David McClellan, *Karl Marx: Selected writings*. New York: Oxford
    University Press, 2000.

McGuigan, Jim, *Modernity and Postmodern Culture*. New York: Open
    University Press, 2006.

Melden, A. I. (1961) *Free Action*. London: Routledge & Kegan Paul,
    1957.

Merton, Robert K., "Three Fragments from a Sociologist's Notebooks:
    Establishing the Phenomenon, Specified Ignorance, and Strategic
    Research Methods," *Annual Review of Sociology* 13 (1987): 1–29.

Mol, Annemarie, *The Body Multiple: Ontology in Medical Practice*.
    Durham, NC: Duke University Press, 2003.

Morgan, Stephen L. and Christopher Winship, *Counterfactuals and Causal Inference*. Cambridge: Cambridge University Press, 2007.

Mumford, Stephen, "Powers, Dispositions, Properties or a Causal Manifesto," pp. 139–151 in Ruth Groff (ed.), *Revitalizing Causality*. New York: Routledge, 2008.

Niven, David, "A Fair Test of Media Bias: Party, Race, and Gender in Coverage of the 1992 House Banking Scandal" *Polity* 36 (4) (2004): 637–650.

"Objective Evidence on Media Bias: Newspaper Coverage of Professional Party Switchers," *Journalism and Mass Communication Quarterly* 80 (2) (2003): 311–326.

"Partisan Bias in the Media? A New Test," *Social Science Quarterly* 80 (4) (1999): 847–857.

Norrie, Alan, *Crime, Reason, and History: A Critical Introduction to Criminal Law*. New York: Cambridge University Press, 2014.

Nussbaum, Martha, *Love's Knowledge: Essays on Philosophy and Literature*. New York: Oxford University Press, 1992.

Oberheim, Eric, "The Incommensurability of Scientific Theories," *Stanford Encyclopedia Online*, http://plato.stanford.edu/entries/incommensurability/#KuhSubDevInc, 2013.

Outhewaite, R. William, *Critical Theory and Contemporary Europe*. New York: Continuum, 2010.

Patomaki, Heikki, *After International Relations: Critical Realism and the Reconstruction of World Politics*. New York: Routledge, 2001.

Patterson, Orlando, "A Poverty of the Mind," *New York Times* (2006). www.nytimes.com/2006/03/26/opinion/26patterson.html?pagewanted=al.

"Making Sense of Culture," *Annual Review of Sociology* 40 (2014): 1–30.

Pearl, Judea, *Causality: Models, Reasoning and Inference*. New York: Cambridge University Press, 2009.

Peirce, Charles Sanders, *Popular Science Monthly* 12 (January) (1878): 286–302. www.peirce.org/writings/p119.html.

Peters, R. S., *The Concept of Motivation*. London: Routledge & Kegan Paul, 1960.

Pickering, Andrew, *Constructing Quarks: A Sociological History of Particle Physics*. Chicago, IL: University of Chicago Press, 1999.

(ed.), *Science as Practice and Culture*. Chicago, IL: University of Chicago Press, 1992.

"The World Since Kuhn," *Social Studies of Science* 42 (3) (2012): 467–473.

Popper, Karl, *The Open Society and its Enemies*. Princeton, NJ: Princeton University Press, 2013.

"Three Worlds." The Tanner Lecture on *Human* Values. Delivered at University of Michigan. www.theeonline.com/Documents/Popper-3Worlds.pdf, 1978.

Porpora, Douglas, "Cultural Rules and Material Relations," *Sociological Theory* 11 (1993): 212–229.

"Do Realists Run Regressions?" pp. 260–266 in Jose Lopez and Garry Potter (eds.), *After Postmodernism: An Introduction to Critical Realism.* New York: Continuum, 2005.

"Four Concepts of Social Structure," *Journal for the Theory of Social Behaviour* 19 (1989): 195–212.

"How Many Thoughts Are There? Or Why We Likely Have No *Tegmark Duplicates* $10^{10^{115}}$ Meters Away," *Philosophical Studies* 163 (2013): 133–149.

The Concept of Social Structure. Westport, CT: Greenwood Press, 1980.

Landscapes of the Soul: The Loss of Moral Meaning in American Life. New York: Oxford University Press, 2001.

"On the Post-Wittgensteinian Critique of the Concept of Action in Sociology," *Journal for the Theory of Social Behaviour* 13 (2) (1983): 129–146.

"On the Prospects for a Nomothetic Theory of Social Structure," *Journal for the Theory of Social Behaviour* 13 (1983): 243–264.

"Recovering Causality," pp. 149–166 in Andrea Maccarini, Emmanuele Morandi, and Riccardo Prandini (eds.), *Sociological Realism.* New York: Routledge, 2011.

"The Role of Agency in History: The Althusser–Thompson–Anderson Debate," pp. 219–241 in Scott McNall (ed.) *Current Perspectives in Social Theory*, Vol. 6. Greenwich, CT: JAI Press, 1985.

Porpora, Douglas, Alexander Nikolaev, Julia Hagemann, and Alexander Jenkens, *Post-Ethical Society: The Iraq War, Abu Ghraib, and the Moral Failure of the Secular.* Chicago, IL: University of Chicago Press, 2013.

Poster, Mark, *Existential Marxism in Post-War France.* Princeton, NJ: Princeton University Press, 1977.

"Introduction," pp. 1–12 in Marc Poster (ed.), *Baudrillard: Selected Writings.* Stanford, CA: Stanford University Press, 2001.

Putnam, Hilary, *The Collapse of the Fact/Value Dichotomy.* Cambridge, MA: Harvard University Press, 2002.

Quine, W. V., *From a Logical Point of View: Nine Logico-Philosophical Essays.* Cambridge, MA: Harvard University Press, 1980.

Word and Object. Cambridge, MA: MIT Press, 1964.

Ravenscroft, Ian, "Folk Psychology as a Theory" *Stanford Encyclopedia of Philosophy Online* (2010). http://plato.stanford.edu/entries/folkpsych-theory/.

Reed, Isaac, *Interpretation and Social Knowledge: On the Use of Theory in the Human Sciences*. Chicago, IL: University of Chicago Press, 2011.

"Justifying Sociological Knowledge: From Realism to Interpretation," *Sociological Theory* 26 (2) (2008): 101–129.

"Maximal Interpretation in Clifford Geertz and the Strong Program in Cultural Sociology: Toward a New Epistemology" *Cultural Sociology*, 2 (2008): 187–200.

Riley, Dylan, "The Historical Logics of Logics of History: Language and Labor in William H. Sewell Jr," *Social Science History* 32 (4) (2008): 555–565.

Ritzer, George, *Sociology: A Multiple Paradigm Science*. New York: Allyn & Bacon, 1975.

Rubinstein, David, "The Concept of Action in Sociology," *Journal for the Theory of Social Behaviour* 7 (2) (1977): 209–236.

Sartre, Jean-Paul, *Being and Nothingness*. New York: Washington Square Press, 1993.

"Existentialism is a Humanism," pp. 345–368 in Walter Kaufmann (ed.), *Existentialism from Dostoevsky to Sartre*. New York: Meridian, 1975.

Existentialism is a Humanism. New Brunswick, NJ: Yale University Press, 2007.

Sayer, Andrew, *Method in Social Science: A Realist Approach*. New York: Routledge, 2010.

Why Things Matter to People: Social Science, Values, and Ethical Life. New York: Cambridge University Press, 2011.

Schatzki, Theodore, Karin Knorr Cetina, and Eric von Savigny (eds.), *The Practice Turn in Contemporary Theory*. New York: Routledge, 2001.

Schutz, Alfred, *The Phenomenology of the Social World*. Chicago, IL: Northwestern University, 1967.

Searle, John, *Speech Acts: An Essay in the Philosophy of Language*. Cambridge: Cambridge University Press, 1970.

The Construction of Social Reality. New York: Free Press, 1995.

"What Your Computer Can't Know," *New York Review of Books*, October 9 2014: 52–55.

Sewell, William H., "A Theory of Structure: Duality, Agency, and Transformation," *American Journal of Sociology* 98 (1) (1992): 1–29.

"The Concept(s) of Culture," pp. 35–61 in Victoria E. Bonnell and Lynn Hunt (eds.), *Beyond the Cultural Turn: New Directions in the Study of Society and Culture*. Berkeley, CA: University of California Press, 1999.

Shalin, Dimitri, "Pragmatism and Social Interactionism," *American Sociological Review* 51 (1986): 9–29.

"The Pragmatic Origins of Symbolic Interactionism" *Studies in Symbolic Interaction* 12 (1991): 223–251.

Small, Mario Luis, David J. Harding, and Michèle Lamont, "Reconsidering Culture and Poverty," *Annals of the American Academy of Political and Social Science* 629 (2010): 6–27.

Smith, Adam, *An Inquiry into the Nature and Causes of the Wealth of Nations*. New York: Modern Library, 1937.

Smith, Christian, *To Flourish or Destruct: A Personalist Theory of Human Goods, Motivations, Failure and Evil*. Chicago, IL: University of Chicago Press, 2014.

    What is a Person? Rethinking Humanity, Social Life, and the Moral Good from the Ground Up. Chicago, IL: University of Chicago Press, 2011.

Somers, Margaret, "We're No Angel: Realism, Rational Choice, and Rationality in Social Science," *American Journal of Sociology* 104 (3) (1998): 722–784.

Stanford, Kyle, "Underdetermination of Scientific Theory," *Stanford Encyclopedia of Philosophy* (2013), http://plato.stanford.edu/entries/scientific-underdetermination/.

Steinmetz, George, "Critical Realism and Historical Sociology: A Review Article," *Comparative Studies in Society and History* 40 (1998): 170–186.

    The Politics of Method in the Human Sciences: Positivism and Its Epistemological Others (Politics, History, and Culture). Durham, NC: Duke University Press, 2005.

    "Toward Socioanalysis: The 'Traumatic Kernel' of Psychoanalysis and Neo-Bourdieusian Theory," pp. 108–130 in Philip Gorski (ed.), *Bourdieu and Historical Analysis*. Durham, NC: Duke University Press, 2013.

Steinhardt, Paul, "The Inflation Debate," *Scientific American* 37 (April) (2011): 37–43.

Stoljar, Daniel, "Physicalism," *The Stanford Encyclopedia of Philosophy* (fall edition, 2009), Edward N. Zalta (ed.), http://plato.stanford.edu/archives/fall2009/entries/physicalism/.

Swedberg, Richard, "Markets in Society," pp. 233–253 in Neil J. Smelser and Richard Swedberg (eds.), *The Handbook of Economic Sociology*. Princeton, NJ: Princeton University Press, 2005.

Swidler, Ann, "Comment on Stephen Vaisey's 'Socrates, Skinner, and Aristotle: Three Ways of Thinking about Culture in Action'," *Sociological Forum* 23 (3) (2008): 614–618.

    "Culture in Action: Symbols and Strategies," *American Sociological Review* 51 (2) (1986): 273–286.

    Talk of Love: How Culture Matters. Chicago, IL: University of Chicago Press, 2001.

    "What Anchors Cultural Practices," pp. 74–92 in Theodore R. Shatzki, Karin Knorr Cetina, and Eike von Savigny (eds.), *The Practice Turn in Contemporary Theory*. New York: Routledge, 2001.

Tavory, Iddo and Stephen Timmermans, "A Pragmatist Approach to Causality in Ethnography," *American Journal of Sociology* 119 (3) (2013): 682–714.

Taylor, Charles, *The Explanation of Behavior*. New York: Prometheus, 1964.

Thomas, Gary and David James, "Reinventing Grounded Theory: Some Questions about Theory, Ground and Discovery," *British Research Journal* 32 (6) 2006: 767–795.

Tilly, Charles, *The Politics of Collective Violence*. New York: Cambridge University Press, 2003.

Tipler, Frank, *The Anthropic Cosmological Principle*. New York: Oxford University Press, 1988.

"Three Visions of History," *History and Theory* 46 (2007): 299–307.

Turner, Jonathan and Alexandra Maryanski, *Functionalism*. San Francisco, CA: Benjamin-Cummings, 1979.

Turner, Stephen, "Whatever Happened to Knowledge?" *Social Studies of Science* 42 (3) (2012): 474–480.

Vaisey, Stephen, "Motivation and Justification: A Dual-Process Model of Culture in Action," *American Journal of Sociology* 114 (2009): 1675–1715.

"Reply to Ann Swidler," *Sociological Forum* 23 (3) (2008): 619–622.

"Socrates, Skinner, and Aristotle: Three Ways of Thinking about Culture in Action," *Sociological Forum* 23 (3) (2008): 603–613.

Vandenberghe, Frédéric, "The Real is Relational: An Epistemological Analysis of Pierre Bourdieu's Generative Structualism," *Sociological Theory* 17 (1) (1999): 33–67.

What's Critical about Critical Realism. New York: Routledge, 2013.

Varela, Charles and Rom Harré, "Conflicting Varieties of Realism: Causal Powers and the Problems of Social Structure," *Journal for the Theory of Social Behaviour* 26 (3) (1996): 313–325.

Vision, Gerald, *Veritas: The Correspondence Theory and Its Critics*. Denver, CO: Bradford, 2009.

Wacquant, Loïc J. D., "Toward a Social Praxiology: The Structure and Logic of Bourdieu's Sociology," pp. 1–60 in Pierre Bourdieu and Loïc Wacquant, *Invitation to a Reflexive Sociology*. Chicago, IL: University of Chicago Press, 1992.

Wallerstein, Immanuel, *The Modern World System: Capitalist Agriculture and the Origins of the European World Economy in the Sixteenth Century*. Berkeley, CA: University of California Press, 2011.

Wellman, Barry, "Structural Analysis: From Method and Metaphor to Theory and Substance," pp. 19–61 in Barry Wellman and S. D. Berkowitz (eds.), *Social Structures: A Network Approach*. New York: Emerald, 1997.

Wells, H.G., *The Island of Doctor Moreau*, Los Angeles, CA: Hungry Girl Books, 2013.

Wendt, Alexander, *Quantum Mind and Social Science*. Cambridge: Cambridge University Press, 2015.

Wight, Colin, *Agents, Structures and International Relations: Politics as Ontology*. Cambridge: Cambridge University Press, 2006.

Wikipedia, "Alex (Parrot)," http://en.wikipedia.org/wiki/Alex_(parrot), 2013. Accessed November 9, 2013.

"Zombies," https://en.wikipedia.org/wiki/Zombie, 2013. Accessed June 29, 2013.

Wilson, William Julius, "Why Both Structure and Culture Both Matter to a Holistic Analysis of Poverty," *Annals of the American Academy of Political and Social Science* 629 (1) (2010): 200–219.

Winch, Peter, *The Idea of a Social Science*. London: Routledge & Kegan Paul, 1958.

Wittgenstein, Ludwig, *Tractatus Logico-Philosophicus*. London: Routledge & Kegan Paul, 1961.

Wright, Andrew, *Christianity and Critical Realism: Ambiguity, Truth, and Theological Literacy*. New York: Routledge, 2014.

Wolterstorf, Nicholas, "Toward an Ontology of Artworks," pp. 229–252 in Joseph Margolis (ed.), *Philosophy Looks at the Arts*. Philadelphia, PA: Temple University Press, 1986.

Woodward, James, *Making Things Happen: A Theory of Causal Explanation*. New York: Oxford University Press, 2005.

Wulbert, Roland, "Had by the Positive Integers," *American Sociologist* 10 (4) (1975): 242–243.

Wuthnow, Robert, *Meaning and Moral Order: Explorations in Cultural Analysis*. Berkeley, CA: University of California Press, 1989.

Zeitlin, Irving, *Ideology and the Development of Sociological Theory*. New York: Prentice Hall, 2009.

Index